SENSŌ

A Pacific Basin Institute Book

SENSŌ

The Japanese Remember the Pacific War

Letters to the Editor of
ASAHI SHIMBUN

Edited and with an Introduction by
FRANK GIBNEY

Translated by
BETH CARY

An East Gate Book

M.E. Sharpe
Armonk, New York
London, England

An East Gate Book

Library of Congress Cataloging-in-Publication Data

Sensō. English
Sensō : the Japanese remember the Pacific War /
edited by Frank Gibney : translated by Beth Cary.
p.   cm.
"An east gate book."
ISBN 1-56324-588-4 (alk. paper). — ISBN 1-56324-589-2 (pbk. : alk. paper)
1. World War, 1939–1945—Personal narratives. Japanese.
I. Gibney, Frank, 1924–   .
II. Title.
D811.A2S43313   1995
940.54′8252—dc20
95-34939
CIP

Printed in the United States of America

The paper used in this publication meets the minimum requirements of
American National Standard for Information Sciences—
Permanence of Paper for Printed Library Materials,
ANSI Z 39.48-1984.

BM (c)   10   9   8   7   6   5   4   3   2   1
BM (p)   10   9   8   7   6   5   4   3   2

Contents

Introduction

On 10 July 1986, *Asahi Shimbun*, Japan's great newspaper of record, ran the first in a series of letters from its readers about their reminiscences of World War II. Since January of that year, readers' letters on various themes had been featured on the op-ed page of *Asahi*'s morning edition, under the heading "Let's Talk About Topics" ("Tēma Danwa-Shitsu"). Predictably, the first topics chosen, "Teachers" and "Men and Women," evoked a good response. As more readers added their thoughts and comments, some interesting exchanges of opinion developed. The letters on both of these subjects were later printed by *Asahi*'s publishing division as separate books.

The *Sensō* series was originally planned to last for three months. Because of the very nature of the subject, however, the response was extraordinary. *Asahi* had succeeded in capturing the attention of its readers far beyond the original hopes of the op-ed page editors. The series was extended several times, ultimately running through 29 August 1987. Some 1,100 letters were printed out of 4,000 received. That year the letters appeared, with suitable introductions, in a two-volume book, *The War [Sensō]: A Testimony Composed in Blood and Tears*. It became a best-seller.

All of the letters related to wartime experiences or opinions about the War. Some of the letters were written by soldiers about their experiences in battle, in military camps, or as war prisoners. Others dealt with civilian life. These included the evacuation of school children from Japan's bombed cities, and descriptions of life under military control by war workers and families. Women as well as men told their stories. The reflections of the wives, mothers, and children of Japan's soldiery proved to be poignant indeed. Most of the correspondents were in their sixties, people who had been in their teens or twenties at the time of the War, but the letters included some childhood reminiscences. All were looking back over the years, an element of retrospection which gave the series a character all its own.

Many were stimulated by the appearance of the first letters to recall incidents or experiences that had been buried within their own consciousness for decades—like people remembering a long-forgotten nightmare. The letters were extraordinarily frank, so much so that the editors were often shocked by their candor. Most wrote of things they would not have revealed at the time they happened—old men and women seemed to want to get something off their chests before they died. Their recollections covered almost two decades, from the early thirties, when the Japanese armies marched into Manchuria, to the repatriation of the last prisoners of war from the Soviet Union in the late forties.

The letters attracted their share of controversy when they appeared in the eighties. Many readers, quite disturbed, wrote to *Asahi* saying, in effect, "Why did you dig up the old evils now? Just when we are trying to expand our friendship with neighboring countries, raking up what happened in the past can be very destructive. We are trying to forget this past. Don't be so cruel as to write about it. Please don't let our memories come alive again."

A member of *Asahi*'s editorial board, Nagasawa Michio set out to answer such complaints. "Of course," he wrote in an afterword to the two volumes of published letters, "where people are thinking of their own personal lives, it is quite natural to want an unpleasant past erased from memory. Indeed, for individuals to forget a bad past amounts to a healthy act of self-purification. But the history of a country is a different matter. Doesn't it hurt our national conscience to try to cancel out the bad parts of the past, as if they never happened?

"The really brave will face up to the negative acts of the past. Above all, even if we think we can forget these things, others will not forget them. At that time, Japanese people—70 million strong—made up one of the world's leading nations. How they acted, the deeds they accomplished, are done, for good or for ill. They weigh heavily on us now. To face up to this without any fear may give us valuable lessons—a compass bearing for the actions of Japan in the future."

His words were prophetic. The English-language publication of this series now, fifty years after the close of the War, comes at a time when Japan, as a government and as a society, has been heavily criticized for what many see as a national attempt to sweep the events of the War under the rug. Unlike the Germans, who very early in the game faced up to the problem of responsibility for the War and did their best to atone for the misdeeds committed during the Nazi era, the Japanese have been slow to come to grips with crimes of the past.

At the end of World War II, the country was seized by a kind of mass shock, in which remorse played a considerable role. There is no question that the Japanese people had participated wholeheartedly in the war effort. By the late thirties, all vocal opposition to the War had been systematically crushed. Stimulated by early successes in China and in the Pacific, the Japanese rallied proudly to support their armed forces. While privately many Japanese had serious doubts about the wisdom and morality of Japan's war policies, the pressure for national conformity was difficult to resist.

The postwar Allied Occupation of Japan, successful in many ways, in a sense made it easy for the Japanese to deal with the question of their guilt. In order to effect a smooth and peaceful transition to U.S. military control, General Douglas MacArthur's Occupation kept the Japanese government intact. This policy—so different from the direct Allied military government in Germany—conspicuously included the preservation of the Emperor as Japan's symbolic if not its actual ruler. The U.S. government overruled the complaints of many who urged that Hirohito be tried as a war criminal, perhaps the leading war criminal of all. Throughout the late forties, the United States, anxious to eradicate wartime militarism, in essence imposed a moratorium on the teaching of recent Japanese history. Ironically, however, this laudable effort to reverse the effect of militarist government indoctrination in fact supported the desire of many in the Japanese bureaucracy to forget the disasters wrought throughout Asia by Japanese colonialism and militarism.

By 15 August 1945, the Japanese public was numb from years of hardship. The Emperor's unprecedented personal announcement of surrender deepened a national consciousness of failure and despair. People wanted only to forget. The desire to forget the War was intensified, on the American side as well as the Japanese, by the disasters inflicted on Japan in the overwhelming military victory of the United States and its allies, which culminated in the ghastly firebombings of Japanese cities and the dropping of atomic bombs on Hiroshima and Nagasaki—still cause for remorse among Americans. Although the memory of Japanese atrocities remained strong, the Allied desire for revenge was considerably softened not only by the conviction of Japanese military men as war criminals, but by the pitiable condition of Japanese civilians at that time and the almost total devastation of their cities.

As a result, the war period became a kind of dead space in Japanese education. The conservative Ministry of Education saw to it that the stormy years from 1937 to 1945 were passed over quickly in the textbooks it sanctioned. In later years, as Japan became prosperous and the memory of the War faded, new generations were taught little or nothing about what really happened. Older survivors of the War, including political leaders who should have known better, went to the point of denying the realities of that period. Japanese invasions of China and Southeast Asian countries, for example, were referred to as mere "advances." Assisted by some revisionist Japanese historians, many politicians even argued that the Rape of Nanjing, among other atrocities, had never happened. Nor was there much discussion about the gross mistreatment of Allied prisoners on the Burma-Siam Railway and the Bataan Death March.* And only recently have the atrocities perpetuated on prisoners by the doctors of the infamous Unit 731 been revealed.

The debates among scholars and political leaders have not died. It is interesting, as the editors of *Asahi* noted, that the reaction of so many was "Why spoil our day by dredging up events from the long-forgotten past? Let's leave the past where it belongs, deep in our memory." In 1995, fifty years after the War, some Japanese officials are still trying to whitewash the militarists' war, calling it a defense by Asians against American and European colonialism. Some Japanese scholars and historians—notably Ienaga Saburō and Irokawa Daikichi—have tried their best to portray the War as it really was, but their efforts have been largely undermined by official disinclination to face an unpleasant past squarely.

All the more credit is due *Asahi,* therefore, for publishing these letters. It was very fitting that *Asahi* was the forum for such frank reminiscences, which the editors presented quite unsparingly. Since its founding in 1879, *Asahi* has through the years proved itself to be one of Japan's most distinguished publishers—perhaps the most distinguished. Publishing magazines and books as well as its daily newspapers, it is a national presence. Each issue of the paper is published simultaneously in Tokyo, Osaka, Kyūshū, and Hokkaidō. Its current circulation of over 13 million (morning and evening) blankets Japan and is second only to that of *Yomiuri Shimbun.* Founded originally in Osaka, *Asahi* over the years has developed its own character. Liberal and fair-minded on the whole, *Asahi* has generally tried to report the news without bias.

During the prewar years, as the militarists gained power, *Asahi* suffered for this. In the thirties its offices were attacked and ransacked on several

---

*In April 1942, after the collapse of resistance on the Bataan peninsula, some 70,000 Filipino and American prisoners of war were marched to camps under brutal harassment by their Japanese captors; almost 10,000 of them died. Between October 1942 and November 1944 some 61,000 Allied POWs and 270,000 conscripted laborers—Malays, Indonesians, Thais, and Burmese—were put to work on Japan's ill-fated railroad planned to link Thailand and Burma. More than 100,000 died as a result of brutal treatment by the Japanese army. Almost 30 percent of the POWs captured by the Japanese in the Pacific either died or were killed by their captors.

occasions by rightist goon squads. During the U.S. Occupation and well into the seventies, *Asahi* assumed a rather uncritical leftist editorial stance. This gradually diminished as the hope among Japanese intellectuals for a Marxist "workers' paradise" proved to be illusory. The present generation of *Asahi* editors probably presents the news as fairly as anyone can in Japan. It stands to *Asahi*'s credit that the editors made no effort to censor these letters, but on the contrary presented them exactly as they were written.

Asahi's two volumes came into my hands in 1989, and I decided to attempt a translation for American readers. It seemed to me then, as it does now, that Americans would profit from a discussion of the War as seen by the people who fought and lived through this terribly difficult period in Japan's history. But it took time to find the financial support for the translation work. This was ultimately provided by the Sasakawa Peace Foundation and the Japan-United States Friendship Commission. For this, the Pacific Basin Institute is most grateful.

Although *Asahi* ran the letters as they were received, I felt that this approach would demand too much knowledge of an American public, which continues to display a surprisingly superficial acquaintance with things Japanese. I decided therefore to present the letters by subject, for example, the China war, the Home Front, and so on, prefacing each section with a brief introduction. In this preliminary work I was assisted by my wife, Hiroko Doi, who read the letters and translated some samples. The bulk of the translation, as well as the even more critical work of selection, has been done by Beth Cary, who has worked on this project with me for several years. Born and raised in Japan, Ms. Cary was exceptionally qualified for this job. A skilled translator, she winnowed her way through all the letters, with some small help from me. Mindful of the limits of condensing these books into one volume, we selected some 300 letters, choosing those that seemed most representative of the original selections.

For the benefit of American readers, I have attempted in the introductions to put the letters in each chapter in some kind of historical context. To many Americans, principally those of the current generation, the struggles of the War are very distant memories, to be read about in history books—if at all—or when newspapers occasionally commemorate wartime anniversaries. The hardships and the heroism of soldiers and civilians on both sides now seem remote indeed. I lived through the War myself, however, and the experiences of those days remain vivid and real. My generation was formed by the events of World War II.

I joined the navy in December 1942, just a year after I had begun college. After fourteen months' intensive study of the Japanese language, I was sent to the Pacific for duty as a language officer in U.S. Navy intelligence.

As such I participated in the major American landings at Peleliu and Oki-nawa. I gained some wider knowledge of general Pacific theater strategy from my vantage point at the Joint Intelligence Center / Pacific Ocean Area Headquarters in Pearl Harbor. Since my particular job involved interrogating Japanese prisoners of war, I ended up a lot closer to the enemy than most Americans did. Through my acquaintance with the Japanese at that time, and later, during the beginnings of the U.S. Occupation, I managed as much as a foreign observer could to live through this period with the Japanese. Reading these letters, I found myself recalling the people I met then and the events of those fateful days.

No effort has been made here to pretty the letters up or otherwise adjust them to our own literary conventions. We have had no personal contact with those who wrote them, although, thanks to the good offices of *Asahi*, they agreed that their letters be published in English translation. The letters remain as they were received by *Asahi* nearly a decade ago—testimony of what the War was like by Japanese who lived through it.

Thanks are due to the editors of *Asahi* and the management of *Asahi*'s Business Development Department (*Jigyō Kaihatsu Bu*), in particular Ms. Mitarai Kyōko, who worked most constructively with me throughout this project, as well as my executive secretary at TBS Britannica in Tokyo, Ms. Honda Yukiko. Finally, let me express my gratitude to Douglas Merwin, my editor at M.E. Sharpe, and his colleagues for their responsive and sensitive handling of this work.

Frank Gibney

SENSŌ

Chapter 1

The Road to War

By the early twenties, the Empire of Japan—already a world power after its victories in the Russo-Japanese War and as one of the Allies in World War I—seemed to be emerging as a representative democracy. Only fifty years before, the young architects of the Meiji Restoration had cleared away the last remnants of the feudal Tokugawa Shogunate and initiated Japan's startling and successful modernization.* Among the Meiji reformers were populists and democrats like Nakae Chōmin and Itagaki Taisuke. By and large, they wished to reshape Japan in the mold of Western democracies, into a nation with a responsible electorate and a sound legal system, whose people would be well educated and aware of their rights as citizens. Of course, the mainstream Meiji reformers were reluctant to democratize too much; some, like Yamagata Aritomo, were strong authoritarians. Itō Hirobumi's constitution emerged as a very conservative document, and it was Itō, prime minister and a close associate of Emperor Meiji, who set Japan's political course. Despite the authoritarian overtones of the Meiji Constitution, however, a trend toward democratic government had begun. Under Prime Minister Hara Takashi, the first commoner to attain that position following a succession of the original Meiji Founding Fathers—later ennobled as counts and princes—Japan seemed to have become a two-party parliamentary democracy on the European model. Indeed, in 1925 Premier Katō Takaaki, another liberal statesman, put through the Diet a law granting universal male suffrage, eliminating the property qualifications of the past. A small but vocal group of women's rights advocates also emerged.

---

*Commodore Matthew Perry's forcible "opening" of Japan in 1853 released opposing currents of modernization and xenophobia. In 1868, led by an extremely talented group of young *samurai* officials, who feared that Japan, like China, might come under the domination of Western colonialists, the Restoration brought the young Emperor Meiji to power. The Japanese began to turn their empire into a new nineteenth century-style nation state.

Backed by an ideological socialist movement, Japanese workers had begun to organize themselves into trade unions. Two hundred unions were active in Japan by the beginning of 1926, almost all of them less than ten years old. Through World War I, conditions in many Japanese factories had been as brutal as in the sweatshops of the early Industrial Revolution in the West. Workers and some liberal capitalists, however, had begun to change these conditions themselves. The government gradually responded by setting up labor standards and promoting legislation like the Health Insurance Law of 1926.

The twenties saw an expansion of trade and industry. Japan, led by the *zaibatsu*—the four diversified family conglomerates of Mitsui, Mitsubishi, Sumitomo, and Yasuda—attempted to gain a place in the world economy. Young university graduates were increasingly anxious to become engineers or businessmen, or to work perhaps for one of the big financial houses in Kabutochō, the four-block-square cluster of new office buildings in downtown Tokyo, which promised to be the Wall Street of Asia.

Motion pictures, vaudeville and baseball now joined *kabuki* and *sumo* as staples of popular entertainment. Parts of Tokyo and Osaka took on the look of European or American urban centers. Hollywood stars like Harold Lloyd and Charlie Chaplin became national idols, while so-called *moga* and *mobo,* "modern girls" and "modern boys," crowded Tokyo's few dance halls, doing the Charleston to imported jazz. A diverse and sophisticated generation of writers—men like Akutagawa Ryūnosuke and Tanizaki Jun'ichirō and women like Hayashi Fumiko—followed Mori Ōgai and Natsume Sōseki as leaders of a vigorous popular literature. A profusion of periodicals grew up beside the big national newspapers like *Asahi, Mainichi,* and *Yomiuri.* Almost every shade of public opinion was represented in a press that was largely free.

Japan was one of the founding members of the League of Nations and in the early days of the league played a constructive role in its proceedings. Its statesmen declared that even Japan's China policy must be based on the "Open Door" principle. On 1 January 1926, Foreign Minister Shidehara Kijūrō told the Diet that Japan should make no attempt to take responsibility for keeping order in China's eastern provinces. "Taking that course," he said, "we should forfeit our national honor and pride." A new wave of international thinking had emerged following Crown Prince Hirohito's visit to Europe—the first time a member of the Japanese imperial family had left the shores of his country. Hirohito seemed to aspire to become a constitutional monarch, reigning over a strong parliamentary government.

Japan's intelligentsia, which leaned to a local Marxist-influenced leftism, was highly vocal. Professors like Yoshino Sakuzō and Minobe Tatsukichi were trying to enlarge the democratic side of the Meiji Constitution. By the mid twenties, it seemed to many as if the hopes of the Meiji revolution's liberal reformers were bearing fruit.

Unfortunately there was another side to the Meiji Restoration. As they grew older, the young samurai who led this cultural revolution began to act like cautious bureaucrats. Without discarding the trappings of representative government, they stressed the principle that Itō Hirobumi had put in the Constitution—that it was a document *given* to the people by the emperor. Public officials thus thought of themselves as servants of the emperor, not of Japan's citizenry. Behind the political leaders in the Diet, a still Confucianist bureaucracy fought quietly but determinedly against the increase of popular freedoms, on the theory that only the officials knew what was good for the public.

There were other ominous forces gathering on the far right: a vast police organization, high-handed conservative capitalists, and above all, the officer corps of the Japanese army and navy. A countermovement toward authoritarianism, which a docile and largely agricultural population was only too prone to follow, gained ground. In 1925, the same year that Japan achieved universal male suffrage, the Peace Preservation Law was enacted. This law gave wide powers to the police to deal with cases—real or fancied—of sedition or civil disobedience. It drew widespread support from the "moral majority" of that time. Conservative people were shocked by the "immorality" of the new urban generation and disturbed by the talk of freethinking intellectuals. Many recalled the High Treason Trial of 1910, at which the prominent socialist (later turned anarchist) Kōtoku Shūsui had been sentenced to death with eleven others for attempting to assassinate Emperor Meiji, part of a disorganized but zealous attempt to destroy the established political system. Union activity brought reaction and ultimately repression as the economy sagged.

The recession of 1927 was followed by further economic troubles in 1929 and 1930, a reflection of faltering economies in Europe and the United States. A nation that lived on trade, Japan was tragically vulnerable to the coughs and sputterings of the world's economic system. The beginning of the thirties saw the country mired in a full-fledged depression. Rural poverty worsened. New and cautious leaders succeeded liberals like Hara and Katō. The so-called "Taishō Democracy," named after Emperor Taishō, Hirohito's father, who reigned between 1912 and 1926, began to splinter at the edges.

One element of the new conservative reaction was the formation of cliques of angry young officers, most of them sons of impoverished farm families, who resented the widening prosperity of the city people and hated the attempts of party politicians to keep Japan on the road to democracy.

Like some of their contemporaries in Germany, they were nationalist social-ists—anticapitalist and antidemocratic. Simplistically, they hoped to solve Japan's economic problems by military expansion. At home they began a campaign of propaganda and terror characterized by sporadic assassina-tions. Hara himself was stabbed to death by a right-wing fanatic in 1925. A series of military plots followed.

Now the dark side of the Meiji Restoration showed itself. Itō and his colleagues had consciously put the emperor at the center of Japan's polity. In a sense they had tried to replicate the limited democracy of Otto von Bismarck's Germany, where the Kaiser could replace prime ministers. But an appeal to popular reverence for imperial rule and Japanese tradition offered an easy cloak for the young officers' zealotry. A poor and restless countryside followed them.

On the night of 18 September 1931, a bomb exploded on the tracks of the South Manchuria Railway near Mukden in an area of China occupied by Japanese troops by long-standing agreement. Within two years, Japanese troops took over all of China's northern province of Manchuria, renamed by the Japanese "Manchukuo." The militarist thirties had begun. Cowed by political assassinations of the 1932 and 1936 "incidents,"* civilian politicians moved even further to the right.

The intellectuals who protested represented a wide political spectrum—from doctrinaire Marxists to liberals like Yanaihara Tadao. They were re-pressed by the swiftly growing police power. By contrast, the big Japanese capitalists quickly perceived in the Manchurian conquest a golden opportu-nity to acquire raw materials. In their view, the conquered territories were as essential to Japan as Britain's colonies, taken in similar fashion less than seventy-five years before, were to its own empire. The sound of drums and bugles took the minds of Japan's rank and file off their troubles.

As the thirties unfolded, a key flaw in the Meiji Constitution became apparent: The chiefs of the army and the navy were required to report only to the Emperor and not to any civilian authority. Yet in practice no cabinet could be formed without active-service generals and admirals as ministers of the army and navy. With this leverage, the military high command, in sympa-thy with the angry young officers, set out to turn back the tide of democracy.

Militarists of the Shōwa Restoration—so called after the official name of Hirohito's reign—strengthened their hold on the country with relative ease

---

*On 15 May 1932, a group of junior army and navy officers killed Prime Minister Inukai Tsuyoshi and other prominent political leaders. The so-called 26 February Inci-dent of 1936, another attempted military coup, resulted in the death of several cabinet ministers, but was finally suppressed by loyal troops, at the Emperor's direct order.

for the simple reason that they were bringing nothing alien to Japan. Democracy and parliamentary government were, after all, "alien" things based on principles understood only with effort by the average citizen. But the latent loyalties of Japan's web society—its cohesiveness and clan spirit—were readily exploited by the generals. What better model to inspire citizens than the advancing Imperial Army's soldiers who soon began to "banzai" their way across the China plains. Senior bureaucrats could only nod their agreement.

By the mid thirties, the rightists had almost totally infiltrated the Japanese school system. Boys and girls now learned the "samurai spirit" as thoroughly as Russian contemporaries were learning sacrifice in the name of Lenin and Stalin. Under the influence of the army, new school textbooks expounded on "The Greater East Asia Co-Prosperity Sphere." Rightist spokesmen revived the old Shintō religious theories of Japan's divine nationhood. The primary schools were not neglected. Seven year olds wearing their first dark school uniforms sat obediently in classrooms throughout the country learning the words of the popular children's song:

> Shoulder to shoulder with elder brother, I go to school today,
> Thanks to the soldiers, thanks to the soldiers
> Who fought for our country, for our country.

Primary school students were supposed to bow to the Emperor's photograph, the centerpiece of a shrine installed at the entrance to every Japanese school. Courses in history and ethics, based on the Imperial Rescript on Education, duly stressed loyalty to the Emperor as the highest good for a Japanese. School holidays—the Emperor's birthday, the anniversary of the first Emperor Jimmu, Army Anniversary Day, Navy Anniversary Day—were introduced by songs and lectures stressing the subjects' loyalty to the throne. After 1937, when Japanese troops swarmed into North China, aggressive militarism was ironically reinforced by international disapproval. The public was treated to a carefully crafted official version of heroic Japan fighting against enemies around the world. One of the first casualties of the now ascendant right was Japan's free press. A rightist mob had attacked the *Asahi* offices in 1936. Outspoken journalists faced harassment or arrest for criticizing the government. The military, exploiting the newfound war fever, cemented its hold on the entire country.

The letters about this period describe how Japan went down the road to war. There is an extraordinary quality of reflection in them. It is the note of people waking up from a terribly bad dream. Unfortunately for Japan and others in Asia, it wasn't a dream at all.

Reasons We Couldn't Oppose the War

There have been demands for explanations about why we didn't oppose the War, and I have been thinking of reasons why we didn't.

The people didn't doubt government policies. The people had been educated not to have any doubts about what governmental authorities did.

The people were not given accurate information. Using such tools as the Peace Preservation Law, information that was embarrassing to the military and the government was kept secret. Only information that had been altered to suit the convenience of the authorities was publicized.

We couldn't oppose the orders of the Emperor. The Emperor was a god. His existence transcended the nation-state. "Consider your superiors' orders as Our orders" were the Emperor's words. Orders from the military were considered by the general populace to be the same as orders from the Emperor. We couldn't oppose the War, not until the Emperor ordered the War to stop.

The people were easily flattered by a sense of superiority. War leaders always incite their people before they begin a war. Hitler used the propaganda of racial superiority to incite the German people. In Japan the people were incited by the claim that the oracle of the Founder of the Empire had pronounced Japan to be a divine land—the crown of the world—with an unbroken line of emperors. Because of its superiority, the Japanese race could participate in these imperial achievements. Both the German and Japanese people were flattered by this sense of superiority, and it made them lose their sense of justice. It caused them to feel that invasion of other countries and annihilation of other races were justified.

Leaders strongly stressed the dangers facing the nation. The flattered people were easily taken in by the theory the authorities advanced that the nation was in danger. Based on the inflammation of their narrow sense of nationalism, they even felt smugness in their role as the power advancing the war of aggression.

The sense of superiority fostered in the hearts of Japanese people through education and propaganda extolled war and promoted contempt for other nations and races, furthering the cause of war.

Kumai Masao, sixty-six
(male, hereafter "m"),
retired, Tokyo

What Experiences Led Us to War?

The War has left wounds, both physical and spiritual, which not even the passage of forty-one years has healed. We Japanese are also aggressors who caused more suffering to many peoples in Asia than we went through ourselves. What should we do specifically so as not to repeat war again? What should our attitudes be as we live our daily lives in order to avoid being unknowingly swept from our seemingly uneventful routine in this era of "peace and prosperity" by powers promoting war?

To avoid war, I would like to hear not only about wartime experiences, but also about details of prewar conditions. What was Japan's situation before the War? How did people live, and how did they get caught up in the events leading to the War? I think knowing about this in detail will train our eyes so that we can see through the skillful methods used by those who promote the cause of war. This will be the first step toward rejecting cooperation with a war effort.

For example, in prewar Japan there was a system of oppressive laws that included the Peace Preservation Law. It is said that there was no freedom of expression then, and people could not advocate antiwar opinions. But were these repressive measures thoroughly in place from the beginning, or did they gradually pressure people, so that by the time they noticed, it was too late to resist? I heard that a well-known scholar lamented that he had no idea, when it was first enacted, that the Peace Preservation Law would later become such a frightening law.

Aoyama Akihiro, twenty-five (m),
company employee, Tokyo

My Antiwar Struggle

In response to the request to know more about the situation before the War, I will tell the story of my struggle against the War. In mid 1931, I led the strike at the Asakusa Movie Theater and was detained for several weeks at the Kikuyabashi police station. On September 18 the Manchurian Incident occurred. On the twenty-seventh, before a large crowd of spectators, over three hundred movie theater workers dropped from the theater roof tens of thousands of handbills that read ... "Oppose worker firings and pay cuts, oppose the invasion of Manchuria—liberate Korea and Taiwan." We dared to wave red flags and hold an illegal demonstration, skirmishing with police troops. Nearly thirty of us were arrested.

On 1 September 1932, over two hundred workers and students assembled at the Ōmura Masujirō statue in Yasukuni Shrine and held a quick-step demonstration to the bottom of the Kudan hill, shouting slogans opposing the invasion of China. In addition, we planned an antiwar general strike by more than twenty thousand workers at large factories in Nagoya, such as Mitsubishi Aircraft, for 2 September. The strike was to protest the manufacture of arms for the invasion of China and to demand wage increases. However, over a hundred people were arrested by the Aichi Prefecture Special Higher Police. I barely escaped.

During my five years of opposition struggles, I became weak from insufficient food and repeated torture. After recuperating, I decided to bide my time and wait for the future. I focused all my energies on becoming an electrical welder. Even when I was arrested, I had kept my membership in an illegal political party a secret, and because I had not written a conversion declaration, I was kept under observation by the military police and the Special Higher Police until the day of Japan's surrender. From the third day after our marriage, my wife was strongly advised by the Special Higher Police to divorce me and return to her family.

On 13 August 1945, Captain Fukushima of the Shibuya military police came to my house to interrogate me. For the first time in several years, I became angry. "We're very close to unconditional surrender," I said. He pulled out his revolver. When I said, "The military police and the secret police in Nazi Germany have been arrested. Shoot me if you want," he put his revolver away and left.

I regret that I wasn't able to prevent the War. We must strengthen the peace movement so that Japan won't get caught up in a nuclear war between the United States and the Soviet Union.

Iwata Eiichi, eighty (m),
former Tokyo assemblyman, Tokyo

A Career Hurt Because of "Bad Ideology"

In March 1941, I was the head of the aeronautics section at Nagoya Technical School. One day, just before the entrance examination, Professor "A," the dean of students, came to my office and said, "Student 'G,' graduate of a middle school in Kobe, is applying for admission to your section, but I have received private communication from my friend, who is the head of that school, that we should be cautious because 'G' has some ideological faults." There was no further specific explanation about the fault of student "G." His grades were excellent, and there was no problem with his interview.

Therefore, with the cooperation of the other professors in my section, I stated at the admissions meeting that as far as our section was concerned, there was no reason not to admit him. My opinion, however, was not supported by the other members of the committee, and I was unable to admit "G."

I learned later that "G" entered the mechanics section at Hamamatsu Technical School the following year. When I checked with a professor in that department years later, I heard that he had graduated with excellent grades.

By the principal's indictment with the single term "bad ideology," a promising youth was hurt. This was one aspect of the tide in Japan on the eve of the Pacific War.

Yamada Haruo, eighty-one (m),
professor emeritus, Nagoya
Institute of Technology, Nagoya

If the Emperor Had at That Time ...

I interpret my generation's unwillingness to pursue the question of the Emperor's responsibility for the War as being due to our feeling that the Emperor's name was merely used. He was not the one who was truly responsible. When, at the beginning of the Sino-Japanese Incident, the Emperor expressed dissatisfaction that the government's localization policy, which limited military action, was not being implemented, the military reshuffled its leadership to smooth over the situation. After that, the situation worsened, as if rapidly rolling down a steep hill, and plunged into ruin. It could no longer be reversed by the Emperor's power alone.

Before then, in 1931, at the time of the Manchurian Incident, the Korean Division had crossed the border at the Yalu River on its own arbitrary decision to reinforce the Kwantung Army. If, at that time, the Emperor had exercised his prerogative of supreme command as the commander in chief, stating, "Movement of troops without my permission is mutiny," and had ordered the retreat of the division, the course of history might have been changed greatly. Since not one person at that time was likely to have foreseen the calamity of unconditional surrender, this suggestion is based on hindsight. But to me it is a disappointment.

Fukushima Tadashi, seventy-two (m), former teacher, Tokyo

The Eve of War

When I read this column on the War, I feel that the War is being talked about now for the first time. Although over forty years have passed, the contents of the letters are graphic and persuasive. Some people have taken up their pens feeling it is now necessary to discuss the truth. War stirs in people such an intensity of spirit. The multifaceted stories based on the experiences of the general public and of former military men are part of a valuable discussion on the War and reveal the true character of war.

I would like to see the theme "The Eve of the War" developed, to focus discussion on this as well. In his letter, Mr. Ōshima concludes by stating, "War is the greatest waste of money and human lives." Why, then, do people keep making wars? Wars do not occur suddenly one day, but rather are deliberately caused by human beings. What processes lead to the road toward war? I would like to hear about experiences in various fields, such as politics, economics, culture, education, and mass media, and about changes in the workplace and in local communities. It is too late to say, "By the time I noticed, I was holding a rifle on the battle-field."

The discussion about the War in these pages will, I think, contribute to Japan's peace by making our people intellectual heirs to their history.

Hiramoto Toshihiro, forty-two (m), civil servant, Atsugi

We Could Criticize in the Tokyo University Newspaper

In November 1937, the Japanese military invasion of north China was progressing, and an "acculturation policy" for China was intensifying day by day. At that time, I was an editor of the Tokyo University newspaper (a weekly). When I heard that a researcher at the Institute of Oriental Culture was participating in the planning of this "policy," I went to interview him. According to this researcher, the military and the Foreign Ministry had decided on policy directions in four areas: education, thought guidance, diagnosis and aid for medical ailments, and academic research. He said that policies had already been partially implemented.

What shocked me the most was the plan to teach the Japanese language to Chinese. He explained, "The plan calls for the thorough dissemination of Japanese. Japanese language courses will be offered from elementary school through university. We will instruct the northern Chinese masses in the Japanese language. We will train many Japanese language instructors and bring about the Japanization of the entire north China district. We will abolish the use of Chinese by Japanese residing in north China, in our push for complete Japanization." Was this not an attempt to introduce to China what had been done in Korea and Taiwan?

My article was published in detail. The next week the university newspaper's top story reported the responses of Tokyo University professors. Chancellor Nagayo stated, "We cannot threaten the lives of the Chinese people just to benefit Japan. We must attempt to raise the livelihood of the people in China." Professor Emeritus Nagaoka of the science faculty said, "What is needed is renewed recognition by Japan that these are Chinese citizens and it is their territory. We must take into full account the greatness of the Chinese people and the history of their contributions to world culture. It might be fine to have Chinese speak Japanese, but Japanese must speak modern Chinese as well. We should get rid of the study of classical Chinese literature and learn modern Chinese language."

At that time it was still possible to levy criticisms and advocate resistance to what was said to be military policy. But with calls for "recognizing the current circumstances" and "purging some elements from the school," liberal professors were gradually ousted or silenced. As the years went on, the "faction that recognized the current circumstances," like the researcher I interviewed, came to exercise great influence.

Hashimoto Masakuni, seventy-one
(m), self-employed, Tokyo

Children Who Had No Doubts About the War

This is what I remember happening in 1935, when I was in the third grade. There was an event at the municipal auditorium called "Judo and Boxing Match and Newsreels." The one-thousand-seat auditorium was choked with an overflow crowd. A Japanese black belt judo expert and an American wearing boxing gloves climbed onto the stage. The crowd, excited even before the match, cheered the judo man and booed the boxer.

During the match, the judo fighter threw the boxer, who retaliated by punching his opponent. Several gongs signaled rounds, and in the end the judo fighter won by using a neck squeeze. The crowd roared approval. The American boxer left dejectedly. Following this fight was a newsreel that showed scenes of fighting in Manchuria. When Japanese soldiers occupied enemy territory and hoisted the Rising Sun, the audience applauded loudly, rejoicing in the victory.

I thought it was a matter of course to go to war. I thought it would be a matter of course to defeat foreigners. That was how I was raised. From childhood, I never doubted that we would win the War or that I would become a soldier. This was how war-waging Japanese were created.

Furusawa Atsuo, sixty-two (m),
former union leader, Kitakyūshū

Japan Avoiding Self-Destruction

Japan is a country lacking in natural resources. In the prewar period, it relied to a large degree on the U.S. and Southeast Asia for oil and other resources. To curb Japan's incursion into China, the U.S. and Great Britain led other nations in the restriction of exports to Japan. They created a situation close to an economic blockade. No oil or materials entered Japan. With something called the ABCD (American, British, Chinese, Dutch) encirclement, they were said to be strengthening their military forces. If this situation were to have lasted for a long time, Japan would have been destroyed.

The U.S. and Great Britain were great world powers. If it turned into a full-fledged war on both sides, there was no way that we could win. The only tactic that might work was to launch a limited attack against them with all our might. Now—when most of their soldiers were engaged on the European battlefront—was thought to be the chance.

In order to ensure the safety of our country, it was essential to secure our interests on the Chinese mainland, including Manchukuo. To lose this security by compromising with the U.S. and Great Britain would be akin to handing them a power of attorney over our country's future. This kind of peace is not true peace. Forcing a decisive battle with the U.S. and Great Britain, protecting our nation's interests, and succeeding in increasing our influence in the area would lead to the beginning of the liberation of the Asian peoples.

This is what we were taught, and this is what we believed. I cannot forget the Socialist who exclaimed in his speech in the fall of 1946, "Japan's assertions regarding the War were correct."

> Iwanami Yasuo, sixty-three (m),
> farmer, Yamagata Prefecture

Uninvited Midnight Guests

Between the spring of 1941 and the end of 1943, I lived as a student on the second floor of a boardinghouse in Minato Ward in Tokyo. There we met with repeated late-night interrogations. The unwelcome authorities always paid their visits at one or two o'clock in the morning.

I woke up at the landlady's knock on my door. Her voice cried out, "Iwata-san, someone's here from the police, so wake up." Then she went around to other rooms. I sleepily got up and found two detectives at my door. One came around and stood behind me, while the other knelt on one knee and talked to me as he referred to his notebook.

"What school do you go to?" "What's your major?" "Your permanent residence?" "When did you come here?" They knew the answers but asked anyway.

"You already know those things."

"Don't complain, we'll ask you as much as we want to."

"Who's paying your tuition? You have it easy." The detective behind me was opening the closet and looking inside. Hidden in the bottom of my wicker trunk were books I had read when I was younger, like *The Flame of the Blast Furnace Is Darkened* and *In the Midst of the NAPF* [Nippon Artista Proleta Federacio] *Battle Zone,* but still I shuddered. They studied the titles of each of the books on my bookshelf.

"You're in the sciences, so I don't think you would have, but have you joined any groups lately?" Pulling out one book, they asked, "What is this book about?"

"It's an original text on organic chemistry."

"I can't tell, but you're sure about that? Sorry to have bothered you."

They left without even closing the door.

I turned off the light but was unable to sleep. From "S"'s half-basement room, I could hear loud voices and the sound of someone crying. He was a night student at a university in the Kanda district. As he cried, I could hear "S" saying, "You're making a fool of me just because I'm Korean."

The next morning, I heard from the landlady, "While they were questioning him, the detective suddenly got angry, overturned his bookshelf, and flipped through the pages of every book. He even opened up his trunk, and looked inside the picture frames. They didn't have to go that far. It's really frightening."

What I discovered after three or four of these raids was that the following day there would always be an official convoy through the area—a high-ranking official who rode through the main street surrounded by escort vehicles headed by a lead car.

Iwata Haruo, sixty-six (m),
retired, Mitaka

The General Public Favored War

Several letters have described people who criticized the military or made antiwar statements before and during the War. If the majority of the Japanese people had been opposed to the War, it would have been impossible, solely by police and military oppression, to mobilize the entire country to fight a war as total as that War was.

During the period of the Japanese incursion into China, before the War against the U.S., we—the general public—rather than being against war, were actually prowar. We supported and cooperated fully with the military and the government.

There seemed to be quite a few people who opposed the military and the government in the early period of the War. But these people were Communist Party members and some scholars, not members of the general public. Of course, we were not well-informed, but the reaction of the general public toward these dissenters was, "Those reds have done something else now. They're terrible to oppose the Emperor."

By the middle of the War there also were people who had personal doubts about the War or opposed the War. These were only a handful of university students and intellectuals. They suppressed their opinions more from the fear of being considered cowardly than from fear of the civil police and military police. The general public was in favor of the War by the time it began. We were brainwashed to idolize the strong Japanese military forces.

To prevent another war, we must investigate thoroughly why we were in favor of the War and why we supported the military. We then have to inform the general public of the results.

Fukushima Toshio, sixty-eight (m),
retired, Chiba

Let's Convey the Spirit of the Times

From the High Treason Incident in 1910 to the Yokohama Incident in 1942—particularly after the promulgation of the Peace Preservation Law in 1925—the denial of freedom of expression accelerated with the promotion of government-sanctioned ideology.* The country sped down the

---

*The anarchist Kōtoku Shūsui and twenty-three others were arrested for an assassination plot against Emperor Meiji in 1910. In the Yokohama Incident, senior staff members of the liberal journals *Chūō Kōron* and *Kaizō* were arrested on charges of being communist sympathizers.

road to War. I think it would be good—indeed we have the duty—to communicate the continually changing shades of the atmosphere of those times. As one method of doing this, I would like to advocate leaving a record of people's impressions of the world they knew in their childhood (what they were told by their parents and teachers, the sights of the towns, what they overheard adults saying—these are materials which we can use) and what they remember as the popular sayings and phrases of the times.

In my case, I remember that Manchuria and Mongolia were called the lifeline of Japan, and that the word *austerity* was very popular. I can't forget that we were forced to believe that Russia was a frightening country where the devil lived. In a single-minded effort to imbue children with patriotism, the shameful prejudice against peoples of other races became part of the education of the Japanese people.

War is by no means something that starts suddenly one day. Preparations for war are made slowly, patiently, carefully, and cleverly. When these preparations start taking on the shape of a system, they take on a life of their own and cannot be reversed. History teaches us countless lessons.

Kimura Takashi, sixty-five (m),
high school instructor, Chiryū

Please Untangle the Threads for Me

The War was an irredeemable evil. I had many personal sad experiences. Before I face death, which must come at some time, I want to ask how that War might have been prevented. A large number of underlying causes overlapped and intertwined in complex ways to cause that War. At each of those times, how might the people in our leadership have dealt with each event in a way that would have prevented the War? I know that it is useless to go over such things at this point, but I don't want to leave the threads tangled as they are. I want explanations that will untangle these threads by tracing them systematically.

This happened during my girlhood, at a time when I could only judge things based on information provided to me. Still, I thought it was inevitable that war would break out. I didn't even suspect that the process of war was evil. (1) The population was growing rapidly, and so was the impoverishment of the agricultural areas. In particular the crop damage from the cold weather in the northeast and the practice of selling into servitude and prostitution girls my own age caused me heartache. (2) The great powers of the world had many colonies far away from their own countries. (3) The harsh treatment of Japan, such as encirclement by the ABCD (American, British, Chinese, Dutch) alliance, incensed even a young girl's heart.

Everyone seemed to think that the only solution was to go to war. That was so pathetic. The few bright people who foresaw certain defeat were tortured and labeled traitors. That the desire to obtain an expanse of land to relieve the plight of poverty-stricken farmers would result in this.... As one who truly believed it to be a righteous war, I want to hear a clear explanation. How could that War have been prevented?

> Haneda Hiroko, sixty-seven
> (female, hereafter "f"),
> retired, Hachiōji

An Unfortunate Misjudgment

In prewar times, the Emperor selected the prime minister. Before issuing an imperial command to form a new cabinet, the Emperor questioned the elder statesman Prince Saionji. (After the prince's death in 1940, the Emperor questioned the Lord Keeper of the Privy Seal as to who should be the next prime minister.) As a trump card, Saionji recommended Prince Konoe. Konoe took up his post carrying the hopes of the people on his shoulders. Unfortunately, this was a mistake in judgment. According to *Prince Saionji and Politics,* Prince Konoe had "a severe weakness of character," "lacked perseverance," and "lacked consistency." Even Prince Saionji finally despaired of him, saying, "I thought Konoe had considerable vision, but it appears that he has no opinions of his own. This is most troubling."

Despite this, Prince Konoe became prime minister three times. During his first term, the Marco Polo Bridge Incident of 1937 occurred. The intended nonexpansionism ended up becoming a very deep penetration into the Chinese mainland, with no way out of this dilemma. During his second term, the Tripartite Pact [of 1940] was formed by Japan, Germany, and Italy. In his third term, the entire cabinet resigned in the face of the initiation of war against the U.S. and Great Britain. Konoe's policies were criticized. "What he does grudgingly is exceedingly irresponsible," it was said.

The other prime ministers were not very different. They took no definite stand against the Fascists who were acting against the Emperor's desires but were pulled along by them. (One example of this was their failure to stop the Japanese ambassadors to Germany and Italy, who were acting on their own to establish the military Tripartite Pact.) The indecisiveness common to all the cabinets can be said to have caused the destruction of the country.

In postwar Japan there are abuses that occur in the process of selecting the prime minister. But this is easier for the people to understand than the imperial-mandate method was, and it is better because the people are free to criticize the government now.

Yonemoto Hoichi, sixty-seven (m),
retired, Kumamoto Prefecture

The Night of 7 December

I was on fire-patrol duty from the evening of 7 December to the morning of 8 December 1941 for the block association of Akafune-chō in the Shiba district of Tokyo. The location of the present Nisshō Hall was then a vacant lot, and we had built a fire-patrol duty shack there. Usually the wide street leading from Kamiya-chō to Kasumigaseki had hardly any car traffic after 11 P.M., and no foot traffic in the middle of the night. On the night of the seventh, however, there were many cars around from evening on, and cars coming and going speedily even late at night. By 2 A.M. the automobile traffic became even heavier. After making our rounds, we returned to the shack and said to each other, "Something strange is going on tonight. So many cars. They're all fancy cars from embassies and ministries." "I hope it's not something bad happening."

When I returned home after my patrol duty, I heard on the radio that war had broken out with the U.S. and Great Britain.

Koizumi Kōtarō, sixty-nine (m),
translator, Tokyo

Militarism Fanned by Mass Media

Shortly after the outbreak of the Manchurian Incident, one newspaper company began a fund-raising campaign for donation of a warplane to the army. An admirable story about a primary school student saving his allowance to contribute to this cause fanned the donation fever of the people. The donated airplane was named the *Patriot*. A model of the *Patriot* was included as a supplement in an issue of *Boys' Club*. I was one of the boys who put together this model and absorbed military knowledge by reading the description.

When the war with China started, one newspaper company held a competition for military songs. The lyrics of the songs that won this competition—"Grasp the punishing rifle and sword" from "Song of the Advancing Troops," and "How can I die without performing a heroic deed?" and "Encouraged to return home dead" from "Encampment Song"—strongly influenced the actions of the Japanese military. These were in stark contrast to the Meiji Era military songs, such as "War Buddy" and "March in the Snow," which were about the sadness of war and the trials of the battlefield. Later, "The Rising Sun March" and "Song to Send Off Soldiers to the Front" also came out of competitions held by newspapers.

When we entered into the Greater East Asia War, words signifying conquest and victory became popular as names for newborns. This was also the effect of newspaper propaganda. I am pained when I see these words in the names of those who are now in their mid forties.

If the mass media, particularly the newspapers, hadn't allowed themselves to become tools of the military, we might not have had the tragedies of the atomic bombing of Hiroshima and Nagasaki, the major Tokyo air raids, and the invasion of Okinawa.

> Yoshida Akio, sixty-five (m),
> former Nippon Telegraph and
> Telephone Corporation employee,
> Ichikawa

Chapter 2

Life in the Military

Any good military must depend heavily on two elements: fighting spirit and discipline. Obviously, training and the handling of weapons play a vital role, but without high morale and discipline, even the best of modern technological armies will have troubles. In the course of indoctrinating recruits and keeping discipline, any army will risk provoking excesses of roughness, brutality or injustice, which often escalate into actions against civilians or prisoners in war zones. In World War II, despite the matrix of a democratic society, acts of brutality and cruelty were often committed by American military personnel. Such incidents may have been the exception, but they occurred in all wars from World War I to Vietnam. From its formation, however, brutality and cruelty were the rule rather than the exception in the Japanese army. It was the last primitive infantry army of modern times. Even through the final disastrous battles of World War II, Japan's "blood-and-guts" generals emphasized fighting spirit and devotion to the Emperor over technological mastery. They lost a war in the process.

In the thirties, the Japanese military managed to intensify the nation's perception of the glory of soldiery. Caught up in the wave of victories, real and apparent, in China and remembering the success of the Sino-Japanese War (1894–95) and Russo-Japanese War (1904–5), the Japanese public was swept up in a perpetual war fever. Recruits were given public send-offs by cheering families and high-ranking officials. Every family was taught that it was an honor to have a boy in the Imperial Army or Navy. Whatever one's private feelings, it paid in Japan, as always, for people to go along with the crowd.

When the recruits arrived at the regimental depot for their first training, however, all the fanfare disappeared. Probably the world's roughest corps of noncommissioned officers literally slapped and beat and kicked their charges into submission. Discipline was administered in the same way in the officer corps. It was not uncommon for a senior officer to slap a junior in front of the men. It was part of the toughening-up process—part of what it took to be a *gunjin*—a Japanese military man.

All the ancient glories of the samurai ethic were brought into play by what was fast becoming a huge national propaganda machine. Traditionally, the samurai was renowned above all for self sacrifice. "Be resolved that honor is heavier than a mountain," the old Imperial Rescript to the troops read, "and death is lighter than a feather." This was the sort of training that produced kamikaze pilots and "human bombs." Soldiers were taught that to be taken prisoner brought disgrace on them and their families. Other than dying in battle, suicide was regarded as the only honorable way to atone for defeat.

One cool fall day in 1938, Emperor Hirohito went to Yasukuni Shrine, the large Shintō establishment on the Kudan hill in Tokyo dedicated to those fallen in battle in Japan's wars. There, while the reedy voices of the priests recited the *norito,* the ritual prayers for the sanctified dead, families and relatives of the slain gathered in a worshipful attitude.

The English-language *Japan Times,* by then under government control, described the ceremonies as follows:

> Enshrined as *Kami* (demi-gods), [the soldiers] become deities to guard the Empire. They are no longer human. They have become pillars of the Empire. As they are enshrined at Yasukuni, they retain no rank or other distinction. Generals and privates alike, they are no longer counted as military men, but as so many "pillars." It is because they are the pillars of the nation that they are worshipped by the Emperor and the entire populace.

Behind such rituals was the conviction of the Japanese officer corps that all of their men had to be imbued with what they called *Nippon seishin,* "Japanese spirit." Troops with Japanese spirit, it was argued, could triumph where all others would fail. It is extraordinary how this view dominated the popular thinking of a whole nation for almost a quarter century.

Going into action, the Japanese soldier, the target of all this propaganda, resembled a kind of emotional pressure cooker. All the brutality and hurt he had experienced, it was felt, could be turned on the enemy. This, as much as anything, it would seem, resulted in the atrocities that Japanese soldiers, from the highest officers on down, visited on prisoners-of-war. Their kind of random, unthinking cruelty was epitomized for generations of Westerners by the brutalities of the Bataan Death March and the horrors of the Burma Railway. It was all "Japanese spirit" and all too often encouraged by Imperial Headquarters.

Undoubtedly, many Japanese submitted to this brutal militarism only unwillingly, but few protested. Minorities, whether dissenters or people who are otherwise "different," are rarely popular in Japanese society. In the hyped-up atmosphere of wartime they stood out even more sharply. Many soldiers, however—not only intellectuals—wrote diaries complaining of the treatment they had received. Such accounts of the horrors of military life were generally kept hidden, for by the mid-thirties, censorship was almost total.

There were of course officers who did their best to mitigate these horrors. They are gratefully remembered, as the letters here show. Beneath the carapace of militarism, human decency was not unknown in the Japanese army. But it was distinctly out of favor.

The conscription system was universal, and very efficient. Recruits were often called up twice or even three times for service in China and in World War II. The conditions in which they lived were almost indescribably bad. Still, some, at the distance of time, remembered kindly the camaraderie of *sen'yū* ("war comrades"), the friends that one made in battle. Others looked back with horror on their indoctrination and tried to drive it out of their minds—one reason reminiscences were so slow in coming.

By the end of the War, some Japanese began to describe these experiences. From starkly moving stories like Ōoka Shōhei's *Fires on the Plain* to the penetrating psychological studies of Yamamoto Shichihei, the horrors of the Japanese war machine were finally being brought to light.

But with the passage of time, a great deal of this was determinedly forgotten. Indeed, in recent years in Japan, there sometimes seems to be almost a nostalgia for the dimly remembered wartime past. Underlying this nostalgia, however, is a basic national revulsion. The War was a terribly bad thing, it is generally agreed, but the best one can do is to forget about it. It is here that the people who wrote these letters show their considerable courage. Reading their words, one realizes that for those who experienced life in the Japanese military, it was never really possible to forget.

We'll Die Tomorrow!

One day many soldiers marched past my home, which faced the road leading to Kashima Shrine. Their boots thudded on the pavement, I remember clearly that they raised their fists high in the air and shouted, "We'll die tomorrow, we'll die tomorrow!" I was still a young child unable to understand what this scene meant, so I asked someone standing near me, "What are those people doing?" A tearful voice answered, "They're going to crash their airplanes into American ships." These members of the "special attack" unit were on their way to say their last prayers at Kashima Shrine.

I heard much later that they were young, only seventeen or eighteen years old. When I found that out my heart was wrenched with emotion. Each time I see my own son, who is the same age as those young soldiers, I wonder if we are unwittingly marching toward a new prewar period. I feel it is important to speak out when we can.

Ōba Mitsuko, forty-seven (f),
housewife, Saitama Prefecture

A Good Place for Learning

In December 1943 I bade farewell to my father on his deathbed and entered the corps of engineers (Central Area Detachment No. 52) as a student soldier. I was never sent to the battlefield. When the War ended, I was in Shinjō.

The first thing we were trained in upon joining the military was swimming. A rope was tied around my body, and just like the cormorants in cormorant fishing, I was thrown into the river from a boat. When I lost consciousness from swallowing too much water, I was pulled up. Once I caught my breath, I would be thrown back into the water. My uniform froze.

During my first year, my head was beaten with green bamboo poles and my face slapped with leather slippers. This changed the shape of my face. I wonder what my parents would have felt had they seen me in this state.

It was a tough life, but not one of us died. This was probably because we were keyed up. I understood why Japanese soldiers were strong. In the military, there is no such thing as an impossibility—if one tries, one can do it. One is only unable to do something because one doesn't try or one doesn't have the will to do it. Life in the military was a hardship, but it was an invaluable place to learn perseverance and to experience with my own body that "if one tries, one can do it."

Itō Shinji, sixty-three (m),
former teacher, Gifu Prefecture

Just Wait Until We Get to the Battlefield

For forty-some years I've suffered from ringing in my ears. This is the aftereffect of severe beatings by higher-ranking privates when I was a draftee. It was the norm in the military that new recruits and draftees were beaten for no reason. The members of the military were ignorant and had lost their humanity. They thought that beatings were a form of education. The private who beat me was in charge of weapons. He was a disturbed person. When he began to beat a soldier, he became excited and continued the beating in a crazed way with no sense of when to stop. I hated that private from the bottom of my heart. I told myself, "Just wait until we get to the battlefield." In those days, draftees whispered among themselves, "Bullets come from behind on the battlefield."

Fortunately, I was released and did not have to seek my revenge on the battlefield. I still get chills down my spine when I think of what might have happened had I been sent to the front. Among those military men honored for a "heroic death" there are no doubt a number who were killed by bullets from behind, shot in hatred. The abnormal psychological conditions of war frequently evoked this kind of disgraceful conduct.

Watanabe Katsumi, seventy-three (m), retired, Ōita

Problematic Solo Plays by Commanders

Relying only on a map, the troop commander made us soldiers silently march without telling us our destination. At such times, local residents were dragged out of their houses and forced to guide us. When they were no longer useful, the commander took his pistol out of his holster and, without a word, shot them. Suspicious that our troop movements would be spied upon, the commander would not set the locals free alive. The life of human beings is fleeting. They keel over from a small bullet and their face drains of color. At the end, their skin quivers and that is it.

Officers were in the habit of bragging about the sabers they carried at their sides. These ranged from what they boasted were heirloom pieces to factory-made swords. Saying they wanted to test their swords, they would bring out a local man and have him dig the hole he would be buried in. He was made to sit in front of this, with his legs tucked under him. With a shout, the sword was brought down, and with a single stroke the seated man's body rose up and collapsed into the hole.

To test the power of hand grenades, the officers would go and grab a nearby man and thrust one against his stomach, after pulling the pin. As the man writhed in protest, the grenade would fall to the ground and explode—just seven seconds after the pin was pulled. The man's legs would scatter like clouds and disappear like mist; only his torso remained on the ground.

The enemy attacked a dozen or so of us who were on a mission to defend a bridge a kilometer ahead of our unit's main body. The metal helmets worn by enemy soldiers glittered in the light of the full moon. They were very close to us. The main body issued a shot into the sky to signal danger. The noncommissioned officer in charge of our unit became agitated about what to do when the moon set and it turned dark. He was wavering, thinking of fleeing. Then a soldier who was a fisherman from Cape Omae in Shizuoka Prefecture said, "The full moon doesn't set until morning. Calm down, calm down." From his own experience, he gave the officer encouragement. Spurred on by his words, I am still alive today.

In the fire fights on the front lines, both sides acted like fools. From my experience of being drafted three times—during the Manchurian Incident, the Sino-Japanese Incident, and the Greater East Asia War—I can accept this as human instinct. What I can't forgive are the individual acts of bad judgment by higher-level commanders, taken against those who were defenseless. This was the main reason why war disasters worsened.

Honma Genzō, seventy-seven (m),
farmer, Niigata Prefecture

A Political Offender Targeted by Veteran Soldiers

As a primary school teacher, he resisted militaristic education and supported antiwar pacifism. Arrested for the crime of violating the Peace Preservation Law, he was stripped of his right to active military service for a short period of time and deprived of his qualification to take the examination to become a military cadet. Five years later, he was thrown into the military again on active duty. The curious looks with which the senior soldiers and noncommissioned officers welcomed the new soldier, who was older and taller than they were, simultaneously turned into antagonism. He was obviously an intellectual. An easy target for their bullying had fallen into their midst. On top of that, he was a political offender and a "traitor." They must have decided that physical abuse, which was already partially condoned, would most likely meet with tacit approval from their officers. He had to endure their abuse day after day.

The abuse by veterans toward new recruits was termed "lessons." "Take off your glasses!" "Stand firm!" Then the clenched fists would strike full force on his face. The following morning's salty miso soup stung his lips. The beatings caused his back teeth to crumble.

Other weapons included indoor military shoes, custom-made with thirty-six tacks, clubs, and wooden rifles. Beatings were not the only "lessons." He was made to present arms in a half-erect posture, standing beneath his kit shelf. Having to bear the cross of being a special target, he was forced constantly to submit to two and three times the punishment given his fellow recruits. There were countless pretexts for inflicting violence. "You're moving too slow." "Your attitude is contemptuous." "I don't like the way you look at me." "Since it's your second time in active service, you're being too clever." And on and on. It didn't matter what the reason was.

"Stand one step apart!" All the new recruits were made to line up, and the club smacked their buttocks. After one round, the new soldiers were dismissed. As usual, he alone was left. The club again struck his buttocks. A second-year soldier wielded it as though he were crazed.

At that time, the troop was housed in tents at Lauheishan, near the eastern Sino-Soviet border. By the time the first-year soldiers were allowed to bathe, there was not enough filthy water left in the tub to reach their ankles. That was why the first-year soldiers hid from the senior soldiers to wash their bodies in the river and kill the lice in their thousand-stitch belts.*
"Hey, what happened to your ass?" a fellow soldier yelled. Seeing the reflection of his buttocks on the water's surface, he shuddered. His buttocks and the backs of his thighs were swollen and purple.

Several soldiers committed suicide. Several soldiers deserted. It was a border area, where the soldiers on guard duty carried rifles with live bullets. One night when he was on patrol duty, he put the barrel of the rifle into his mouth a number of times. But then, "This war will be over eventually," he told himself. He was determined to see the day when peace and democracy would come to his country. This desire would not permit him to die.

I was that soldier. It was 1938, still a long way from the end of the War.

Inanaga Hitoshi, seventy-four (m),
former junior high school teacher,
Sasebo

---

*A thousand-stitch belt was an undergarment painstakingly stitched by women on the home front, which soldiers superstitiously believed might ward off enemy bullets.

A Deserter Who Didn't Return

New recruits, we had entered the military with the intention of offering our lives to our nation. But when we found out that the military fed us only watery rice gruel, overworked us like beasts of burden, and beat us, our impulse to sacrifice ourselves faded. We felt like escaping. Realizing that our families would be called traitors if we did, we could only grit our teeth and bear it.

In this situation, one new recruit really did escape. There was nowhere he could go. Ordered to stop our work immediately and split up to search for him, I paired up with "A," who had entered the military at the same time I did, and we searched the tobacco field near where our 1942 Akatsuki Detachment was stationed on Shikoku. When "A" and I happened upon the deserter hiding among the tobacco leaves, he brandished his sword and wailed, "I beg you, let me die. That's the only way I can be saved now."

"Whether you live or die is up to you, but saving yourself by dying is a wasted death. It's much better to be shot once by the enemy!" I shouted at him, as I made "A" sheath the dagger he had drawn. In those times, when all of our lives were wrapped up in the War, death was close enough to everyday life. One needn't seek out suicide. There was an intense silence. We panted, our shoulders heaving.

Finally he said, "I'll think it over a while longer. So please don't capture me." With a sad face, he threw his sword down.

He needed to decide whether to desert, to commit suicide, or to return to our unit. "Come back soon," we said. "When the military police start searching in three days, you won't get off with just heavy imprisonment. We'll all be waiting for you."

His shoulders sagged and he looked down at his feet without saying a word as he wiped away a teardrop. My relief turned into joy and I was happy for a moment. I turned around and waved to him over and over as we walked away. But after three days he had still not returned.

Shimojō Tetsu, sixty-one (m),
freelance writer, Yokohama

Return Home Tomorrow

After being led by the foreman to the shrine in a corner of my workplace to pray for my well-being, I made some impressive parting remarks in front of all the workers assembled in the auditorium. I ended by saying, "Just like the cherry blossoms that are in full bloom right now, I will scatter my life for my country." Early the next morning under the large clock at Nagoya station, I was seen off by people from my workplace and by my relatives. I rode a special military train to Kanazawa to join the infantry. It was 2 April 1945.

At the physical examination, I was told by the military doctor to "go back home tomorrow." It was a surprise to me. I asked him, "Is there something wrong with me? It will be very embarrassing to return now." He responded, "This is an order." I was so shocked I thought my head would fly apart.

Two of us were ordered home. The train was to arrive in Nagoya at around 10 P.M., after dark. Thinking I could return home without being seen by anyone, I boarded the train. I was educated to think that someone who couldn't join the military was not a true Japanese man. Although at my draft physical I had received a second-class designation, I had gone to join up, happy that I was finally able to become a soldier. I was so mortified about being sent home, I thought that it would be better to commit suicide by jumping off the train. Over and over again, I stood on the rear deck of the passenger car trying to decide whether to jump.

Eventually I fell asleep, and woke up at Shizuoka station, way past Nagoya. I took the first train back the following morning and reached home at 8:30 A.M. As I entered the house wanting to cry, my mother said, "I'm so glad you're home." However, a fellow worker had seen me at Nagoya station on his way to work, and I was contacted to return to work at once. I was so embarrassed, I couldn't go out of the house for a week, and I hid in the closet when guests visited. After much urging from T-san at my workplace, I finally went back to work reluctantly.

Despite my poor health, I was able to continue working for forty years until my retirement in 1981. Each year at the time when the cherry trees bloom, I recall this incident. I also think about the influence of education and my late mother's strong motherly love.

> Nagaya Yoshio, sixty-one (m),
> former civil servant, Aichi
> Prefecture

A Farewell Visit From the Sky

In 1943 I was in the fifth grade in Sumoto on Awaji Island. This was the year when the Japanese forces were routed from Guadalcanal and annihilated at Attu. But the Japanese people were not told the truth. They still believed in victory.

When war conditions worsened, appeals to the people by the government and military became more and more hysterical. They inflamed feelings of hatred toward the enemy. The Americans and British were savages that "ate raw meat and had mouths dripping with blood." When Genghis Khan attacked from the north, Hōjō Tokimune had defeated him; Prime Minister Tōjō can triumph over the Americans and British attacking from the east.

This is what we were taught at school, and we were eager to beat the Americans and British.

One day we were told by the neighborhood association that Kawano-san's son was on his way to the front. He would be flying overhead, so we should go outside to wave at him in his airplane. On the day this was to happen, we went outside and waited for him, looking up at the sky. The *Hayabusa* fighter plane that flew toward Sumoto from Osaka Bay plunged down over our heads and then swept upward. This was repeated several times. I could see the pilot's face clearly as the plane skimmed the power lines. Some ten minutes later, seemingly reluctantly, the plane rose slowly into the sky and circled overhead several times. Dipping its wings to either side it flew away to Osaka Bay.

My young heart was excited at the thought that I might soon fight the enemy in a fighter plane like that. I wonder what the pilot thought as he looked down upon the familiar mountains and rivers and what heartrending sorrow his parents must have felt as they bade farewell to their son. I have not been able to remember this event without tears welling up—since I have come to understand the essence of war and the inner workings of human nature.

On his gravestone is carved, "Army Air Corps Captain Kawano Masaaki, deceased. Died on 28 October 1944, while on a mission to Tacloban, Leyte, Philippines; age 23." Next to this stands a gravestone inscribed "Navy Air Corps Lieutenant Kawano Hiroaki, deceased. Died on 12 April 1945, while on a mission to Southeast Asian islands as student conscript for special attack force, special promotion of two grades; age 23."

Kubota Hisajirō, fifty-five (m),
attorney, Yokohama

What I Have Kept in My Heart Until Now

In October 1942, while I was in the Number 62 Western Area Detachment in Matsuyama, I was ordered to receive the remains of some of our war dead. Along with about twenty of my fellow soldiers, I went to the port of Ujina in Hiroshima Prefecture to accept wooden boxes identified with the names of the South Seas war dead whose remains were placed inside. The condition of the remains told graphically of the situation at the front. The remains of those who had died in field hospitals distant from the front were white bones that had been carefully cremated; for the men near the front, the fragments of bones were blackened. Of the men closest to the front, probably because there was not sufficient time, all that remained were simple keepsakes such as their name seals.

One box held a tin can. Checking the inside of the can, I found it stuffed with a waxy substance surrounding something strange. When I looked closely, I saw that it was a little finger that had been cut off. Those of the men closest to the front were merely empty boxes.

Our problem was what to do about these empty boxes. When we thought of the feelings of the members of the dead soldier's family, we couldn't bear to hand them an empty box. After discussion, we concluded that since the soldiers had died together, praying over another soldier's remains should be the same thing. Unable to face the greater sadness of families with no remains inside the boxes and believing that the heroic war dead would rest in peace better, we decided to take a few fragments of remains from other boxes. All the while fearing that it was wrong to deceive the bereaved families, we divided the fragments of bones into different boxes, our hands trembling as we did this.

I have yet to determine whether what we did was right. It has remained a hurt inside me that will never ease. The soldiers who were with me at the time were annihilated in Okinawa. Their families received not one fragment of their remains.

Izumi Tōru, sixty-six (m), former
civil servant, Beppu

Instruction Book on Psychological Tactics

On 13 August 1945, just before the War ended, I went from Nagoya to the Department of Military Education in Tokyo's Ichigaya district. Shown to the warehouse, I was told to take any books that interested me. Inside the wooden building with its leaky roof there were piles of rain-soaked volumes, including military texts from various nations.

Browsing through these books, I came across a postcard-size volume on "tactics to stamp out antiwar feelings" put out by the military police headquarters. I was astounded at the cleverness of this instruction book on psychological tactics. Using its strategies of mob psychology, it would have been an easy task to drive the people of the entire nation to suicide. I was amazed that this volume, stamped with a series of numbers indicating that it was top secret, was mixed in with the other books. If I took it out with me, I would surely be sent to prison. So, in fear, I gave up the idea.

A religious group used exactly the same methods as those in this small volume to increase membership rapidly in postwar times. I heard that one of the leaders of this sect had been high up in the military police.

If someone who has this volume made it public, it would solve the puzzle of why, although they knew one hundred percent that the War was a lost cause, our citizens were driven so far.

Koizumi Kōtarō, sixty-nine (m),
translator, Tokyo

"Across the Sea" That My Father Sang

From the time my father became captain of the destroyer *Kamikaze* in 1936 until he died in battle on 18 December 1943, he lived as a dedicated destroyer sailor. There are those who say that aircraft and destroyers shouldered the burden of the navy's battles during the first half of the Pacific War, so my father was extremely busy. I was about ten years old at the time. I liked to stay close to my father when he relaxed at home during his occasional leaves. I would prepare the ink for him to use when he drew black-and-white paintings [*sumie*], and I would talk to him while he fussed over his Japanese orchids on the veranda.

One of these times my father was singing "Across the Sea" in a low voice. He sang a different melody from the one I had learned at school. It was more like a march and lighter, rather than solemn, but it sounded infinitely mournful. "Would you sing it again?" My father looked at me suspiciously but sang it for me again in a low voice.

The last line was "We will not die an ordinary death," not "We shall not look back," the phrase I had been taught. In later years I learned that "We will not die an ordinary death" was part of an imperial edict written by Emperor Shōmu [reigned 724–749] and "We shall not look back" was in a long poem in response to this edict by Ōtomo Yakamochi [d. 785].

I suspect that the version of "Across the Sea" that my father sang was the one sung in the navy.*

My father fought in the battle of Midway. He also fought offensive and defensive troop-ferrying battles at Guadalcanal before he became a "corpse soaking in the water" off the southern coast of Okinawa, along with his crew of 220 "swamp wind" sailors. Not one survived. The last word from the ship was a telegraphed message, "Discovered a surfaced submarine; ordering its attack." The American submarine *Grayback* was also sunk by the Japanese on 26 February 1944, so there is no way to find out what the scene of my father's last battle was like. I would dearly like to hear his "Across the Sea" one more time.

Toriizuka Noriko, fifty-four (f),
housewife, Koganei

---

*"Across the Sea" ("Umi Yukaba") was the anthem of the Japanese Navy. The verse went:

Across the sea, water-drenched corpses;
Across the mountains, grass-covered corpses.
We shall die by the side of our lord,
We shall not look back.

A Lieutenant Who Valued Prisoners' Human Rights

My parents' house was located near an army barracks. It was across the street from the present athletic stadium at Heiwadai in Fukuoka, in a district now called Ōtemon. Since the Meiji Era, the Twenty-fourth Infantry Regiment had been stationed there. Most recently the Western Area Detachment No. 46 was stationed at that location. It was known as a regiment undefeated through the Sino-Japanese and Russo-Japanese wars.

Originally my family were booksellers, but over the years we started selling all sorts of military goods as well. Along with the publicly available items, such as service bags, reservist notebooks, bags for valuables, identification tags, infantry drill books, and internal military order forms, and operational requisition forms, we also handled replacement parts for the smaller weapons that were needed by the regiment. The crack troops of the

46th Detachment were decimated as they fell victim to defeat: among them the Okabe Company in Guadalcanal, the Matsui Company in Yunnan, and a company attached to the Mutaguchi Corps in Imphal.

Lieutenant Shirabe Masaji left me with an incredibly vivid memory among those events. He was a Christian, a graduate of Dōshisha University who had been a military cadet. He was a pale-complexioned, calm and gentle man. My older sister, who was engaged to a navy officer, even said, "I wonder how such a gentle person can go to war."

I think it was in 1943 that my older sister and brother and I were chatting with Lieutenant Shirabe after he had finished buying something in our store. My brother must have been in the fourth year of middle school. I was in the second year.

At that time a special antitank artillery shell had been developed, which could instantaneously gas the soldiers inside a tank. A sergeant who had just returned from Manchuria told us about it. He said that they placed bound Chinese prisoners of war inside the tanks to test the effectiveness of this weapon. He bragged that now there was no way of losing to America. We were more curious about this new weapon than about the prisoners who were killed.

Lieutenant Shirabe was different. He said, "No matter how important the development of weapons is, it is unforgivable to use live people for experiments and kill them." That wasn't what an officer on active duty would normally say. If this comment had been heard by the military police, even his rank of lieutenant would not have protected him.

My sister protested, "Wouldn't it be impossible to win the war if the military behaved with compassion?" My brother added, "That's why Christians aren't effective." To this, Lieutenant Shirabe showed no anger. "No, regardless of whether one is a Christian or not, human life is invaluable," he argued. "We mustn't kill those who have put down their arms and are defenseless."

Later, Lieutenant Shirabe was posted to head the prisoner of war camp in Yamaguchi Prefecture. Father said, "With him as director, the prisoners there are fortunate."

After the War, many former military men were executed as class B and C war criminals for abusing prisoners. Whenever I heard these reports, I thought of Lieutenant Shirabe.

I want people to remember that there was a military officer who could take such a strong stand even during the War.

Hirose Isao, fifty-eight (m),
company executive, Suwa

For Me a Time of Shame

I was in the second class of a special officers' training course. Those of us who had enlisted as cadets in the military division at Tonoshō on Shōdo Island in the Inland Sea had done so because we were stirred by tales of the heroic exploits of young soldiers in the past. When we learned that we were to man the human torpedoes, called *Maru-rei* [zero] boats, we became alarmed. Graduates of the first class had died in the sea battles off the Philippines. A cadet who tried to desert was placed under military arrest. Another cadet, believing that staying alive was the primary concern, put in for a transfer to the communications corps and was attached to the information division in Nishinomiya. There he was trained to operate a sound-wave detector from a caisson protruding from the bottom of a ship. There seemed to be no way any of us would return alive.

The headquarters office, which consisted of those who had managed to avoid becoming human torpedoes, was overrun by toadying, opportunistic men who knew how to play the game. The cadets on weekly duty would hide their own piled-high trays of food and fight over the squad leader's leftovers. As soon as training exercises were completed, they would swarm like locusts around the squad leader and the assistant instructor to help take off their equipment and loosen their puttees.

The commanding officer entertained women in his office; I was punished at the company meeting for questioning one of his women when I was on night guard duty. The area outside the company barracks had been burned out by air raids and was full of hovels and starving people, but within the company quarters we saw the gluttony and untidiness of the superior officers and noncoms. Men on kitchen duty held sway. In such a state, the transformation of naive middle-school boys into cunning sycophants was no different from brutalization by superiors in broad daylight.

The first I heard of the reunion of this special squad, which was for me a time of shame, was in the letter from Mr. Kimura of Chiba. I wonder if those men still perceive that time in the same way as they did then? That would be adding shame to shame.

Segawa Futarō, sixty (m),
local newspaper reporter,
Kitakyūshū

"Yes, I'm Army General Yamashita"

The internal medicine ward I served in was severely damaged by the enemy's cumulative bombing so I was working at the reception office of the dental section of the Number 74 Supply Hospital. I had no time to look at the faces of the patients who stood at my desk. I asked if they were new patients or old patients. In the case of new patients, I noted down the unit they were attached to, branch of service, official rank, and name and gave out a patient number. For old patients, I looked up the record of their previous treatment using their patient numbers. When treatment was over, the officer in charge called out, "Number so-and-so, treatment completed." For example, if the lower left wisdom tooth had a cavity and was extracted, a voice would call out, "Lower left jaw, number eight, simple cavity extracted, mercurochrome applied." I would repeat this and quickly note it down. As soon as one patient left the chair, I would relay clearly the next patient's previous treatment and patient number. All the while, more patients kept coming.

Someone stood at my desk. I asked whether he was a new or old patient. "Yes, I'm a new patient," came his languid response. I fired off further questions, "Your company, rank, name?" "Yes, I'm Yamashita." In my loudest voice I said, "I can't tell from just Yamashita. State your rank and name." "Yes, it's Army General Yamashita Tomoyuki." At that instant Lieutenant Nakamura's voice crying "Attention!" rang out over the entire room. I had jumped up as soon as I'd heard the first syllable of *general.* "Please excuse my ignorance, sir."

"No, no, stay as you were."

I broke out in a cold sweat as soon as His Excellency had left. When the patient load lessened, Lieutenant Nakamura teased me, saying, "Hey, Ino, you've really done it now. This will mean a demotion or heavy imprisonment for you."

The next day, I was extremely alert. At about 10 A.M., the general's aide arrived ahead of His Excellency—unlike on the previous day—and placed a large cardboard box in front of me. "Thank you for your hard work. His Excellency purchased this with his own money from a store in town. Please accept it." The general came to my desk. As I tried to stand up, he raised his hand to restrain me. "No, no, thank you for your hard work. You carry out your duties just as seriously as my officers and soldiers who charge into enemy troops with swords drawn." I felt his words sink deep into my soul.

Ino Masamichi, sixty-eight (m),
medical technician, Ibaraki
Prefecture

Brutality and Dandruff Rice

I had completed my duties as a nurse in sick bay and was on my way to my sleeping quarters when I heard a loud voice issuing from the first-year soldiers' barracks. I peeked inside.

"I am punishing you to set an example for all first-year soldiers," a man who seemed to be the squad leader said, calling out a soldier's name. "Stand with legs apart, mouth shut tight." The instant he said this, he slapped the soldier across both cheeks several dozen times. The soldier's body swayed back and forth. It was all he could do to withstand the blows. "Next, do 'the bush warbler crossing the valley,' ten times." The soldier had to slide under and jump over the first-year soldiers' beds, stopping at times to warble, "*Hō-ho-ke-kyo.*"

When that was over, "Go on to the next thing. You know what that is." The soldier, panting and out of breath, replied, "Yes sir," and went over to the rack where the rifles used in training were lined up in order. Pretending this was the latticework on windows in the pleasure quarter, he reached out from between the rifles and called out, "Say, soldier, why don't you come inside?" His voice was soft, due to embarrassment. The squad leader shouted, "Your voice is too low. Say it louder so everyone can hear."

I was so shocked that I stopped breathing for a moment. I left the spot quietly and returned to my quarters. I wept in my bed at the cruel methods of the officer.

The next morning I saw the first-year soldier, who was on kitchen duty, intently scratching his head so that his dandruff flakes would land in the miso soup and rice on the tray. Offering them "dandruff rice" seemed to be the customary way to even the score with the commanding officer and the squad leaders. The night of our surrender, I witnessed many soldiers beating up several of the mean-spirited officers, who were screaming, "Forgive me, forgive me!" This scene was also so fierce that I wanted to cover my eyes.

> Fukuda Michi, sixty (f), former
> nurse at Utsunomiya Number 1
> Army Hospital, Tochigi Prefecture

He Who Was Placed in the Psychiatric Ward

It was at the height of the heat in September 1944. Forty of us recruits recently drafted into the air corps were receiving intense training in Mie Prefecture, day after day, from a tough old soldier who was from that area. I remember being outside in the morning's glaring sun.

For one of the daily training exercises, each of us had to recite in front of the group a passage of the Imperial Rescript to Soldiers and Sailors. The turn came around to "O," a diminutive art school student. He seemed to have forgotten the words and got stuck. The older soldier rushed over to him, his face red, and, yelling "You're slack!" knocked him to the ground. "O" was unable to get up. He was carried to the hospital.

I was sidelined by pleurisy and also had to be hospitalized in the army hospital. "O" and I got along, and during rest periods we'd exchange words in a friendly way about his family in Hongō and other topics.

One day I asked one of the medics about his whereabouts. A few days later, a medic I didn't recognize came and told me, "'O' wants to see you, so come with me." I followed him.

I could see iron bars deep in the recesses of another ward. I was surprised to see that "O" had been placed in a private room in the psychiatric ward. It was painful to see how his appearance had changed. He talked to me with a vacant look.

"Japan can't win over America. I hate the War. All I want to do now is to paint."

Hearing this, I mistrusted my own ears. This was because I had been forced to believe that there was absolutely no way that Japan could lose. "O" was the only son of an artist.

> Komuro Kaoru, sixty-three (m),
> former civil servant,
> Higashi Yamoto

I Hit Reserve Soldiers

My fellow soldiers used to tell me, "Even if there was a day when the crows didn't cry, there wasn't a day when Kumai wasn't beaten." I still don't have any hearing in my left ear. It was no wonder that when I, of all people, became a private first class at the front, the older soldiers all raised their voices in dissatisfaction. The following year I became private first class in charge of the education of reserve soldiers. At that time, I vowed to myself that I would not hit them, nor would I let them steal. I knew the ineffectiveness of education-by-beating when one has no knowledge of when, where, or why one is being beaten.

In the military, stealing is called "obtaining the supplies required" and is praised. There is no way of replenishing items in the military other than by stealing. Yet I told my men, "Don't ever steal." On the day we were returning from billeting exercises, one soldier reported, "I'm missing the shoes I wear inside the barracks." I took this soldier with me to look at the shoes gathered by each unit and found his name on a pair of shoes in the unit next to ours.

"Who stole these? Come out and honestly admit it. If no one comes forward, I'm going to hit all of you with these shoes." No one came forward. Praying that someone would stop me, I began to hit the men with the shoes. Finally, to my relief, the private first class of that unit asked me to stop. I had tried to rebel against the method of learning how to shrewdly use the ropes taught by that unit's soldier in charge of education, as well as the method of education-by-beating of the military itself. I was venting my revulsion toward these methods on these reserve soldiers. This wretched memory of military life will probably never leave me.

> Kumai Masao, sixty-seven (m),
> former private first class, Tokyo

Request for Draft Deferment: My Case

I was in charge of testing and adjusting secret weapons at a munitions factory connected to the navy. My superior had assured me, saying, "I've requested that your conscription be deferred because you have specialized skills. No matter where you work, it's for the country." I received my "red paper" draft notice, however, early in June 1943, and I was notified to report for duty on 15 June. "There must be some mistake. I'll resubmit my request right away, so you should be able to return home the next day. You'd better go without telling your block association," my superior told me. So I went.

Upon joining our unit, we had to undergo a physical examination and a personal background investigation. We were to note if we had suffered from any illness recently, had special family situations that might cause hardship, or were needed at our place of work. I was young, excited, and unwilling to be sent back, so I submitted my form without entering anything. A week later, leaving behind just a few soldiers who were inducted at the same time, we were sent to Manchuria. I joined the Soviet-Manchuria border patrol forces.

About a month later, I was called in by the sergeant in charge of personnel and scolded soundly. The request from my factory had come through from my base unit. He said, "Why didn't you say anything during the personal background investigation? This is a battle zone, and we need our full complement of soldiers. If I let you go back, your war buddies will have to bear a heavier burden." It was decided that I would be sent back along with the next group of soldiers to be discharged, but war conditions worsened and there was no demobilization. So I remained with the unit.

In July 1944, our main force was dispatched south to the Philippines along with an army division. Just before then, it was decided that those of us in the heavy-weapons company were to remain, and I was reassigned to a new unit. During this confusing time, another deferment request seemed to have come from my superior. I heard at my factory after I returned from the War that it had been returned as "Current post unknown due to southern movement of that unit." My easygoing attitude ended up causing trouble in various ways.

Seki Senzō, sixty-seven (m),
business owner, Kawasaki

A Suicide Barely Avoided

I joined an antiaircraft artillery unit in Tokyo in January of the year before the surrender. We received intense training at the Yoyogi drill field. One day, after drill exercises that trained us for attack by crawling on our hands and knees in the rain, we were ordered to have rifle inspection. I hadn't noticed until then that the firing pin on my rifle had broken off. Since joining the military, we had been admonished that "the chrysanthemum crest etched in your rifle signifies that it is a gracious gift from the Emperor. Treat it with greater value than your life." There was a heavy punishment for damaging a rifle. Imprisonment was certain. Such a punishment would be noted on the "awards and punishments" line of one's military record. It would not be wiped out for the rest of one's life.

I felt my blood freeze. In a daze, I staggered toward the tracks of the Yamanote line, which ran next to the field, I attempted to climb over the fence. It was then that I heard the order to assemble. I came to myself with a start and fell in. If the order had come a little later, I would have surely thrown myself onto the path of the oncoming train.

The commanding officer asked if there were any problems. I frantically rushed to the front of the line. "I'm very sorry, sir, but I broke my firing pin." Caught off guard, the commanding officer only told me, "Come see me later." When the group returned, I went directly to the commanding officer's office. "It's good that you admitted this honestly. Leave it to me," he said. That was the end of the incident.

Fortunately, I narrowly escaped suicide. It pains me even now to think that there were many soldiers who lost their lives under similar circumstances.

Ikeda Renji, sixty-seven (m),
former high school teacher,
Matsumoto

Special Attack Force Members Who Came to Bathe

I was never more angered than when I read in a letter the words of the air squadron commander of the Heroic Volunteer Air Corps: "Following in the tradition of the *seppuku* of the Forty-seven *Rōnin* of Akō,* I have given you

---

*The famous Forty-seven *Rōnin* [masterless samurai] gained everlasting fame in Japan by killing the persecutor of their master, the *daimyo* of Akō, in 1703, then committing ritual suicide (*seppuku* or *hara-kiri*) to atone for their actions.

a chance to die an honorable death." To think that those brilliant youths were buried with this meager phrase.

In April 1944, when defeat seemed imminent, the public bath that my father operated was forced to remain closed day after day because of fuel shortages. In compliance with military demands, it became a bath exclusively for soldiers, who brought their own fuel. Among the several hundred soldiers was a group of a dozen or so young men with especially muscular bodies. After their bath, they would step into our living area and spend some time playing *shōgi* [Japanese chess] and *go,* teaching me, a middle-school student at the time, *kendō* [Japanese fencing], or sitting my younger brother and sister on their knees to tell them stories. Then they would leave, saying, "We're off to night training."

I think it was 24 May. They were outfitted not in their usual shabby clothes but in military uniforms with the hilts of their swords wrapped in bright white, and they looked very dignified. This was the first time that they told my parents they were members of the special attack force known as the Heroic Volunteer Air Corps. They thanked my parents for their kindness and gave them the large sum of 100 yen, saying, "We who are going to die don't need money. Please use this to hold memorial services for us." My parents were dumbfounded when they requested of my mother, "Please burn some incense in our memory." They raised their hands in military salute and quietly departed.

When the War ended, as she had promised them, my mother ordered a statue of Kannon [goddess of mercy] from a stonemason and recited sutras in the soldiers' memory every day. On the base of the statue of Kannon was the inscription, "Offered to the Valiant Souls of the One Hundred Thirteen Members of the Heroic Volunteer Air Corps' Okuyama Troop." My mother died of illness in 1979. Since then my wife has prayed for their souls.

If they had survived, they would have no doubt been leaders in various fields in postwar times. When I think of this, it seems to me that it is the wily ninety-five-year-old former air corps commander who should have immediately committed *seppuku.* The names of the brave youths that remain in my memory are Sergeant Major Tanikawa from Miyazaki Prefecture, Corporal Nakagawa of Gobō, and Corporals Kawasaki and Arama.

Tsutsumi Kenzō, fifty-eight (m),
public bath operator, Kumamoto

Boy Soldiers Allowed to See Their Parents

The Number 13 coast defense ship attached to the Number 1 marine security squad docked for refueling at Funakawa Port, Akita Prefecture, on 5 August near the end of the War, while it was on maneuvers to escort a convoy of ships in the Japan Sea. Due to the special kindness shown by the captain, three boy soldiers whose families lived in the area were granted bathing and shore leave and spent the night away. The next morning we all became anxious, as one of them had not returned to the ship at cast-off time. Then from far off in the bay a motorized sailing boat filled with well-wishers waving flags approached at full speed, with banners raised. Among them were the red-faced soldier and his parents. The entire ship welcomed him aboard with thunderous applause. We immediately left port. We were deeply moved by the warmheartedness of the captain, who turned the joy of the young soldiers at seeing their parents into happiness for the entire crew.

This captain had always instructed us, "In case all crew members must abandon ship at sea, use anything that floats to help maintain life and prevent fatigue. Each wooden case for a dozen large bottles of sake has enough buoyancy to withstand two or three men hanging on to it in the sea." He also instructed us to keep logs tied up in various places on deck, to be used in the event of the ship sinking from a torpedo attack. On 14 August, the day before the War ended, our ship was sunk in a torpedo attack by an American submarine off Kasumi town in Hyōgo Prefecture. Because of those preparations, almost all of the crewmen, including a nonswimmer like me, were saved. Captain Mizusawa of our ship is still living in Fuchū City in Tokyo.

Taguchi Tetsuji, sixty-four (m),
company employee, Yokosuka

The "Cherry Blossom" Human Bombs

I have not been able to forget the human bombs we called "cherry blossoms" [*ōka*]. From about April 1945, when American troops landed on the main island of Okinawa, we could see the low-level flights of special attack units heading toward Okinawa nearly every day. In mid-April, one of our large planes, pursued by several Grumman fighter planes, crashed into the sea north of Okinoerabujima. The five wounded men who were rescued (one died shortly thereafter) were crew members of one of the eleven planes of the navy's special Shinrai attack unit which had taken off from Kanaya air base. The first time I knew about the cherry blossom human bombs was after they had been picked up, when I heard the senior member of the crew, whose wounds were light, report the circumstances at the base. He stated that the "cherry blossom," piloted by a navy lieutenant junior grade, had been released from the main plane and had slammed into an enemy ship less than a minute later.

My job was nursing the wounded. After I met these human bombs and became aware of their sense of mission, I felt awe and had a deeper understanding of the severity of war than I had ever had before. By that time, air supremacy over the southwestern islands had been attained by American forces. During the day there was a large number of U.S. bombers flying northward. Even in the evening and the early morning, it was nearly impossible to break through their heavily patrolled defense cordon. Despite this, youths of about twenty, with futures full of promise, fought in special attack units. Their lives were scattered over the water's surface as if they were rice hulls.

Suematsu Toshio, sixty-four (m),
retired, Ōita

The Waste of the Aircraft Carrier *Shinano*

By the end of 1944, severely damaged naval vessels were arriving one after another at the docks of the naval arsenal in Yokosuka. Those iron warships had such large holes in their sides that it was as if they had been made of tin. They were so splintered it was a wonder they had made it back to Japan. Sometimes we would find the body of a sailor caught behind a shattered wall of steel.

In the cities, most people believed that Japan's combined fleet was intact. At the arsenal's shipbuilding section, however, we received orders from fleet headquarters on almost a daily basis to incinerate entire sets of plans for warships that had been sunk.

The keel was laid for the aircraft carrier *Shinano*—a Yamato-class battleship with a displacement of 72,000 tons—in May 1940 at dock Number 6 of the Yokosuka arsenal. Plans were changed during production to turn it into an aircraft carrier, and it was referred to as a "Number-110" warship under secret military classification. The *Shinano* was launched on 5 October 1944, and had its official trial run on 11 November. On 28 November, it left the port to sail to its home port, Kure. On the next day, the twenty-ninth, four torpedoes from a U.S. submarine off Shionomisaki ended its short life.

I had been one of the workers on board during the *Shinano*'s official trial cruise around Tokyo Bay. When I stood at the stern on the paved flight deck, the people standing at the bow looked as small as peas. I remember crying out in admiration. On the starboard side, toward the middle, the bridge towered up, and to its right soared a huge funnel. Heavy revolving artillery surrounded the flight deck like porcupine quills. The *Shinano* was the greatest aircraft carrier in the world.

This ship took an enormous bite out of the national budget, and dockworkers toiled incessantly round the clock to complete it. Less than two months after its launching, and without engaging in a single battle, it was swallowed up by the sea, taking over 1,430 victims down with it. War is the greatest waste of human lives and money.

Ōshima Morinari, sixty-one (m),
former civil servant, Tokyo

I Was Labeled a "Bad Soldier"

I was marked as a "bad soldier." It seems that a detailed record of each soldier's family and his preenlistment background and activities follows him around. Several years before I was drafted, I participated in some cultural activities which were still going on, though in a diminished state, after the destruction of the leftist movement in the greater Tokyo region. As a sympathizer and member of this movement, I was detained. Perhaps because this was close to the time I was to be drafted, I was released and told to get retrained in the military. One of my friends died in prison.

After entering the army, I gradually realized that I was being discriminated against. I remained a private second class while soldiers who entered the detachment at the same time I did were promoted, even though they had been taken off duty because they were hospitalized. I carried out my duties adequately and fought in many battles, but I was not promoted. When I reported as "Army Private Second Class Kagawa," the warrant officer in charge of personnel feigned surprise, saying, "Oh? You're still a private?" My group leader felt sorry for me and finally put in for my promotion to private first class, but his repeated requests came to nothing. Instead, I was awarded stripes for diligence.

The discrimination was not confined to promotion. My duties consisted almost entirely of extremely dangerous assignments in watchtowers with three or four other men, guarding barracks or railroads. We were occasionally attacked, and I was almost killed. In the end I was shunted off to a special unit with no name. We all had long hair and soft caps, and our uniforms were just like those of Chinese soldiers. It was a small company that went into enemy territory in disguise, without using Japanese, in an attempt to work on destroying the enemy organization from within. Many died during this operation. The unit consisted of problem soldiers from various companies. As a result we all felt a strong sense of kinship.

It was First Lieutenant Kugimiya who commanded our motley company. It is not meant as flattery when I say that he was a good commanding officer. He considered himself to be the eternal platoon leader and protected us, saying, "What do they mean by discriminating, when dying is all the same?" I was willing to die as long as I could do it in the service of this commanding officer. First Lieutenant Kugimiya is the one who told me about my "preenlistment record." But he patted me on the back and told me not to worry about it.

On the day of Japan's surrender, I cheered that I had been right, and I was hit by an officer. I hit him back.

> Kagawa Haruyoshi, sixty-three
> (m), former company employee,
> Chiba

On the Banks of the Isuzu River

In the spring of 1945, a special company, not directly related to the war effort, was organized. This was the Ise Guards Troop, formed from selected infantrymen of the Konoye [Imperial Guard] Division. As the name suggested, members of this unit were to guard the Ise Shrine. They say that there was a unit of the same name during the Russo-Japanese War. Company members displayed the symbol of the sacred mirror on their chests. [The three imperial treasures enshrined in Shintō myth were the mirror, jewel, and sword.]

The Number 1 Company, arriving in Ujiyamada (the present Ise) on 15 April, was put in charge of the security of the outer shrine while the Number 2 and Number 3 companies protected the inner shrine.

My company, Number 3 Company (Hosoda Company), was housed at an inn on the banks of the Isuzu River. The first platoon stood at key religious spots, guarding the inner shrine. The second platoon was held in reserve and dispatched to various smaller shrines each time a siren sounded. The third platoon was posted as the antiaircraft control unit on Mount Kamiji. We rotated duties with the Number 2 Company (Hoshino Company).

Military security guards were stationed separately from the specialized shrine patrol. At times we stepped inside the prohibited sacred fence in our military boots. Of the three sacred treasures, the mirror had already been placed in an underground imperial treasure storehouse. Preparations had been taken so that if necessary, the main hall of the shrine could be collapsed by pulling on thick ropes and using ladders on its roof. In the 28 July air raid, all the material placed in readiness for the rebuilding of the inner shrine in four years* was burned, and much of the surrounding town of Yamada was razed. But not one bomb fell on the inner shrine.

On 15 August, sweat stained my uniform. Once we realized that the War had ended, we threw down our type-99 rifles and sank to the ground. The kamikaze [divine wind] had not blown. Yet we could say that a heavenly wind with a different meaning blew that 15 August.

> Anzai Masaru, sixty-two (m),
> high school teacher, Yokohama

---

*Every twenty years the buildings of the Ise Grand Shrine are reerected on an adjacent site.

Machine Gun's Wooden Barrel

Until 1944 I worked as a lacquerware technician at the Gifu Prefecture crafts training center in Takayama. Toward the end of the War, it became difficult to continue making crafts due to the lack of materials such as lacquer. As difficulties mounted, the military ordered us to do various types of experimental research. One such project was production of a gun barrel for machine guns that were to be attached to the wings of airplanes. The section embedded in the wing would be metal, but we were to make the protruding part from a material that would be undetectable to radar. It was explained to us that the body of the aircraft was covered in special paint that radar would not pick up. We made many experimental models of shafts from wood layers stuck together and strengthened by hardened lacquer, and then we tested their capability to withstand the shock of firing. Although no one voiced his opinion, I doubt that any of us thought we would succeed. I heard later that these models tore apart after a few rounds.

It is frightening that war leaders who thought up things that were even more absurd than bamboo spears and paper balloon bombs held in their hands the fate of the nation. At that time, however, we couldn't even voice our sadness at not being able to sustain hope. In reality, almost everyone had to follow orders no matter how skeptical they might have been.

> Iwajima Shūichi, sixty-eight (m),
> craft artist, Gifu Prefecture

"Prince Yamatotakeru" Operation

"The company commander is asking for you," the commanding officer's aide informed me. I was on the clerical staff, and I stopped work immediately and went to the commanding officer's room.

"Private Nakamuta, we've got a big plan."

"What big plan?" I asked, surprised. What he said next shocked me thoroughly.

We were in a small town in Miyazaki Prefecture, where the landing of American troops was thought to be inevitable.

"Listen carefully, now," he began. And this was what the company commander told me. "I want you to find some veteran soldiers in the company who would look believable dressed as women and form them into a shock unit. When the fighting with the American troops begins, our men, dressed as women, will approach the enemy officers' camp, surrender as prisoners, and use hand grenades to blow themselves up along with the enemy."

He said that I had been chosen to be one of this special Prince Yamatotakeru troop.

I replied, "You must be joking. As the company commander knows, I fought for four and a half years with the army in China. This is the second time I've been called up, and this time I've made my own resolution about my end. You've been particularly kind to me since I entered this company, sir. But if I am to die, I would like to die a soldier's death at the company commander's side. I don't want to die dressed up as a woman. I respectfully refuse."

"That's what I thought you'd say. I didn't think this operation was such a great idea myself," the company commander, in civilian life a middle-aged banker, responded calmly to my refusal.

About two weeks before this talk, our regiment had put on a performance in the village square and had invited the local residents, to thank them for billeting our soldiers in their houses in the defense zone. Before the War, I was a newspaper reporter interested in drama and film. I had written a script for the performance and gathered an ensemble together to perform a historical play about the wandering life of gamblers. I played the part of a woman.

During the performance, I could see from onstage that the audience thought I was a professional actress. Our play was a great success. We received thunderous applause, and even the Commander in Chief's Award. This seemed to be the origin of the division leader's idea to form a "female" shock troop. As the proverb says, "Poverty dulls the wits." Such was the state of the Imperial Army a month and a half before the end of the War.

> Nakamuta Katsūsaburō,
> seventy-two (m), retired,
> Tsukushino

264 Blows

Until the end, my military life was filled with training and beatings. Training began as soon as the reveille sounded. The senior soldiers would stand in wait at the entrance to the peak-roofed barracks with bamboo swords at the ready. The bamboo swords were used on those who were tardy. After roll call and the completion of our fatigue duties, we returned to our barracks. Sometimes we found that an "earthquake" had occurred, and our blankets and neatly folded clothes were strewn all over. On these mornings, we had to go off to training without time to eat even half our breakfast.

As the days passed, we found out what the internal situation was like. We learned that the senior soldiers were gods. These senior soldiers had time on their hands. Some of the disciplinary actions were actually intended to educate the new recruits, but we were also punished according to the senior soldiers' whims, because it was a way for them to while away the time. Before inflicting punishment, they always said they were indoctrinating us with the military man's spirit. We were made to form a single line and stand at attention and then ordered to clench our teeth. Then they hit us with their fists. This was better than the occasions when they struck us with the leather straps of their swords or with their leather indoor shoes. At the limit of the human body's endurance, greasy sweat pouring from my forehead, I nearly fainted in agony.

Some forms of punishment degrade human nature. The senior soldiers looked on, laughing. They justified it by saying we should consider it an act of kindness. I asked myself about the meaning of this groundless punishment. The military is an organization created to fight wars. In a war, it matters only whether you kill the enemy or the enemy kills you. In a normal state, people cannot kill others. This method of inflicting brutal punishment without any cause and destroying our power to think was a way of transforming us into men who would carry out our superiors' orders as a reflex action. The number of blows I received, which I vowed I would never forget, was 264.

Sakata Tsuyoshi, sixty-two (m), retired, Gōtsu

Feelings of Youths Ordered to Die

The model-99 higher-level training plane was unarmored, an ungainly airplane that carried only a 250-kilogram bomb. In July 1944, I was deployed to an airfield in southern Kyūshū, not knowing when I might be ordered to take off as a member of the special attack force of the army's Furitake Detachment. We had concealed the airplane in a potato field baked by the midsummer sun.

A Grumman attacked the airfield. It blasted machine-gun fire from an ultralow altitude of fifty meters or so. Craning my neck as I threw myself down, I could see the red face of the shirtless gunner.

"The bastards. When will we get our orders to fly? This must mean that the enemy is really close. We should get our orders soon.

"I'll have to decide what to do quickly. That's it, that's what I'll do. When we get our orders to make our sortie, I'll take off nonchalantly and then, at the right time, I'll close the valve to the fuel tank so that the other crew members won't notice. Then, because the engine will be out of fuel, the plane will have to make an emergency landing in the ocean. I may lose a leg or an arm or two, but I will still be alive. I just don't want to plow the plane into an enemy ship. It's too frightening. I can't possibly die as a member of a special attack force when I don't even know by whom, when, or on what basis this was decided. I want to stay alive. I'll stay alive no matter what."

This was the way I thought at age twenty-six. We surrendered before I was ordered to take off.

Nakata Kazunari, sixty-eight (m),
retired, Shiojiri

My Squad's Battle to Steal Okinawas

Our squad was billeted in farmhouses, and we agreed on designating ourselves "sweet potato thieves." Ibaraki Prefecture grew a sweet potato called Okinawa. The abundant crop of these potatoes was extremely attractive to us hungry soldiers. After midnight, the chosen potato thieves took a mere thirty minutes to fill the baskets on their backs with the fruits of their sneak attack and returned triumphantly. This was in July of the year the War ended.

More intent on satisfying their hunger than on sleeping, the soldiers built a fire and steamed the Okinawas right away. Eight squad members, including the squad commander, ate until they were stuffed. If we had only foraged that one time, there would have been no problem. But two soldiers, unable to forget the taste of the potatoes, went out on a mission in daylight without permission from the superior officer. They returned brazenly carrying muddy clumps of the fruits of their battle. It was inexcusable for soldiers to be walking in broad daylight with stolen potatoes in their hands. What was worse was that the fruits of this battle were from a field belonging to a house where the commander of another troop was billeted. The two soldiers were followed by the owner of the field and were caught just as they were about to eat the potatoes.

Discovered by their superior officer, the soldiers were scolded. When the squad commander heard about it, he yelled at them too. The group commander and then the commanding officer also were told of their violation. As a result, the commanding officer lectured the squad leader and all the squad members. For punishment, we were put on twenty-four-hour guard duty for the detachment and twelve-hour guard duty for the company.

Even though we were caught red-handed, we couldn't simply throw away the Okinawas, which had been steamed and were ready to eat. We were upset, but we ate them anyway. They tasted just as good.

Honchi Eiki, sixty-two (m),
drama critic, Komae

Live Bullets to Use Against Comrades

On the day the War ended, after the noon radio broadcast by the Emperor—so full of static that it was impossible to understand what was being said—we were instructed to gather at the seacoast. This was at Wagu on Tōshi Island, offshore from Toba. A group of over forty navy men was stationed there under the command of a petty officer who had been promoted to the rank of lieutenant. Not yet eighteen years old, I was a naval airman first class. There were about ten of us with the same rank. Besides the unit commander, student officers-in-training, and us, there were thirty-some reservists who had been drafted and who were all over the age of forty-five.

There was a watery cave that could conceal special attack boats, but not one boat existed. Our weapons consisted of one submachine gun and training rifles gathered from the local middle school and training schools. When we shot at empty cans, flames would spew out of the back of these rifles. Except for a few type-38 infantry rifles, our guns were useless.

What could we have done under those conditions? The commanding officer could not have had any plans. He liked to hear the song of the Japanese white-eye, and, using an ice axe made for him by one of the soldiers who had been a blacksmith, he went up into the mountains on a daily basis to try to trap these birds. There was nothing to do all day, so we also had a lot of time on our hands.

The commanding officer began his instructions to us on the seacoast with "It is my great honor to obey respectfully the august words of His Majesty," and he went on to tell us to be prepared to receive further orders. At the end, he said, "Live ammunition will be supplied to soldiers guarding storehouses, to prepare against attacks by local residents." Though this seemed like a strange order to me, I stood on guard with live ammunition. Thinking that no one would attack the storehouse, those on guard duty would light a candle and pilfer the tin cans and other foodstuffs inside. This was at a time when everyone was suffering from hunger. If someone had come to steal something, I would probably have shot him as ordered. The victim would have been one of the local residents we had been indebted to on a daily basis.

The commanding officer did not hesitate to pass out live ammunition. Until yesterday it was meant for the Americans, today it was to be used against the local residents. Later I realized the essence of this order: the military is a tool which follows the will of those in power.

> Okuyama Yūji, fifty-eight (m),
> director, Ise Consumers
> Cooperative, Mie Prefecture

Chapter 3

The China War

In 1931, taking advantage of the disunity of China, the Japanese Kwantung Army, already entrenched along its South Manchuria Railway concession, brushed aside local warlords and began the formal occupation of Manchuria. By 1937, Manchuria—renamed Manchukuo—although nominally independent was for all intents and purposes a Japanese colony. Japan's single-minded military leaders hoped to use it as a kind of industrial base plus granary, and as an outlet for Japan's surplus population. Emigration to Manchukuo was encouraged; by the mid 1930s more than a million Japanese colonists were in the region.

As the thirties rolled on, with Japan's trading economy still crippled by world depression, the military became even bolder, trying to add north China to their list of conquests. In July 1937, while practicing night-action tactics near the venerable Marco Polo Bridge (Luguoqiao) on the outskirts of Beijing, a reinforced company of Japanese infantry had a firefight with some Chinese troops in the area. Exactly who provoked the shooting remains obscure, but the militant "young officers" clique running the Kwantung Army was quick to seize on this minor skirmish as an opportunity to further aggression. The small Japanese force of some 7,000 troops in north China was quickly augmented. More regiments proceeded to occupy the Beijing–Tianjin area. With the encouragement of the high command in Tokyo, the Kwantung Army set out to conquer and occupy north China.

In an effort to strike at a weak point, China's Generalissimo Chiang Kai-shek retaliated by sending his best German-trained divisions to assault the Japanese navy's landing forces in their long-established Shanghai enclave. The Japanese army and navy fought back with overwhelming force. Ultimately, almost 250,000 Chinese troops were killed and wounded as the fighting spread beyond Shanghai. The civilian government in Tokyo was as powerless to intervene as it had been earlier in the case of

Manchukuo. In fact, the new Konoe cabinet shifted its support to the military. The Kwantung Army extended its conquests to most of north China, establishing bridgeheads in Shanghai and elsewhere along the coast. The China Incident, as it was now called, had grown into a full-scale war.

Ironically, Japanese diplomats and semiofficial missions continued attempts to make some sort of settlement with the Chinese, despite the ultimate refusal of Prime Minister Konoe Fumimaro to negotiate with the government of Chiang Kai-shek. Many Japanese still believed that China could somehow become assimilated as a kind of supercolony. They hoped that the Japanese would develop a closer relationship with the Chinese than the colonizing Europeans had in the past century and well into this one.

The Kwantung Army had no such peaceable intent. As early as 1931, some army majors and colonels had attempted a massive assassination plot to destroy the entire civilian government. They were only dissuaded by the intervention of a senior general. Anticapitalist as well as antiforeign, they felt that Japan should go through a "Shōwa Restoration"—so called after Emperor Hirohito's Shōwa reign—which would result, ultimately, in a "purified" Japan dominating all of East Asia. The brief but bloody military revolts by young officers in 1932 and 1936, in which government leaders were assassinated, were enough to silence antimilitarist opposition.

The army that marched into China in 1937 was loyal, competent, and indescribably brutal in its performance. Called "the divine sword" by home-front propagandists, the armed forces were destined to conquer China in the interests of what the Japanese people were told was their divine mission. Discipline was administered by the same rough cadre of noncommissioned officers who had beaten and kicked their conscript charges into a tightly run military force back in the regimental depots of the homeland. Yet it is hard to imagine Japanese soldiery running amok in any of the wartime atrocities they perpetrated without either the orders or the tacit encouragement of the officers in charge. With few exceptions, the Japanese officers corps from the generals down trained its men to regard the Chinese they encountered— soldiers and civilians alike—as subhuman enemies. Troops were ordered to live off the land; bringing fire and desolation to Chinese cities and villages, while systematically looting the country for their subsistence. The Imperial Army was called *kōgun;* Chinese referred to it as *kōgun [hungjun]*—the same sound with another character meaning "army of locusts."

Toward the close of 1937 a large Japanese force moved out of Shanghai and up the Yangzi [Yangtze] River toward Nanjing. By 13 December the city was taken. For several weeks after, the victors carried out a program of mass killing and looting that has few parallels in modern history. While some Japanese units began methodically to massacre Chinese prisoners of war, others fanned out through the city in an orgy of rape, murder, and pillage. At least 100,000 Chinese soldiers and civilians were killed. Evidence strongly suggests that some 20,000 women were raped. In commemoration ceremonies in 1994, the Chinese, who have long memories, set the death toll in the Rape of Nanjing at 300,000.

Whatever the exact body count, the capture and spoliation of the city offered a scene of horror. American and European missionaries and businessmen who were caught in the city later gave eyewitness reports of these acts of thuggery. (One of the witnesses was General Alexander von Falkenhausen, the German general who had been on loan to Chiang Kai-shek to train troops.) Photographs were surreptitiously taken while the massacre was going on; considerable film footage survived. Given the tight discipline of Japan's military, one must conclude that the Rape of Nanjing was not simply the result of soldiery suddenly gone wild but a deliberately planned program of terror devised by Japanese military commanders. Among them was Lieutenant General Prince Asaka Yasuhiko, a regular army officer of thirty years' service who happened to be Emperor Hirohito's uncle. General Matsui Iwane, the nominal commander of Japanese forces in the area and an advocate of Japanese–Chinese cooperation, was shocked by the deeds committed in his name. Ironically, it was Matsui who was hung for the crime after judgment by the International War Crimes Tribunal in 1946.

Although they felt at first that the War would soon end in their favor, the Japanese army command was increasingly frustrated—first by the refusal of the Chinese to surrender, then by the delaying tactics of Chiang Kai-shek, who ultimately brought his troops back into the western interior and set up a new capital at Chongqing (Chungking). Guerrilla groups sprouted behind the Japanese lines. Atrocity begat counteratrocity. Japanese commanders, provoked by unexpected Chinese resistance, grew ever crueler in the revenge they took on prisoners and civilians who fell into their hands. Their anger was exacerbated by several serious defeats inflicted on them by the Nationalist armies, notably at the battle of Taierzhuang in 1938, and by persistent attacks of Chinese guerrilla troops.

Probably ten million Chinese civilians were killed by the Japanese during this war, which lasted from 1937 to the enforced peace of 1945. Roughly one and a half million Japanese troops were sent to China in those years. Japanese strength on the ground was never less than 850,000. Japanese casualties were heavy, although the care given to the Japanese wounded held down the number killed in action.

As horrible in its way as the Holocaust was in Europe, the Japanese occupation of China continues to this day to spawn bitterness and recrimination. As some of these letters reveal, Japanese soldiers were systematically ordered to commit atrocities ranging from bayonet exercises performed on Chinese prisoners to the vivisection experiments conducted by the infamous Unit 731 in Harbin, whose ghastly work rivaled that done in Nazi concentration camps. Chinese men who survived were drafted by the thousands into the Japanese army to serve as laborers—or more aptly, beasts of burden. The fate of the women was worse. While thousands were impressed, like Korean women before them, into the officially sponsored army "Comfort Corps" (*Ianbu*)—itself nothing more than a network of brutally run brothels—others were indiscriminately raped and killed by soldiers on the march.

The men who perpetrated these deeds were ordinary conscripts. Most of them were farmers, city factory workers, or tradesmen who had never expected to be in China in the first place. Accustomed over the months to the tight discipline of the military and imbued with the idea that the Emperor's army could do no wrong, they blindly followed orders. Many found what they had to do horrible and distasteful in the extreme, but in the climate of that time, few felt brave enough to protest. As the letters make clear, to speak out against this institutionalized cruelty was sure to bring severe punishment on the protester.

The entry of the United States into the Pacific War seemed for a while to bring hope to the Chinese. Yet, faithful to its policy of concentrating on the European theater, Washington did not at first commit too many resources to the China front. When Claire Chennault, the U.S. Air Force general of "Flying Tigers" fame, vowed that he could beat back the Japanese with airpower alone, General Joseph Stillwell, then commander in chief of the Allied forces in China, strongly advised Chiang Kai-shek against it. "The first thing the Japanese will do," he warned, "if the air raids begin to hurt, is to advance further and capture the bases. Then you will be pushed back even further than you are now."

This is exactly what happened. In early 1944 the Japanese army started its sweeping Ichigō (Number 1) Operation; Japanese troops surged out from their coastal bases in south China to make inroads deep into Guangxi, Guizhou, and Hunan provinces. The Nationalist armies sustained terrible losses in the course of this operation. But the guerrillas, both nationalist and communist, kept up the pressure. Each raid made local Japanese army commanders angrier and more determined to wreak bloody and indiscriminate vengeance on the Chinese population.

By 1945, when the Russians, by mistaken American invitation, entered the War, Japanese troops found themselves taking a good bit of their own medicine. Although some soldiers returned to Japan from the China War boastful and arrogant, most brought with them a crushing sense of defeat and a permanent feeling of guilt for the atrocities in which they had partici- pated. No one was anxious to talk about what had happened. Over the years, however, the troops who took part in these punitive expeditions had ample time to reflect on what they had done. The memories were not pleasant ones. The tendency of postwar Japanese citizens and governments has been to play down or even deny the fact that atrocities occurred; to write these letters required courage as well as candor.

The Red Circle Is the Heart; Don't Ever Stab It

In March 1942 a post was fixed in the ground in a corner outside the town in Shan County of Shandong Province. In a hollow next to the post cowered five captured Chinese soldiers, their hands tied behind their backs. They were painfully emaciated and absolutely filthy. Their faces twitched and their bodies trembled.

These prisoners were to be used as targets for bayonet practice by twenty-some raw recruits. During my training period with the Kōfu Regiment we used straw dummies as targets. Here on the battlefront they used live human beings. About to stab a human being for the first time in their lives, the new recruits were terrified—their faces sheet white. The tips of their bayonets quivered as they stood ready.

The prisoners were blindfolded and tied to the post. A circle was drawn in red chalk around the area of the heart on their grimy clothes. As the bayonet training began, the instructor bellowed out, "Ready? The red circle is where the heart is. That's the one place you're prohibited to stab. Understood?"

I had thought that the instructor had marked the area to make it easier for the new recruits to stab the heart. But that was my misunderstanding. It was to make the prisoners last as long as possible.

Several minutes later, shrill war cries echoed continuously outside the town. The prisoners, their bodies honeycombed with bayonet stabs, crumpled in a pool of blood.

War had transformed the instructors and the soldiers into frenzied murderers. This abnormal state of mind must be unfathomable to today's young people who haven't experienced war.

Kawano Masato, sixty-seven (m),
restaurant owner, Yokosuka

The Burning of Interpreter Chen: Chinese Eyes

In 1941 our platoon was stationed in a village called Fuzhuang Zhen in Hebei Province in China. I was a second-year private at that time. The platoon leader, Sergeant "A," was using as his personal interpreter a Chinese named Chen. Chen had previously worked in Osaka as an electrician and was good at speaking the Osaka dialect. Small of stature and round of face, Chen made a good impression.

With the outbreak of the Greater East Asia War, army personnel were pulled out of various posts to form a mixed company. This unit was sent out to occupy the British concession in Tianjin. One night when the defenses were thin, our barracks was attacked with trench mortars and machine guns by the Communist Eighth Route Army. The flashes of explosives bursting in the dark were terrifying. With the coming of dawn, the Communist enemy abandoned the attack and retreated.

Around eight o'clock, interpreter Chen came to work as usual. Sergeant "A" called Chen to his office. Binding Chen's hands behind his back, he repeatedly tortured him, insisting that the previous night's attack was due to Chen's passing information to the enemy. The sergeant paid no heed to Chen's protestations that he had been home with his two children. Chen's face rapidly turned purple and swelled up. The sergeant calmly ate his breakfast in front of his disfigured prisoner.

Chen was dragged out to the open space next to the barracks. The local people, worried, watched from a distance. Ordered to guard him, I stood there, bayonet fixed. The sergeant shouted at the peasants, ordering them to gather around. He made an announcement: in reprisal for last night's attack and Chen's betrayal, Chen would be burned at the stake.

The sergeant always carried his revolver in his right hand. Any attempt at escape and he would shoot. Chen was at his mercy. His ankles were tied with rope and he was hung upside down from a log portal. Beneath his head some wood was piled and kerosene was poured on to it. The sergeant ordered soldiers to set fire. Chen hung there, his head and arms dangling down.

As the flames rose, his body twisted and his arms danced like grilled squid legs. That lasted for about thirty seconds. The local people's eyes seemed to be burning with rage at the barbarity of the sight, as Chen's blackened body hung in the smoke. The peasants wept as they placed his body on a plank and carried it away.

In those days the Chinese thought of the Japanese forces as "fearful Eastern devils" [*Dongyang kuizi*]. I heard later from the locals that Chen's two sons had lost their mother as well. They became orphans.

Matsugatani Toshio, sixty-seven (m),
retired, Chiba

The Devil and Buddha Coexist on the Battlefield

Both the Devil and the Buddha exist in war. The Devil enters into people's souls, but human beings must find the Buddha for themselves. The main character in the book *The Harp of Burma* was someone who found the Buddha.

Five years ago we held our first reunion of wartime buddies. One man who was a new conscript in 1942 commented, "I was grateful to you, the squad leader, for telling me not to go back then." I had forgotten all about the incident.

One day, just after lunch, the private first class on duty notified us, "Assemble the new recruits for roll call." There was to be a stabbing execution of a prisoner on the outskirts of the city. All new recruits were to gather to observe this as a means of building up their nerve. As squad leader and assistant training instructor, I saw no need for this, and didn't allow my men to observe it. This man had recalled that incident to tell me he was grateful. Here was a soldier who had not lost his humanity.

I participated as a company headquarters signals NCO in the Taihang operations of autumn 1943. Thus I was often at battalion headquarters away from my company. I had to lug around with me a large case containing communications instructions and maps. I was armed with a bayonet and 1939-model pistol. Although the night temperatures on the border of Shanxi and Hebei provinces dipped low in September, the sun during the day was as strong as in midsummer.

Entering a village after our forces had passed through, I was about to deliver orders from the battalion commander. I stopped dead in my tracks. A boy about ten years old had fallen down, hit by a rifle bullet. Blood stained the whole front of his body from his chest to his stomach. He was foaming from his mouth. The harsh sun was beating down on his face. No one from the village was in sight.

"I'll make you feel comfortable," I said. I aimed my pistol at his temple and gave him a finishing shot. After making sure that the boy no longer moved, I ran at top speed to catch up with our troops as they moved out. As I ran, I muttered to myself, "It was for the best, it was for the best."

I wish that those who grow up without knowing war can develop a resistance to war.

Mori Ishichi, sixty-seven (m),
company employee, Sendai

"Where's Daddy?" the POW's Child Asks

While I was in Ronghe County in Shanxi Province the execution of prisoners of war always took place in a particular spot outside the city gates. There was no one around by the muddy Yellow River. In the spring, red flowers bloomed forlornly on the single remaining aronia tree.

The season was still chilly in 1939. Our first prisoner from the Eighth Route Army was pulled into our compound, prodded by the bayonet of a grim-faced Japanese soldier. The young Chinese man appeared to be less than thirty years old. He was leading a three- or four-year-old boy by the hand. The man's swollen lower lip was dirty from the dust, but his wide forehead and deeply set features seemed to indicate he was a man of learning. The little boy, wailing at being pulled away from his father, had a rice ball put in his little hand and was taken piggyback outside the town by an old conscript on the orders of the company commander.

Even when sentenced to execution by a firing squad, the man's expression remained aloof. Silently he groped·inside his inner pocket and pulled out an old pocket watch. He attempted to hand this over to the commanding officer with some sort of request. It was rejected. He looked around. Aiming at a broken gravestone, he raised his right hand up high and hurled the watch against it with all his might, smashing it. When he was tied to a thick pillar by a burly soldier, he cried out with a fierce expression on his face and yelled out his insistence that he not be blindfolded. Glared at by eyes flaming with anger, the young first-year private faltered.

At that moment, a noncommissioned officer dashed up energetically, in a probable show of bravado in front of his fellow soldiers, and took aim with his rifle from about three meters away. One shot. Two shots. The sound of the shots echoed in the quiet of the desolate field. The smell of gunpowder filled the air. The prisoner's face pouring out blood was like a punctured pomegranate. He fell limp.

That evening when I returned in a roundabout way to my office in the state government agency where I worked, I found the little boy leaning against the white wall of my room, playing alone with a bamboo toy. Looking up at my face, he muttered in a lisp, "Where's Daddy?" This little bird in distress had come to the bosom of the hunter to seek to live. For over six years until the end of the War, this orphan was always at my side and came with me wherever I was posted as a civilian official.

Hirakawa Zenzō, seventy-two (m),
university administrator, Narashino

Germ Warfare and Human Body Experiments

In the autumn of 1943, while I was working as a pharmacologist at the Linfen army hospital in Shanxi Province, Major General Ishii Shirō came to inspect the hospital. He was then the surgeon commanding the First Army Medical Section and was also commander of the infamous Unit 731 of the Kwantung Army in Manchuria.

After the inspection a dinner for Major General Ishii was given by the hospital director and other officers. A documentary film from Unit 731 was shown at the dinner. This film presented a succession of graphic data from experiments on human beings, for use in germ warfare and the treatment of frostbite in cold districts. One wanted to avert one's eyes. Major General Ishii proudly explained his data to us.*

Also depicted were scenes of the wretched condition of the decimated Japanese forces in the Nomonhan Incident. We saw the surge of Soviet tanks as the sky darkened with Yakovlev fighter planes. We saw the exhumation of the body of Japanese ace pilot Chief Warrant Officer Shinozaki from its burial on the steppe.

Major General Ishii reportedly boasted that he would become a full general as an army surgeon.

When I look back at the brutal treatment given to military prisoners of war and the whole population of China after the invasion of China, I cannot but feel that the time-honored courteousness of the Japanese people and our sense of chivalry had sunk so low that Japanese soldiers had been reduced to a group of madmen. It is true that the state of mind of those involved in a kill-or-be-killed war is abnormal. Japanese, however, were particularly prone to flaunt a sense of superiority over the Chinese. Even in hospitals behind the lines there were cases where suspected Chinese spies were subjected to experimentation in surgical operations. The purpose was to improve the clinical skills of unseasoned young army doctors! For some reason, while flattering themselves that they were the world's best peoples, the Germans and the Japanese were capable of outrageous behavior.

---

*Ishii's Unit 731 performed a ghastly series of vivisections on Chinese captives throughout the War, for the alleged purpose of testing human endurance in a variety of situations. Equally appalling were the experiments on American POWs and others conducted at Kyūshū Imperial University by Japanese army and civilian doctors.

Regrettably, not once were we taught about the International Red Cross Convention during our military service.

Kimizuka Kiyoshi, sixty-seven
(m), corporate advisor, Narashino

Mystery of Atrocity on Zhujiang Riverbank

At the end of 1944, we departed Guangzhou and headed for Liuzhou in a fleet of small boats going upstream on the Zhujiang, five or six men to a craft. Our unit was an aviation detachment charged with staking out a position on a mountain and spotting enemy aircraft. We planned to obtain our equipment in Liuzhou and take up our posts. We passed by after the infantry units had been through. All the hamlets on the riverside had been laid waste. Most lay in ruins. The bodies of Japanese soldiers had been dumped on the riverside, and the combat dead floated in the slack water.

We were just about to reach our campsite for that night. Rocky mountains ranged along both sides of the river, making it look just like a Chinese ink painting. We made quick progress, telling each other that we would be helpless if we were shot at by machine guns from any of those rocky peaks. Just then we discovered what looked like the bodies of a dozen or so Japanese soldiers on a sandy hill on the right bank. Putting our boat ashore, we saw that there were a total of sixteen Japanese soldiers placed about a meter apart in two neat rows. Around them were scattered hats, torn coats, and cartridge cases from infantry rifles.

It looked as if two or three months had passed since their deaths. What made us catch our breath were the signs of violation on the dead bodies. All of the bodies were naked, their eyes gouged out, their noses and ears sliced off, and their stomachs cut open with their entrails pulled out. What was even more grotesque was that about ten centimeters of the flesh of their thighs had been cut off, exposing their white bones. Uniformly their left hands were cut off at the wrists and wrapped in white bandages. A short distance away on the sand were the dead bodies of a young Chinese man and woman, but they were dressed. The only wound on each was a single stab in the heart.

Feeling the eeriness, we quickly went back to our boat and followed our fellow soldiers. That night our conversation was full of theories about the atrocity we had seen. Those soldiers must have been killed on the sand by enemy fire. Their flesh must have been sliced up in the hope that they wouldn't be able to walk even if they were to come back to life. Their left hands were missing because Japanese soldiers who came across the bodies cut them off to perform a memorial service. And the young Chinese man and woman must have worked for the Japanese forces. These were our conclusions. What I will never forget is the name Kurokoma embroidered on a hat left on that spot.

> Nishimura Susumu, sixty-nine (m),
> high school teacher, Shizuoka
> Prefecture

Arranging for a Prisoner Couple to Meet

It was before the start of the Pacific War. During the operations in Shanxi Province in northern China I was working on routine matters in the rear area. One day I was called over by the first lieutenant of the information section. Some prisoners had arrived from the front, and one of them was asking for something. The lieutenant said that he had no interpreter and no way of finding out what the prisoner wanted.

I started by trying to communicate in writing, but I soon found out that the prisoner could speak English. My English wasn't too reliable, but it was better than my Chinese. I was able to find out the following.

He was a communications technician married to a woman doctor and had a loving family. When he went into military service, his wife became a military doctor, taking along their one-year-old child. He sobbed that he had lost sight of his wife and child in the disarray following the night attack. He was beside himself. He constantly heard the sound of his child's voice in his ears.

I also had a wife and child. "Shouldn't you have prepared yourself once you were called to duty?" I asked. He replied, "Your family is in Japan. If you die in the War they will get proper compensation. This is a war zone. There is no protection. Have you thought about that difference?" His way of speaking was blunt, but his expression showed no fear or hatred.

"I can understand your position," I said. "I am just a low-ranking soldier, so I will report what you said to my superior officer and do what I can for you." He nodded and calmed down.

Several days later, the woman military doctor and child arrived. The Chinese prisoner had already been transferred. When I told the first lieutenant that I wanted to take them to him as quickly as possible, he made an immediate decision. Armed with a single bayonet and a special-issue handgun, I was given the duty of transporting five prisoners.

This first lieutenant was a man of few words. But his casual way of getting to the heart of others' feelings while not showing off his rank let his men know they could rely on him.

Blessed with good weather, we safely reached our destination. After delivering my charges, I stole a brief glance at the emotional reunion of the prisoner's family before I turned back to return to my unit. I felt grateful for the peace of mind I gained in setting down my burden. That day's sunset was beautiful.

I was concerned about the later whereabouts of the prisoner and his family, but my fate was also in doubt. No matter what incidents were to occur, my impression of the sunset would not change, I was sure. I wonder if we can't bring about a world in which as many people as possible can live in ease and die with a sense of fulfillment.

Kuribayashi Itarō, seventy-five (m),
former high school teacher, Otaru

Don't Ever Get Caught Again

A prisoner of war was sent all tied up to Baofeng in Henan Province, where I had been posted from regimental headquarters in Lushan. We low-grade noncommissioned officers had received no word on this prisoner. For the time being we sat him down on the earthen floor of the noncommissioned officers' room. When suppertime came around I sent to the mess for the same food as mine. Telling the prisoner to taste for poisoning as he ate, I loosened his bonds. He must not have eaten for quite a while, for he gobbled up his food. Expecting some order to come the next day, I posted a night watch so that he wouldn't escape—I told the prisoner not to even think of escaping.

The next morning, I received orders from First Lieutenant "T" to execute the prisoner. If I took the prisoner to the outskirts of the village, the local residents would see us. As this had been enemy territory until a few months ago, there might be some enemy soldiers among the local inhabitants. It was obvious that executing the prisoner would incite the negative feelings of the inhabitants. At that time there were fifty soldiers under First Lieutenant "T" in the Baofeng garrison. These were all castoffs or rejects collected from each company. The three noncommissioned officers, including myself, had all been wounded and just released from the hospital. So we were in no condition to be sent to the front lines.

Among the prisoners were two Koreans, one of whom couldn't speak Japanese. With the first prisoner in a horse-drawn cart, we went outside the town. Many of the local inhabitants lined the road, watching us with hatred in their eyes. It sent a chill down my spine. I thought I could take care of the prisoner by a large tree and moved ahead toward it. As I asked the prisoner where he was from, how old he was, and why he was captured, I felt compassion for this man, who was my own age. I decided to let him go. My self-justification was that by letting him go I'd be getting the local inhabitants to calm down. This might insure the safety of the Baofeng garrison.

I told the prisoner that I was letting him go, so he should never return to this place again. He should go and live a healthy life elsewhere. He wept as he repeated his thanks, "*Xie xie.*" I aimed my rifle at the sky and shot three times and made my way back. When I turned around, the prisoner waved and bowed to me over and over again. Then ran off like a streak of lightning.

When I reached the village, everyone welcomed me with smiles, saying, "Gentleman, thank you for your trouble." I don't know how they had seen what I had done.

This happened in March 1945.

Uchida Keiji, sixty-six (m),
camera shop owner, Odawara

Unforgettable—the Blood Spurting From That Chinese Boy's Chest

I was doing Christian missionary work in Rehe Province in Manchukuo in May 1945 when I was drafted and posted to a guard unit at Shanhai Guan. A single company of about a hundred men was posted to a place with facilities for a permanent regimental station. Thus we had everything in abundance in terms of food and equipment and could eat as much as we wanted. Each day was uneventful, with no enemy attacks or punitive expeditions.

One day, two peasant boys were captured and brought to our post. There had been no trouble to speak of. Yet the garrison commander tried to create an incident so he could claim credit for his actions. At that time I had been assigned to be the interpreter for the unit, so I was ordered right away to interrogate the two boys. I found out that they were only local peasant boys—two brothers aged eighteen and sixteen. They had no ideological leanings, and it was obvious to me that they were not underground activists for the Eighth Route Army. I told my sergeant that the commander should release them.

But the commander's idea was to punish them as underground operators for the Eighth Route Army, whether they were or not. In this way he could have it noted as an achievement for him and his company. My suggestion was rejected. That night the boys were held in a cage hastily built to serve as a detention cell. It was in the crawl space under the guardhouse. Guards were put on duty day and night, but the guard on night duty, accustomed to peaceful conditions, must have dozed off. Late that night the two boys broke out of their cage and ran away. The flustered guard chased after them and captured the younger boy, but the older brother escaped into the darkness.

Angered by this, the commander called all the troops to the back yard early the next morning and ordered the boy's execution in the presence of the entire unit. Under the baking hot rays of the August sun, the boy was made to strip to his waist and sit on the edge of a deeply dug pit. Suddenly the commander said to me, "Give him his last words in Chinese." I had been staring at the commander, desperately trying to keep from loudly shouting out, "He's not an underground activist! He's just a naive peasant boy. He should be released!" A strong voice called out in my head, *You're a missionary, aren't you? You should save this innocent boy.*

But if I had raised my voice it was a sure thing that the frenzied commander and the other officers in charge would immediately execute me as a traitor as well. My mind was in disarray. My body shook. At the commander's voice, I staggered like a sleepwalker to the boy and knelt down.

During my interrogation of him the previous day, I had given my word to him, saying, "You are innocent. I'll do my utmost to get you released." He fixed his eyes on me. What was I to tell him? In Chinese, I said, "I was powerless and couldn't save you. I'm a coward and can't do anything. All I can do is pray to my God. You should pray to the god you believe in, too." Until then he had been calling out "*Maaya! Maaya!*" [Mother! Mother!] but now he closed his eyes and fell silent.

The youngest soldier in the company was ordered to stab the boy to death, but holding his bayonet at the ready, he was unable to move. "I'll do it," said a sergeant, and jabbed the point of his bayonet into the boy's naked chest. The boy's face paled, and blood spurted from his chest.

I still feel a deep sense of grief and guilt, and I am unable to forget the vivid color of the boy's blood.

Futabashi Masao, seventy-two (m), preschool director, Numazu

Stories About Nanjing Shocked a Young Girl's Heart

In the early fall, just after Japan's surrender, I was a third-year student at a girls' middle school in Kishiwada. It was the most difficult of times. School was closed. There was no more food left in the neighboring farming community. We were barely staying alive by eating the vines of squash and sweet potatoes that we cultivated beside the road. My mother and I went to Niigata to buy some rice. After riding a train so crowded that even the lavatories and luggage shelves were jammed with people, we finally arrived at a farming village. Because there was no glass left in the windows of the train, soot from the locomotive blackened the passengers' faces when we went through tunnels. We traded some money and our best kimonos for a little rice.

That night we stayed in a cheap village lodging house. Everyone slept in one large room under a huge mosquito net. I was beginning to fall asleep, exhausted, when five or six men started drinking. They were all recently discharged soldiers who were now professional black marketeers. Each bragged about his exploits in the War.

It was unbearable to listen to them. They laughed coarsely about the many Chinese women they had raped, and one told about seeing how far into a woman's body his arm would go, pushing his arm all the way in up to the armpit.

I shot up off the mat like a windup doll and tried to rush out of the room, tearing at the mosquito netting. In a panic, my mother grabbed me, warning me to stay quiet because who knows what might happen. I kept quiet. And still the men went on and on.

"Where was that?"

"Nanjing, we had the most fun in Nanjing. We could do anything we wanted and steal anything we wanted."

They said that when the soldiers got tired and hard to command during marches, their superior officers would urge them to persevere a bit more, promising them that they could do anything they wanted in the next town.

I remembered joining in the parade to celebrate the fall of Nanjing, waving a handmade flag. Now I couldn't bear it. I had used things we needed dearly to fill comfort bags to send our soldiers; I had made talismans and thousand-stitch belts; I had written letters nearly every day to thank and encourage our soldiers. I was so shocked by what I heard that I couldn't sleep at all that night. I don't think all our soldiers were like those men. My uncle was a kind man who died young at Guadalcanal.

Those soldiers who did such terrible things in Nanjing and in other places are now probably traveling and enjoying themselves, playing croquet in seniors groups. I beg of you, please write the truth about the War.

Ozaki Junko, fifty-five (f),
housewife, Yokohama

Death in the Water During Night March

On 14 May 1944, our Twenty-seventh Army Division was continuing its march toward the crossing point at Changtai Guan, by the Huai River, along the Beijing-Hankou line in Henan Province. Torrential rains had fallen since that morning. The roads had turned to mud and the route toward our destination was made extremely difficult. Having won many battles in some twenty days as part of the Beijing-Hankou action, the soldiers were all exhausted.

The night march in the pouring rain was conducted in pitch darkness. It might have been possible to take refuge during daytime had the commander so decided, but orders are coldhearted. As the companies ahead bogged down, the companies at the rear were brought to a standstill, overflowing the highway. The water from the break in the embankment of the Huai River flowed over the road. It was hip-deep in the low-lying places. The temperature normally reaches summertime levels in May in central

China, but the abnormal weather caused near-freezing conditions. Valuable time elapsed. By the time each rear company started to evacuate the area, it was too late.

A mere few lines in the war history tell of this event in which 166 men were lost, drowned and frozen during one night's march. This incident was reported in the newspapers, but these deaths were treated as deaths from disease contracted at the front.

It was unbearable to look at the bodies like mud dolls on the road and in the lowlands the following morning. There wasn't a single officer among the dead. Most were new recruits and soldiers who handled the horses, those who were most exhausted from being driven the hardest. Overwork caused their deaths as much as the flood and the cold.

Matsumura Tatsuo, sixty-eight (m),
former company employee, Tokyo

Two Women Soldiers With Musical Instruments

I think it was about June of 1943. A reporter in the Jinan bureau of *Asahi Shimbun* newspaper, I was stationed as a war correspondent during operations on the Shandong Peninsula in a village in Sushui County. The commanding officer in Jinan was Lieutenant General Dobashi of the Twelfth Army Corps.

We were told that some women soldiers had been captured and that we should attend their interrogation by the company commander. Two girls were held in a room in a shabby mud-walled house. When we arrived, they were brought out to face the commander. They appeared to be about twenty years old and had fine-featured faces. These girls would be quite pretty if they wore normal clothes, I thought. As it was, their light blue uniforms were dusty and dirty, and their faces lacked color.

"Where and how were you captured? Which unit are you with? As women soldiers what were your duties? You don't even have any rifles, but do you still call yourselves soldiers?"

Among the war correspondents was a fellow whose Chinese was good, and he interpreted. The women soldiers showed no timidity and answered readily without any appearance of fear. Their voices were lovely.

"We are with the Eighth Route Army and our commanding officer is Xu

Xiangqian. We belong to the XX squad of OO company. Our duties are to perform drama and music. We carry no weapons because our duties are to entertain and encourage the soldiers in the unit and to win over the masses. We carry musical instruments." They showed us their Chinese flute and fiddle.

"Commander, it's best to release them. I can't see that releasing them would have any effect on the overall situation," I said. The commander answered, "You're right." The two women soldiers said, "*Xie xie*," and pressed their palms together in thanks.

I must have heard the women's names, but I have forgotten what they were. I wonder if they were able to return safely to their unit.

> Takahashi Rentarō, seventy-eight
> (m), former newspaper reporter,
> Hanamaki

A Memorial to Three War Buddies

On 28 December 1937, a force of twenty-five men led by a platoon commander was dispatched to a village in Lingshi County, Shanxi Province, for pacification activity and to scout enemy movements. While we were resting, we were suddenly hit by a concentrated attack. Enemy soldiers from a mountaintop to the west strafed us with machine guns. The enemy numbered over a hundred. Deciding that we were at too much of a disadvantage to counterattack, the platoon leader retreated and assembled his men in a safe location.

A roll call indicated that three were missing. The interpreter stated that "A" and "B" were standing guard, while "C" was returning fire from the roof of a house. We waited for them, but they didn't return. Dusk was falling. Fearing that staying put might lead to more casualties, we started back. We took a long detour without stopping to sleep or rest and reached our defense post the next morning.

At battalion headquarters, a rescue unit of three hundred men led by the battalion commander was assembled and immediately set off. Reaching the village where the attack had occurred the day before, they made a search. They found out that our three fellow soldiers had been taken prisoner by the enemy and their weapons and ammunition had been snatched from them. In the −10° centigrade cold, they were stripped of their army uniforms and, hands tied behind their backs, they were massacred. It was unbearable to look at the numerous scars of beatings and stabbings on their bodies.

Their war buddies knelt down and wept at how painful and wrenching it must have been for them. This killing of human beings who are close together—this is what war is. Though they were fighting for our country, I wonder if any of the soldiers who witnessed this had a liking for the War. Didn't they feel at heart that, if they could, they would like to quit and go home? I'm sending this in as a memorial for the repose of the souls of the three soldiers.

Tanaka Norio, sixty-eight (m),
retired, Mie Prefecture

As Proof of Repentance

"Stories About Nanjing Shocked a Young Girl's Heart" [pp. 75–76, above] was a reproach, as well as a demand for some response from the generation that experienced the battlefield. Finding out the shameful reality—such a far cry from the image of the imperial forces cherished in her pure girlish heart—she must have been greatly shocked, particularly during the unsettled time after Japan's defeat.

I was also sent to the Chinese front in 1939. We were told that we were to give up our lives for our country and not expect to return. I was attached to a unit full of veterans. They had taken part in many engagements in various places since their unit had landed in Shanghai in the face of the enemy. The following three points were immediately impressed on our minds: (1) if we don't kill, we will be killed; (2) the lives we have today we may not have tomorrow; (3) even if we can eat today we may starve tomorrow—one night a prince, the next night a pauper.

Although there may have been some differences due to an individual's rationality and nature, I think this instinctive way of thinking was held in common by all soldiers. No one dressed it up as a holy war for peace in Asia. It was a place where impulsive acts and massacres were committed. It was only natural that the propaganda directed at the homeland, which glorified militarism, was in sharp variance to the reality of military forces invading another country. War itself is most brutal and wretched.

Even so, by the time I was sent to war, military discipline had become strict, so there were no cases like the stories of Nanjing. Yet battlefield surroundings change people. Don't we all have things, whether many or few, that we don't want to recall? We are probably thinking that at this point we not only don't wish to brag about our experiences, but we also don't want people to pick at our old wounds. People may think that we take this casually. But my proof of repentance is to pledge my opposition to war with emphatic feeling and to search my soul about the war of aggression that caused such immense damage to another country.

Inoue Hitoshi, sixty-eight (m),
company owner, Tokyo

Imperial Army Comfort Women

In 1938 I was conscripted in an emergency call-up to the transport regiment in Hiroshima. In the following year, 1939, I was assigned to the Thirty-ninth Division, took intensive training in the Chinese language, and joined the invasion battle of Yichang. Each troop movement was almost always followed by a group of women from Korea. Tucking their hems up high, they balanced their single suitcases on their heads and trudged along, trailing after the marching forces.

When there was a break in the fighting, it was time for the engineers to rig up a rush-mat enclosure. Practically all of the houses were destroyed. It seemed strange that only the tobacco fields were bright green. The long queue of soldiers outside the rush huts contrasted weirdly with the roving sentries carrying fixed bayonets. After an hour or so passed, there would be a trench mortar attack from the Chinese forces. A trumpet would sound the general alarm. Trousers still lowered, soldiers would run helter skelter. The women in the rush-mat huts, used to these attacks, immediately threw themselves face down on the ground, using their suitcases for cover. Some were killed by stray bullets, but the military took no notice.

Their armbands reading "Imperial Forces Comfort Women" still dirty, once again they would trail silently behind the marching troops. The soldiers put a bit of their dreams in their brief interludes with the comfort women between battles. While our forces were on standby status in Jingmen, I reported this scene in a mimeographed newsletter called *Advance Guard*. The next day I caught hell from the military police, but the comfort women read it avidly. The women who survived the War must be grandmothers by now.

Kaneko Yōichi, sixty-nine (m),
retired, Yamaguchi Prefecture

After Live Experiment

With the start of the Sino-Japanese Incident in 1937, I landed in Shanghai in the face of the enemy as a raw recruit. Since then I was part of the central China operations, literally walking one step of 75 centimeters at a time, pushing into Nanjing, Xuzhou, Dankou, and Yichang. This happened when I was a member of the pacification unit in Xinyang, north of Hankou. I was gathering intelligence on the enemy and working on pacification of the local inhabitants. One day, a Chinese who was thought to be an enemy spy was sent to our unit. He was said to have been caught on the advice of a local informant. He was tortured but refused to confess. Finally, he was used as experimental material for the military doctors and veterinarians. They injected air into his blood vessels.

In a cave halfway up a mountain medics injected air into his vein. We watched the air bubbling in as the blood vessel bulged out. He just lightly coughed and didn't die. The veterinary officer cocked his head, saying that a horse dies right away from this. After about thirty minutes, they decided to stab him to death.

The Chinese man said something before he was stabbed to death. I asked the interpreter later and found out that he had said, *"An hao ren."* These words meant that he was a good person and not a spy.

Yokoyama Tsuneza, seventy-two
(m), former civil servant,
Shizuoka Prefecture

The Chanting MP Buddhist: My Grandfather's Teachings

I was born in a family of successive generations of fervent followers of the Nenbutsu Buddhist sect. As my father had died when I was very young, I grew up under the influence of my grandfather. When I was departing for the Wuhan front as a reserve conscript, my grandfather came to see me off at the station and handed me an envelope, saying, "Read this with care after you have a chance to feel settled." I took it out to read when I was alone on the deck of the troopship as we crossed the East China Sea.

"Fate allowed us to be connected as grandfather and grandson for twenty-some years," he had written, "but we must be prepared for this to be our parting in this life. As we have had the good fortune to be born in a family of believers of this blessed sect, it would be most regrettable if we are parted in the hereafter. Let us intend to go together to the Land of Happiness by believing in the Original Vow of the Amida Buddha. . . . Consider the place you fall to be Paradise and advance along with prayers to Amida."

My view of life and death during my military service was determined by these words. I had no need for a thousand-stitch belt or a sacred amulet. Running over to the first enemy soldier I sniped at, I saw that he was a naive-looking raw recruit clutching some communications gear. What came rushing out of my mouth were the words *"Namu Amida Butsu"* ["I take my refuge in Amida Buddha"]. As a member of the military organization, I dutifully obeyed the Imperial Rescript to Soldiers and Sailors and the Field Service Code, but I was never able to believe in them. This was because since before that time my belief in the Buddha transcended life and death as the foundation of my soul.

When I was reassigned to the military police and was given a private room in Nanjing, I copied the Nenbutsu onto a piece of straw paper with brush and ink, put photographs of my parents below it, and tacked this up on my wall. Using this as a substitute for a Buddhist altar, I offered my morning and evening prayers. One commander on his inspection tour even bowed deeply before my paper altar when he greeted me. I did not succumb to the temptations of money, women, or desire for glory so readily available to military police in an occupied territory. My grandfather passed away shortly after I left for the front.

Ishii Hisao, seventy (m), farmer, Gifu

Despicable Acts Against an Old Woman

My unit was the fourth platoon of the 108th Independent Infantry Battalion's Machine Gun Company in the Fifty-eighth Division. We were posted to the first company in May 1942 and entered Zhangjiagou, central China. On New Year's Eve that year, the main force of the company led by first company commander Captain Kōriyama was suddenly mobilized on a punitive expedition. The night air was piercingly cold after a rainfall.

About 5 A.M. the following morning, New Year's Day, we arrived in a village three kilometers from the enemy position. We immediately prepared for battle. The heavy-weapons unit left the packhorse unit there and mounted an attack. But not one shot was fired back. The enemy camp was deserted. It was a silvery world of heavy frost as far as the eye could see. We were instructed to bow in the direction of the Imperial Palace to pay our New Year's respects from afar. The company took a long rest period of one hour, during which we had breakfast.

However, the packhorse unit of our machine-gun squad was nowhere around. The packhorse unit follows directly behind the advancing attack unit; the attack unit loads equipment not immediately necessary for the attack onto the packhorses just before it goes into action. The machine-gun platoon was disgraced. The normally smiling face of our platoon commander, Second Lieutenant Tsurutome, turned red with rage. That face looked like three monkeys' red rear ends bunched together.

He gave me orders, saying, "Private Kushige (my former name), lead those guys over here, on the run." Carrying my revolver with me, I began to run, slipping on the frozen puddles. When I finally reached the village, I could hardly believe what was happening there. "Hey, Kushige, since you've come all this way, see what's going on." The platoon orderly led me to the doorway of a house.

The soldiers had dragged an old women from her sickbed and had pressed her to undress. It appeared that the old woman had stayed alone in the village in order to protect her house even if her life depended on it. The soldiers threatened to set fire to her house and, in the bitter cold, took the clothes off the lower half of her body. Making her sit on a chair, they picked at her private parts with their swords. As she bled, the old woman trembled with fear.

I became agitated and yelled out, "You idiots! How would you feel if she was your mother?" At the same time, I handed her the trousers that they had taken off. The color returned immediately to her face.

It was New Year's Day, but thanks to the behavior of the five soldiers in the packhorse unit, the platoon leader ordered us to fast all day. Of course he also fasted. All of us felt about to faint.

> Uehara Masao, sixty-six (m),
> retired, Ōmuta

Death in Battle: A Korean Squad Commander

I pray every morning and evening to a small memorial tablet on the Buddhist altar in my home. This has gone on since my demobilization in December 1947. On that handmade tablet is written "Army Sergeant Suzukawa Natsue." He was my subordinate and he was from Korea.

On 2 March 1945, our unit encountered the Chinese Nationalist forces at a village called Daxin Zhuang in Shandong Province. Getting the jump on the enemy, the Japanese forces laid siege to the main force of the enemy detachment in the village. At about 3 P.M. my company charged their position as Suzukawa, the squad leader, climbed onto a roof to give his commands. Just at that moment his chest was struck by a single bullet, which killed him immediately, and he fell from the roof. In that instant the late afternoon sun shone on the brilliant red streaks of his fresh blood seeping into the mud wall. His body lay below.

Someone said, "Squad Leader Suzukawa was fond of Ishii, wasn't he?" Ishii was a first-year recruit under Suzukawa's command. He had trained Ishii, who had died in battle early in the War. I could well understand Suzukawa's feelings of loss and rage.

For over forty years I have not been able to forget Suzukawa. Of course I remember the circumstances of his death, but also branded in my mind are his everyday expressions. And when I think of his emotions at having to carry a gun and die fighting for another country, I am haunted by a complex sense of remorse. I wonder how his parents lived. No doubt they received no compensation for his death.

> Hirata Yūichi, sixty-six (m),
> former elementary school teacher,
> Kumamoto Prefecture

"Neither Side Wants to Kill the Other"

In response to a request—"pleasant memories and experiences from the battlefield"—I would like to provide an anecdote showing a human touch.

Soon after the outbreak of the Sino-Japanese Incident, the South Manchuria Railway Orchestra received orders to entertain the troops at the front lines and entered a village near Datong that was famous for its stone Buddhist images of Yungang. Although this was the most advanced position of the Japanese forces, near Inner Mongolia, it was only a small unit of thirty or forty men. The unit commander was a slightly built man about thirty years old who had been a schoolteacher. The village comprised a mere fifty or sixty houses, located on a slight rise. About forty or fifty meters below was a small unit of Chinese Nationalist troops. Despite the fact that each side knew of the other, they had not shot at each other for over half a year. It was a surprise to me that if our forces threw down some cigarettes to them, they would throw some fried sweets to us. The unit commander smiled guilelessly, saying, "Neither side wants to kill the other."

A performance featuring the orchestra was organized. A stage was erected in the village square from desks and boxes covered with straw mats. Several mats were laid out for the audience. The local residents streamed out with pleased faces to sit on the mats. Children, women, old people—the entire community no doubt—showed up. Our soldiers had to stand around the edges to watch.

"I wanted to show these unusual musical instruments to the local people," the commander said in a moving way.

I have no way of knowing what happened to this unit and the village. But I put this heartwarming scene in the context of the War that I experienced.

Fushimi Yoshio, seventy-nine (m),
former South Manchuria Railway
employee, Kasukabe

A Warmhearted Commander

In 1938 our infantry unit prepared to be sent to the battle front on the continent. We were reviewed for tactical efficiency by the platoon leader.

Our second lieutenant was a conscript officer just out of cadet training. About eight years older than the men, he looked irritatingly clumsy, even to those of us who had barely managed to learn what we were taught as first-year conscripts. In front of his subordinates, who were lined up at attention at dusk on the snowy drill ground, he was vehemently reprimanded for his lack of leadership ability by the battalion commander, a man noted for his courage and initiative. Our lieutenant's epaulettes trembled and his saber quivered. A wave of apprehension flitted across the minds of the soldiers who were about to head to the battlefield under his command. We wondered what would happen to us under such a commander.

We were sent to the front in China. Here also, our platoon, led by this mild-mannered lieutenant, was viewed askance by the careerist company commander and shunned by the other platoons. Yet in battle, the soldiers showed fearless bravery. In each battle, we soldiers, led by our squad leaders, would leave our lieutenant behind and storm the enemy camp to foil the company commander. Complaining in his heavily accented voice that "my soldiers won't obey my commands," our lieutenant had entirely lost his dignity as a superior officer. But we subordinates had seen through to his true state of mind: he did not want to get any of us killed.

During the forty-some years since the War's end, we have been overjoyed at his attendance at our annual reunion of wartime buddies. Having been promoted to captain by the end of the War, he remained an officer who was incapable of being pompous. He was just a good fellow soldier. Forced to wear a stiff military uniform, even though his command abilities as a military officer were clumsy, he held his subordinates together by his warmheartedness. It was this that enabled them to display boldness in action.

Senga Tōjū, seventy (m),
company executive, Nagoya

Told to Grasp a Living Heart

Going up the Yangzi River, I alighted at Jiujiang. Like Arita in Kyūshū, it was a pottery town, but the roofs of the buildings had been blown off by Japanese bombs. Pieces of pottery were strewn everywhere as if military boots had trampled on them. Crushing the pottery shards, I walked for twenty minutes and arrived at a building said to have been the barracks for Chiang Kai-shek's forces. Across the large training ground from the nurses' quarters where we were housed was a series of target circles, and further beyond rose Lushan.

Taking my orders from the medical corpsman, I started providing treatment and giving injections. When the bandages of the evacuated wounded were taken off, we found that their flesh was full of pus and maggots. On the mornings after night duty, I would go to throw out the contents of the lovely flower vases picked up from the town, which we used as bedpans.

An old man was brought to our quarters. We all took to calling him Ni-ni. He brought us our meals by the bucket and cleaned the hallways and stairs for us. In the barracks a woman helped with the soldiers' laundry and cleaning. She had a six- or seven-year-old boy, and reminded of the children they had left behind in Japan, the soldiers would give the boy caramels from their care packages. They fondly called him Li-li.

There was always a soldier with a fixed bayonet guarding the entrance to the barracks. If he thought that the Chinese who entered didn't bow properly, he would give them a double slap in the face. As this was an everyday occurrence, I became numb to this behavior.

One day I received a notice to go to observe heart surgery from the person in charge of the emergency operation room. Told by the army surgeon to feel the heart, I realized for the first time how strong a heartbeat is. When I left the operating room, there were two more Chinese covered by blankets and seated on chairs. I couldn't tell their gender. This was vivisection. My heart aches each time I recall this. I wonder if I should have written this; perhaps I should have kept it in my heart forever.

> Yamaki Tamotsu, seventy-four (f),
> former nurse, Hachiōji

Tomorrow's Mountains in Steep Taihang

In May 1941, my first posting was to the battle at Zhongyuan. As a mountain artillery soldier in the attack forces, I crossed over the Taihang mountain range by foot, leading a horse carrying a caisson loaded with ammunition. I was a first-class private in the spring of my twenty-second year. The newspapers of the time reported, "Mountains yesterday, mountains today, and mountains tomorrow in the steep grades of Taihang." To fight meant to walk. I scrambled up one mountain and then another, biting my lip. My army boots tore. When it rained I covered up with a poncho and continued to drive forward.

No matter how far we penetrated, we didn't encounter the enemy. A mere foot soldier, I had no way of knowing what the big picture of war operations was, but the Japanese army was slowly tightening its iron ring encircling the enemy. As the drive across the mountains was so hurried, our supplies couldn't catch up to us. The unit gradually began to starve. We would slurp up a handful of rice made into gruel and dissolve powdered miso paste in hot water to stave off starvation. Burdened with their loads of disassembled heavy gun carriages on their backs, the army horses stood with difficulty, shaking from salt deprivation.

We were single-minded. Dismissing all other thoughts, our hearts were emblazoned with just one word: *homeland.* As we got close to the front lines, the heavily wounded from the infantry units were brought down by stretcher one after another. Those who had died in combat were covered by a tarp and carried on the swaying backs of horses to the rear.

Our unit finally pushed our way deep into Shanxi and charged into a hamlet called Xiyangcun, if I recall correctly. We were astonished by the many rifles that were dug up from the ground in that village. These had the chrysanthemum crest clearly carved into them: they were the weapons of Japanese troops. A unit had advanced into this remote area of Shanxi before us and had met a crushing defeat. One of our units had returned to earth along with their rifles without anyone knowing about it and without making a mark on history. Looking up to the heavens, we prayed for the souls of those unfortunate fellow soldiers.

Narita Takeo, sixty-nine (m),
company employee, Kawasaki

The Forceful Last Will of a Fallen Enemy Soldier

At the end of May of 1940, Japanese forces massed on the eastern bank of the Hanshui tributary to the Yangzi River. Undaunted by the enemy's barrage of heavy mortars and machine-gun fire, Japanese troops began a furious charge to cross the river and head for Yichang, their destination. The advance was so sudden that some units were bombed by mistake by our own aircraft.

Three or four days into the push across the river, I came across the dead body of a fleeing Chinese soldier, lying face up on a footpath between paddy fields. An infantryman right behind me shouted, "Hey, this one's still alive." I turned around as he said, "Hell, I'll put him out of his misery," and aimed the bayonet attached to his rifle at the heart of the Chinese soldier. At that moment, the Chinese soldier grabbed the blade pointed at his own heart and, summoning up his last bit of strength, refused to let go. The infantryman could neither push forward nor pull back. Taken aback by the force of will of the Chinese soldier in his death agony, the infantryman lost his spirit to stab him.

Loosening his grip on the bayonet, the Chinese soldier, still grasping the blade with one hand, shook his other hand and pleaded in a moaning voice that his life be spared. We were in the midst of pursuing the enemy unit, so we couldn't dally. Leaving the scene as it was, I followed the rest of our detachment.

We charged into Yichang on 12 June after a desperate struggle. A short while later there was a phenomenal flooding of the Yangzi River. From upstream of the splendid natural stronghold of the Taihang gorge, countless bodies of massacred men and women, old and young, floated down on the torrents of water, giving off a foul stench. I wonder what had gone on in the territory not occupied by the Japanese forces.

Honda Kōtarō, seventy
(m), shop owner, Tokyo

Without Even Confirmation of Names

A middle-aged man came to see me. He had read my account of military service during the war and said he wanted to hear in detail about conditions at that time. His father, who had been sent to the China front with the Hinoki Unit, had died from malnutrition at the supply base hospital near Ishu River in Hunan Province.

As a noncommissioned medical officer I took part in the battle at Xiangkui which began in May 1944. At the time of the Yangjiao battle in July, I was evacuating wounded and ill patients of the Hinoki, Hiro, and

Arashi units* to the field hospital set up in the Yangjiao suburb. That was where the tragedy occurred. Supplies from the rear area were cut off, and basic food needs were not met. In this situation, in which none of the hospital functions could be met, cholera broke out. In less than a month most of the patients died. The death count has been said to be four thousand or even five thousand, but it is not known. Desertions and suicides occurred in this extreme situation, and men died without confirmation of their names.

The dispensary where I was, a hastily built ward of straw mats laid on the earthen floor of a private house, held about six hundred patients. They died a week after cholera broke out. The six medical corpsmen who had looked after the six hundred patients were ill themselves from malnutrition and in no condition to move. The dead were left behind, their bodies rotting. I don't recall preparing an official record of the names of the dead patients or death reports to send to detachment headquarters. The other aid stations must have been the same. Under such extreme conditions, even the identification tags that all soldiers should have had could not be put to use.

My visitor said his father was a noncommissioned officer in the Hinoki Unit. I feel sorrowful at the thought of my visitor who, even after forty years, still wishes to find out something about his father's last moments.

> Tobita Toshio, sixty-seven (m),
> company executive, Kyoto
> Prefecture

---

*Japanese units of battalion strength were often identified by code or generic names, e.g., the Hinoki [Cypress] unit or the names of their commanders, e.g., the Yamamoto unit.

Shoot Even Without Confirmation

This happened in January 1939 during security patrol at Hanshui on the central China battle lines. The previous night there had been a river crossing, suggesting an enemy attack. The response to our desperate communication requesting support from company headquarters was that support was impossible; orders were to defend our position to the death until the following morning. The platoon commander instructed the sentries to consider all who came from ahead to be the enemy; we were told to shoot or stab without challenge, not to yield an inch. With these strict orders, two men from each squad stood on sentry duty two hundred meters apart on the forward embankment.

In the deep darkness the sound of dogs barking far away was eerie. Sounds and lights that seemed to be signals crossed each other. Menacing gunfire echoed from the opposite shore. Early in the morning there was a loud rustling in the grasses beyond the fog-covered embankment, as if a large army force were approaching. However much I looked, I could see nothing, and only heard the noise. *Shoot!* As I got off two shots, the soldier ahead called out "*Aizu!*" to which I replied with the password, *Byakko*. From ahead I heard a pained shout, "I've been hit! I've been hit!" It was the company commander and two fellow soldiers.

"Are you first-year conscripts?" "Yes sir." "Why did you shoot without challenging?" "We were taught that in emergency cases it was all right to shoot without challenging." "Idiots, where did you hear such a regulation?"

Weak-kneed, we eventually went on guard duty. We were shocked that we had wounded three men with two shots. If, risking our lives, we had downed the enemy as ordered, we would be considered heroes, but our firing on our own troops would lead to a court-martial. It was regretful, but it would be better to commit suicide than live with the shame. Just as I poked my rifle muzzle against my throat, my squad buddies, who had found out about the accident, came rushing over. They took away my weapon until my agitation subsided, and I was shut up in a room. They put me under strict guard. My buddies said that since the company commander hadn't received the communication, and the platoon commander was the one who had issued the order, if I were to die, they couldn't live either.

One week later I was told to go outside, where I found a buddy from my hometown. When I gave him my account, he counseled me saying, "It's not unusual to be shot at from behind. If you kill yourself over something like that, you'll run out of lives, no matter how many you have." His words helped me get back on my feet.

Tanno Midori, seventy (m),
farmer, Nihonmatsu

Assailants and Victims

From the spring of 1942, as a soldier I spent harried days in punitive expeditions against the Chinese Communist army in Shandong Province in

China. One of our regular operations was what could be called the labor procurement operation.

We surrounded a village at dawn and made wholesale arrests among the peasants. Setting aside women, old people, and children, we handed over all the men to our commanding headquarters. It was only after I was repatriated that I found out that these men became the Chinese forced laborers who faced tragedy in the mines in various locations.

The operation was ruthless and terrible. Not even a single ant was to escape the tightening circle of us soldiers, some carrying lights—large bottles whose bases had been sheared off by heating the glass, which we held upside down with candles stuck in the necks—and others loudly banging oil cans or washbasins. But at that time we thought in a matter-of-fact way that this was what war was like. Later, I was interned in Siberia. My four years of forced labor, I think, was a measure of atonement for my wartime actions. We were assailants as well as victims.

> Yamada Ichirō, sixty-seven (m),
> dye works owner, Tokyo

Strike by One-Star Privates

According to the phrase "consider superior officers' lives as the Emperor's life," soldiers were expected to give up our lives if so ordered. Yet there was one time when the lowest-ranked, one-star privates went on strike.

The Fourteenth Division Medical Corps Motor Transport Company was made up of transport soldiers with hardly any training. When we were sent to the front some of us didn't even know how to cook the rice in our rations. The company was divided into three platoons. Each platoon's first squad was the stretcher unit, and its second squad was the horse wagon squad. The wagons transported stretchers hung on two levels. This was in 1937, at the start of the Sino-Japanese Incident.

The company commander was a vicious drunk and often behaved disgracefully in front of the soldiers. When we were in march formation, he would make us walk extra distances, insisting that we overtake the unit ahead by taking a side road and circling around in front. On foot and carrying their heavy equipment on their backs, the soldiers suffered great pain. The frequent boos from the rear and calls of "You idiot!" fell on deaf ears.

One day we were lying on the ground, totally exhausted, on standby alert. The commander rode up on horseback, ordering us to help the engineers with bridge building. Not a single man stood up. There is nothing more pitiful than a superior whose orders are not obeyed. The unit commander came over on his own horse and, from his saddle, whipped the company commander. Then he departed.

The company commander of the infantry stretcher company rode up. "The infantry is engaged in battle on the front lines. We must quickly build a bridge so that we can send reinforcements. I'm sorry to put you through all this trouble, but please help us out." One after another the soldiers stood up and waded into the river. That company commander was worldly-wise, and his concern for the men—in the mornings, he called out, "Have you eaten?" even to those of us in a different company—made him popular among the troops.

Maruyama Kōshirō, seventy-two
(m), farmer, Nagano Prefecture

The Tank Swayed Like a Small Boat

In June 1942, Japanese troops with the Number 4 Cavalry Brigade as their main force planned an operation to outflank and exterminate the Number 28 Combined Force of the Chinese army in northern Henan Province. I participated in this operation as driver of the brigade tank commander's tank. Our forces began our movements at midnight, and, engaging in fierce battle at every point, we encircled the town where the enemy command post was located. The tank forces were deployed near the town's western gate.

The foot soldiers of Number 72 Cavalry Regiment carried out several daring assaults but were unable to achieve results. The enemy consisted of crack troops under the command of General Gao Shuxun. It was an opponent not easily resisted. Eventually the sun tilted to the west. Changing our tactics, our forces attacked by opening up the eastern gate enclosure. With tanks accompanied by infantry, we crashed against the city gate to break through. Acting in concert with the units standing by, we charged. The enemy was finally routed, and they surged through the eastern gate in retreat.

The tank force was immediately ordered to give chase. We hurried to change our course. When we neared the eastern gate area, ahead was a mass of foot soldiers and cavalry rushing for their lives in retreat. On the road ahead lay the dead bodies of many Chinese soldiers. We progressed around these bodies but were unable to avoid them all. The only way to go was over the bodies of the war dead. Making up our minds, we passed over them. I gripped the drive shaft and closed my eyes. There was a soft impact. The tank swayed gently. It felt like being on a small boat as it plowed through the waves. In my heart I prayed *"Namu Amida Butsu"* to the Buddha and went ahead.

When we had been in pursuit for a while, we came across a worn-out Chinese soldier kneeling on the ground, his hands pressed together. We stopped the tank. Our commander directed the soldier to hang his rifle on the radio antenna. When he had done so, the commander said, "Go off, you're free." He stood to attention, saluted, and made an about-face to the right. Then he dashed off. It must have been fifteen or twenty minutes since we had run over the dead bodies.

In the special circumstances of a battlefield, we could not afford to reflect on the situation with humanity. All we could do was act as we were commanded.

Suhara Seiichi, sixty-eight (m),
labor association member, Inasawa

China's Mata Hari, the Girl
With the Hair Ornaments

Fourth Company commander First Lieutenant Yoshida, a seasoned officer who had landed at Hangzhou Harbor, was known for his operational skill. As platoon commander of the Second Company at the time, I was often with him, and many times I copied his battle tactics. During the turning point of the first Changsha battle, we were chased by enemy forces several dozen times larger than ours. Volunteering his unit to bring up the rear, First Lieutenant Yoshida got into hand-to-hand combat against the Chinese forces' volunteer unit. The flesh of his rear end was blown off by an enemy grenade and he was sent to the Hankou army hospital.

This hospital employed many Chinese girls to help care for the patients who had difficulty moving about. First Lieutenant Yoshida was cared for by a girls' high school graduate who spoke good English, was bright, kind, and a rare beauty to boot. Her clothing was simple, but he said she always wore elaborate hair ornaments. After recuperating for some three months, Lieutenant Yoshida was released from the hospital and resumed his command of the Fourth Company. The girl found it hard to part with the lieutenant, and, resigning from the army hospital, followed his unit, to the envy of us young men.

She settled into our encampment. When asked to do something, she immediately answered, "*Mingbai*" ("I understand"), and accomplished the task with efficacy. We took to calling her Mingbai. Here also Mingbai always wore hair ornaments and went about her work so diligently that she made herself highly useful.

In December 1941 the second battle for Changsha commenced. Lieutenant Yoshida and I advanced to Changsha once again. But Mingbai had disappeared. No one knew her whereabouts. This battle turned into a series of difficult struggles from the start. Although we finally took Changsha, it was only after we'd suffered extremely heavy casualties.

In analyzing the reasons for the failure of this battle, one of the causes given was that the enemy's ninth battle section chief, Xue Yue, had detailed information about our forces. The reasons for this were investigated. Mingbai's name surfaced as a possible source of the information. Lieutenant Yoshida was accused of engaging in acts aiding and abetting the enemy, demoted to private and sent back to Japan. Later gossip pegged Mingbai to be a brilliant spy from Chongqing who was called the Mata Hari of China. When I recall that she always wore hair ornaments that she didn't let anyone touch, I wonder if she was hiding a microphone there.

> Kawakami Tokio, sixty-nine (m),
> former civil servant, Tochigi
> Prefecture

Devil Sergeant's True Heart

I was drafted on 1 February 1945. Enrolled in the Nishiyama Company of an independent garrison in the Kwantung Army, I was placed under the command of a tough "devil" sergeant from hell. After three months of arduous training consisting mostly of antitank attacks, we had our first target practice with live shells. Two out of three of my bullets hit the target, and I was made a light-machine-gunner.

My hardship increased after I became a gunner. Six-kilometer marches lugging a light machine gun were difficult, and during exercises I had to run at the head of the troop. I was also exhausted from the time it took me every night to keep the machine gun in good working order. If we were lax in our care, the devil sergeant would slap our faces and scold us, saying, "I can replace you draftees with a single red card, but I can't immediately replace a light machine gun. It's a valuable weapon."

On 8 August, upon reports that the Soviet Union had entered the War, we were ordered to the Soviet border. On the way we passed evacuating [Manchurian] colonizers. Our courage was boosted by their saying, "We're counting on you, soldiers," as they waved to us.

We neared the front. Suddenly, a voice shouted, "Enemy air attack!" and the devil sergeant yelled, "Take shelter in the sorghum field." I jumped into a creek, but with the weight of my machine gun, my feet slipped, and I tumbled down. The gun sank into the muddy water and I couldn't retrieve it. It was then that I heard the sergeant say, "Hey, Nakamura, what are you doing? Hurry up." "My gun has sunk into the water and I can't reach it." "Get the gun later. Hurry up, you'll get shot." I crawled up the bank of the creek and ran to the sorghum field. Behind me was the sound of machine-gun strafing. *Da-da-da!* it chased after me. Just as I ducked for cover, the bullets landed close to my body, *busu, busu!*

When humans come face to face with death, we finally learn their true nature. To me the devil sergeant from hell turned into a Buddha, a saintly sergeant from heaven.

Nakamura Toshio
seventy-two (m), retired,
Shimonoseki

Shot—Thought of Time Left Me

It was about 4 P.M. on 15 August 1945. I was clinging to a riverbank, breathing the sickening fumes of the grasses, in battle against Soviet troops across the river. The location was near the Yusong Bridge on the outskirts of Chongjin in north Korea. (The cease-fire order had not yet reached the front line units.)

I had been leaning out to scout the movements of the Soviet troops when suddenly I felt excruciating pain along with a great bursting. It felt as if hot tongs were gouging out my right ear. I had heard that if a bullet hits you above the neck you have an eighty to ninety percent chance of not surviving. "Damn it," I thought, resigning myself to unavoidable death. I was amazed that this made me feel serene.

I slumped down on the spot. The fleeting time I had left seemed infinitely valuable. Bleeding heavily, I was trying to think with my muddled senses. Having to die at the young age of twenty-six had never seemed more regrettable than at that time.

A medical corpsman rushed over to treat my wound. As he bandaged me up, he assured me that the bullet had missed any vital parts. I would be all right. At this, I was immediately revitalized. My nerves grew tense. The gunfire from the Soviet forces suddenly subsided. Instinctively I sensed that this battle would end at sundown. A feeling of ease and equanimity welled up inside me.

I looked at my fellow soldiers. Relief spread over their fear-strained faces. The sound of gunfire stopped. The battle was over. Two or three cigarettes glowed in the dusk.

When I think back on that time, having been near death, I am keenly thankful for the happiness of being alive now and of having peace.

Katō Shunroku
sixty-six (m), union officer,
Ichikawa

Chapter 4

The Greater East Asia Co-Prosperity Sphere

The Greater East Asia Co-Prosperity Sphere (*Daitōa Kyōeiken*) was what the Tokyo propagandists named it. As the Japanese Armies marched first into China, then advanced into Southeast Asia and the Pacific Islands—which the Japanese called *Nan'yō,* "the South Seas"—many thousands of civilians came with them. Some of these were the dependents of military men, for in some cases officers at least were able to bring their families to their posts in China and elsewhere. Others were civilian employees of a Japanese military occupation that soon grew a bureaucracy all its own. Japanese-language newspapers sprouted up in the occupied areas. Local newspapers were taken over by Japanese editors and military censors. Japanese businessmen went overseas in the wake of military conquest. Local Japanese started businesses, first to provide supplies for the troops, then to offer a variety of services. Japanese companies for their part were quick to set up branches and subsidiaries in the new Greater East Asia.

Then came the colonists. Families were encouraged to migrate from Japan to settle in the occupied territories. They did so firm in the conviction that Japanese rule was there to stay. Japanese schools were founded everywhere the Occupation reached. Japanese children grew up in China, Korea, and Taiwan, living the rather cushy existence of colonialists among a subject population.

When the War ended, all these people were cut adrift. Some were lucky enough to be in port areas, whence they were repatriated quickly to Japan under Allied control; others spent months or even years in Soviet-occupied regions of China and Manchuria before they could return. While in China they fell under the jurisdiction of rival Nationalist and Communist armies. Their treatment varied. Many did not come back at all, for the hardships visited on Japanese civilians were severe. Suddenly transformed into hunted fugitives, they straggled through Japan's former colonies desperately looking for food and clothing. Thousands of children perished in this time. Many were killed by their parents when there seemed to be no hope of survival.

Names like Hong Kong, Harbin and Beijing had once sparkled like exotic signposts on the perimeter of the Greater East Asia Co-Prosperity Sphere. They now began to ring dolefully in Japanese ears as the battered survivors returned. Some came in boxes. Trains began to go through the Japanese prefectures bearing the ashes of soldiers who had perished on far distant islands defending what they thought was theirs to keep. Thousands of families were broken up by the War and its aftermath. Their anguish remains.

Some of the letters in this section are from people who were colonists or officials and other civilian workers in the occupied lands, while others are from those who had tried through the War to keep in touch with fathers, brothers, and sons overseas. Some scattered families were never brought together again. Many children were left behind in China. It was not until the 1980s that the Japanese government began systematic efforts to repatriate these lost "orphans," who arrived, most speaking only Chinese, desperately looking for the Japanese relatives who had abandoned them decades before.

Wandering Around Saipan

I was in the first grade when the American military forces landed on Saipan. Born and raised on the island of Saipan, I had spent a peaceful life surrounded by the beautiful South Seas.

That peace was shattered by the bombs from American planes, followed by a naval bombardment and then the landing of American forces.

The five of us, my parents, my older sister, my younger sister, and I, wandered around the jungle along with other refugees. The greatest hardship was living without water. We were pouring sweat from the hot summer sun. We had no water. It was very hard. Along the way, injured Japanese soldiers and island natives begged us, "Please take us with you."

My father left us and went to forage for food. As he went, he shouted out to us in a loud voice, "I'll be back for sure, so don't move." He came back with berries, sugarcane, and food left by Japanese soldiers.

They say that after two months of living in the jungle it becomes hard for people even to think. Our senses had become numb to the mountains of dead bodies of Japanese and island natives, and we felt nothing. Those of us who were alive must have looked like the refugees in Africa that we now see on television.

No longer able to move, we were captured by American troops and evacuated to a camp. Ours was the only family whose members all survived. It was a miracle that we did.

Komatsu Megumi, forty-nine (f),
school staff, Heda

In Penang at War's Outbreak

During the last War I experienced more than I cared to both sides of the proverb "The winning army is called the government's forces; the losing army is called the defeated forces." I operated a store in the city of Penang, in the British Straits Settlements. Before dawn on the day the War broke out I was suddenly detained by the British authorities in Penang Prison with fifty-three compatriots as resident enemy aliens. But in just over two weeks the local representatives of the various ethnic groups visited us and beseeched us for help. "The city is now in a state of panic and in complete anarchy; we want you immediately to take charge and maintain public order." They said that in the face of the continual bombings by the Japanese army, which had landed at Kota Baharu, the Anglo-Indian troops defending the island of Penang had fled toward Singapore without putting up a fight.

This was how the residents, without stirring, were able to effect a bloodless occupation of Penang, a city of 400,000. We nominated the chairman of the local Japanese residents' association as the mayor. As economic department chief, I exerted myself in securing distribution channels for food and procuring goods needed for the occupation. Wielding absolute authority, we lived like royalty.

In the following February of 1942, soon after the fall of Singapore, the Penang Province Government Office was established under military administration. We formed a union to ration goods and worked toward stabilizing the lives of the residents. Later, Japanese military police entered the city and purged a great number of anti-Japanese Communist Party elements. As interpreter I attended their interrogations by military police in Penang Prison.

At the War's end, I was an interpreter attached to the Thirty-third Army Staff imprisoned in Rangoon Prison as a suspect in the Tsuji staff incident. I withstood daily torturing and was finally released half a year later. Immediately I was sent back to Penang, my old stomping grounds, as a suspect in the Penang military police incident.* But I didn't make it in time for the combined group trial. As I had already spent over two years in detention awaiting trial, I was released under the principle of double jeopardy. It was a major incident in which all of my colleagues were declared guilty. Twenty-three of them were executed by hanging.

Yoshida Tamekichi, seventy-seven
(m), retired, Kanagawa Prefecture

---

*Both incidents involved wartime Japanese army atrocities in Malaya.

Beheaded Bandits on Horseback

During my childhood in the former Manchukuo, where I was born and raised, the region was overrun by mounted bandits. We often heard the sound of gunfire, day and night. The town where I lived was a marshaling area for all kinds of military forces, making it seem like a military outpost.

There were many punitive expeditions against bandits. The military would capture several prisoners and execute them in front of a firing squad on the outskirts of town. Others were beheaded. I went with several friends to the execution spot to watch. I now shudder to think that I must have been quite inured to such brutality.

"The severed heads are out in the open." I was swept up by the voices of those who ran to see them, and I ran as well. Some of the faces had lips clenched in resentment. Lined up were such ferocious heads that I had to avert my eyes. Nearby a large crowd of Chinese had gathered to see the heads. I wonder what they felt as they watched this ruthless form of execution.

> Shiobara Suzue, sixty-one (f),
> housewife, Shimane Prefecture

Arrogance of Top Military Officers

When I was working at a shipbuilding yard in Shanghai during the War, my supervisor's wife was the daughter of an army lieutenant general. Her mother occasionally came to visit her. This mother purchased a handbag with a gold metal clasp at a store run by a Chinese in the international concession. She claimed there was a scratch on the clasp, and I was ordered by my supervisor to go with the lieutenant general's wife to negotiate the return of the handbag. The negotiation was carried out in my halting Chinese and the storekeeper's halting Japanese.

The shop owner refused to acknowledge the problem, saying, "I can't take it back. You looked it over thoroughly before you bought it. You must have dropped it or something and scratched it after you took it home." The lieutenant general's wife glared at the shop owner and said, "Perhaps if I was the wife of a lieutenant colonel or a first lieutenant it would be all right, but I can't be seen with a scratched handbag like this one." I had a bad conscience about it, but I told the shop owner, "This person is the wife of a lieutenant general, the highest-ranking army officer in the central China area," and kowtowed to him to get him to accept the return. The words of the lieutenant general's wife still sting my heart some forty-five years later.

At that time there were lectures in each workplace for the wives, on what to do in case of air raids. After one of these lectures the daughter of the lieutenant general boasted, "If we have an air raid, I'll just fasten the congratulations we received from Mr. Tōjō on my child's head and hold my child's hand and evacuate." When I heard this, I asked my wife, "Wasn't there any older person who could have taken her to task?" My wife said everyone was silent and cast their eyes down.

The sense of arrogance of the families of the high-ranking military officers of the time was repulsive. But not to criticize such behavior was also a fault. The fact that most women now have acquired a critical cast of mind, I believe, acts as a major brake against war.

Hase Hideo, seventy-five (m),
union official, Kumamoto

Securing Chinese Laborers

By 1943 the shortage of labor had become the most pressing problem at war plants. That April, along with three colleagues, I was ordered by the Mitsubishi Nagasaki Shipbuilding Works to transport 820 Chinese factory workers from north China. When I visited the North China Factory Workers Association in Beijing, representatives from thirty two war plants all over Japan were crowded into the office. We waited at our inn until we received orders to pick up the laborers in Changjou.

When I asked the Japanese army captain who was the commander of the Changjou region how the laborers had been gathered, he said they had been forcibly captured as delinquent young men who were out on nighttime sprees. The next day fifty of them were tied up with cord, and I led them on the two-kilometer march to the station, flanked by Japanese and New Government soldiers with bayonets. Among those watching this march were people who glared at me in anger and women with their hands pressed together who seemed to be mothers. When the freight train stuffed with laborers started off, these mothers cried, hitting the platform with both hands.

A Japanese coal ship transported the laborers who had been gathered in this way. When we reached Shimonoseki, the policy had changed. These laborers were sent to coal mines, where I heard they were brutally treated.

I was following company orders, but even now my heart aches at this memory.

Haseba Sueto, seventy-five (m),
former teacher, Kumamoto

One-Man Class Reunion in Harbin

"The Harbin that I dream about. My second homeland. The Sungari flowed gently, and the White Russians enjoyed themselves on summer holidays on Taiyang Island. The beautiful Western European–style buildings and cobbled streets. The flowers that bloomed abundantly. In winter it changed completely, into a frozen world. The cold weather turned the entire town into a crystal room. The river and pond were frozen over and became icy fields, and all the traffic was by sleighs. The winters were severe. But for us children, we enjoyed skating to our hearts' content on the school playground, which had turned into a natural skating rink."

In the seventeen years since our marriage, I heard my husband talking many times about his childhood memories as we looked at his old photos. To me Harbin was only a city in my imagination, the place I planned to visit with my husband on our trip abroad after his retirement. Our entire family was blessed with an unexpected chance to visit Harbin last summer. As if in answer to my husband's hope, cherished for forty years, he was able to communicate with citizens in the Chinese he hadn't used since his return to Japan. Relying on a map, we visited his elementary school. Through the kindness of the school, the gate was unlocked and we were allowed to see the school grounds. The name had been changed to Majiagou Primary School, but there was no doubt that the building was the one I had seen so often in the photo. Standing in the same spot he had stood in those many years ago, my husband muttered, "This is my one-man class reunion," as our teenage son took his picture.

There they were—the fifth-grade, number-two class, of Hakubai National Elementary School. What kind of lives have the teacher and classmates in the photo led since then?

We were able to find the house where my husband's family had lived. It now had two separate entryways and seemed to be a dwelling for two families. A lovely woman who appeared to live there happened to come home when we were there. She looked suspiciously at these foreigners who had suddenly arrived. But she seemed satisfied with my husband's explanation, which was aided by his gestures, and nodding, she smiled gently and asked, "Would you like to see the inside?" My husband declined, saying, "Thank you, but we don't want to bother you." While we were unaware, Chinese people appeared at the neighboring doorways. They called out, "good-bye," and waved as we left. The summer day came to an end.

The city's development was progressing rapidly. Many high-rise apartment buildings were completed just behind the house. We turned back for one last look at my husband's old home before it, too, would be torn down.

Ōno Yumiko, forty-three (f),
housewife, Nagoya

Article on First Snow Forbidden by Japanese Military

Toward the end of 1943, I was a reporter at the *Manshū Nippo* Jiamusi branch bureau in the city of Jiamusi, capital of Sanjiang Province, Manchukuo. Major news items were sent to the national edition at the central bureau in Xinjing. My work mainly consisted of writing articles for the local daily, *Sanjiang Nichi Nichi Shimbun*. One morning when I arrived at the office, I found that bureau chief Mizoguchi was surprised at being called in by the military. The cause was an article I had written on the first snowfall of the season, which had appeared that day. News censorship was strict and any defiance of the military would result in immediate suspension of publication. The bureau chief was riled up that a report on the first snowfall would be cause for suspension of publication.

The stubborn bureau chief returned exhausted and told me, "Articles that can give the Soviets information about the weather in northern Manchuria are anti-War. All such articles are prohibited in the future as well. That's what they said. They wouldn't listen to my arguments at all."

The Amur and the Sungari rivers freeze over in the winter, allowing spies free crossing of the border region. The Soviet troops were not so naive as to get their information on the weather conditions by reading a Japanese newspaper. Rather than being angry, I was frightened to find out about this unexpected weak spot of the Japanese military.

I don't know if that was why, but soon afterward I received my red card draft notice and was shipped out from the news group staff on the Japan-Soviet front to the front lines in Okinawa.

Enomoto Shōtarō, sixty-six (m),
writer, Tokyo

A Present from the War

Having lost my father before the War's end, I should curse the War. My father was a career soldier. He was hardly ever home, and I have no sense of the reality of my father's love. During the transitions of my life—school commencements, employment, and marriage—I felt the misfortune of not having a father. But recently my way of looking at things has changed.

Although there certainly are shortcomings to a fatherless family, I was raised freely with little repression by a mother and grandmother whose sole purpose for living was to raise a child. Bewildered by the sudden change to a democratic society and pressed by the demands of everyday living, they may not have sharply disciplined me. But from our adversity I gained the strength to observe things with my own eyes and to act according to my own will. If my strict father had lived, he would no doubt have said girls should be feminine, and I would have been raised to be a woman unable to assert herself.

My mother, over seventy now, looks after her store while caring for her bedridden mother. Because she lost her husband, my mother was able to grow into an independent and self-supporting woman. Even though elderly, my mother is still able to provide for herself; and I have been able to think for myself. Perhaps these are presents that the War gave us.

Hiroshige Kiyoko, forty-four (f),
housewife, Yamaguchi

I Want to Go to Beijing

We found out thirty-six years later that Grandpa's ashes—he died in 1950 in Beijing—are at Guanyin temple. Grandma was very surprised and overjoyed and says she wants to go to bring him home, but her blood pressure rose and she took to her bed. She can't walk around on her own, so I want to quickly learn Chinese and thank the Chinese people who looked after Grandpa's remains for so long.

Grandma became a woman military doctor during the Chinese civil war. She was in her last month of pregnancy with my father, so until dark she was carried around on a litter to take care of the sick and wounded. At night she was called to deliver babies. There was no food in the area because it had been burned out. My father was born when there wasn't enough to eat, so he suffered from malnutrition. Even now he doesn't have the use of one of his eyes and can't work.

Grandpa's name was Iwamura Genjirō. He lived in Beijing for about ten years. Before the War ended, he became a civilian army employee. Earlier he had worked as a reporter for the *Kahoku Shinpō* newspaper. He once taught at a girls' high school in Tokyo; maybe his students might know more about him.

I would work part time or do anything to make money to pay for a trip to Beijing.

> Iwamura Enji, twelve (m),
> elementary school pupil,
> Yokohama

Sad Trip to Deliver Soldiers' Remains

The first term review completed, the soldiers I had lived with in the same unit departed for the front on the continent one early spring day. I was in officers' training and left behind, assigned to the awards section when I was ordered to deliver the remains of the war dead. I was happy about the unexpected chance to be liberated from the strictures of barracks life and go to the port of Kobe on official business, and all the more so because Kobe was where I spent much of my childhood. But this trip was full of sadness.

A passenger ship loaded with the remains of the soldiers who had died all over the continent quietly docked at the pier. This was their silent return to the homeland that they had dreamed of. All the ships in port sounded their horns in condolence. It was a moment of grief.

It was late at night that the train arrived in Shiga Prefecture. Having received word from the village military affairs section, the families of the war dead were gathered at their local train stations, waiting tearfully for the moment of their meeting with the dead. A soldier wearing a mask covering his mouth and gloves gently passed the box of remains wrapped in white cotton cloth through the train window. Family members rushed to the box. Elderly parents and young wives holding children's hands or carrying babies clung to the box and wept. "This is your father." Thinking, *This will be us tomorrow*, we soldiers cried also and could only stand silently at the window.

This is my memory from the third year after the start of the Sino-Japanese War, in the early summer of 1939, when I was with the Tsuruga Nineteenth Infantry Regiment.

Kimura Fumio, seventy-two (m),
former company employee, Chiba

Standing Still in a Strong Blizzard

January 1943. Despite a strong blizzard that day with visibility of only five or six meters, it was my first leave in a while, so I went out to Qiqihar. To a first-year soldier warmly bundled up like an Eskimo, the weather didn't present a hardship. But there were very few people out and about in the largest city in northern Manchuria.

In the swirling blizzard I spied a couple standing still. I could tell they were Japanese right away. After curtailing our sight-seeing of the city, we hurried back and saw that the couple was still standing in the same spot. Seeing how they were dressed, I couldn't help staring at them. The scrawny man didn't even have a hat on and wore only a summer cloak. The woman, quite noticeably pregnant, was dressed in a thin, fluttering kimono with a summer shawl wrapped around her shoulders. I felt awkward about the great difference in the way we were dressed, but I called out to them. They were members of a settlement group waiting for a bus.

I was at a loss for words on seeing members of the Manchuria and Mongolia settlement for the first time. These were people who had been sent off with cheers and who were said to be cultivating the great earth. If the War's end had occurred in the bitter cold of winter, these people might all have become corpses strewn on the wastelands. These were people in the weakest position in Japanese society. Our past history is one of seeking to solve our domestic and foreign stalemate through war. And now people seem to dare privately to anticipate the coming of another war. Are human beings so weak and sinful that they are unable to come to their senses unless they experience for themselves the tragedy of war?

> Takizawa Kinji, sixty-six (m),
> company employee, Akita

Teachers and the People's Trial

They say that there are two ways to win over people: the carrot and the stick. I have finally come to realize that I played the role of the carrot. Growing up in Manchuria, there was no way for me to see through to the real essence of Manchukuo, touting "harmony of the five races" and "peacefully governed land" under the Imperial flag. Having deprived Korea and Taiwan of their native languages and forced the Japanese language on them, Japan made great efforts to spread Japanese as the language of the Greater East Asia Co-Prosperity Sphere. I spent my youth teaching Japanese language to Chinese girls. These pure and innocent pupils studied hard and trusted in me.

In 1945, in the name of a unified Japan and Manchuria, labor mobilization started. Day after day the students had only meager meals and worked at sewing machines. As I exhorted students who complained, I felt I wanted to cry as well. Japan's imminent defeat was being secretly whispered among the Chinese, and some students returned to their hometowns, using illness as their excuse. And then came 15 August. In the continuing chaos, Harbin was put under the control of the Chinese Communist forces. Suddenly one day I heard of the arrest of two teachers who were my former colleagues. When I heard that during the people's trial many of the students threw stones at the teachers, shouting that they were guilty, I was so shocked my heart felt a deep chill. Their appeal for clemency was rejected. They were executed in front of a firing squad. I understand that several teachers at other schools also met the same fate.

How can hard work and loyalty to the country's policies become crimes of exploitation and contempt? These people had become victims when the long-standing anger of the Chinese masses exploded. I certainly have no confidence that the reason I wasn't caught was because I loved my students.

After my visit to China last year I have received letters from several of my former pupils. Some of them write in very good Japanese. I wish that words can be taught and learned in a peaceful manner to be used to communicate what is in our hearts.

Ono Michiyo, sixty-five (f),
housewife, Mie Prefecture

Tearful Days in the Old Capital of Kyongju

Until the end of the War I spent my boyhood in the old capital, Kyongju, in the southern part of Korea. Those were dreamlike days, but as the War intensified, they turned into days of tears.

One afternoon my mother wept as she changed her clothes. Yoshimatsu, my classmate, had cried and clung to his father, who had been drafted and had left from the train station. My mother said, "It was so sad I couldn't bear to look at them."

My homeroom teacher, "M," seemed to be one of those old soldiers stationed on the homefront. Wada, the class president, was beaten merely because he didn't stand up straight when he saluted. He was forced to salute over and over and was beaten again and again. Higashitani, who commuted by train, was beaten until he fell over, each time he was tardy because his train was late.

The War got worse, and even teacher "M" was drafted. Only the women teachers remained to teach in the school. The older brother of Ms. Yamada, who lived in my neighborhood, died as a kamikaze pilot. The women teachers sang his praises, saying there was no greater honor.

Yoshimatsu's father was killed in the War. His eyes full of tears, Yoshimatsu returned home to Japan.

The Soviets entered the War. They landed in Wonsan and were said to be headed south. My mother pulled out a small bottle and said that if the Soviet troops came she and my sister would take the poison and die. I was desperately sad and unable to understand why only she and my sister had to die.

Ōba Tatsurō, fifty-three (m),
company employee, Machida

The Manchuria-Mongolia Youth Volunteer Corps

As a civilian attached to the Kwantung Army's Quarantine Division (later Unit 731), I was posted to Harbin in 1938. It was the autumn of the year I turned eighteen. During the first half of 1939, two friends of mine from grade-school days who had settled near Dongjingcheng as members of the Manchuria-Mongolia Youth Volunteer Corps were sent to the hospital in Harbin. I went to visit them in the hospital as soon as I could. I heard from them that the actual conditions in the volunteer corps were very different from what had been publicized in Japan. I could not help feeling disillusioned.

I found out that the lands allotted to the volunteer corps and the colonization groups were not only unclaimed territories, but also included much land already cultivated by the local peasants, which was bought up by force. They said some of the peasants who had lost their farmland had turned into groups of armed bandits.

The Nomonhan border incident of May 1939 was settled when a cease-fire agreement was reached with the Soviets, but it resulted in a crushing defeat for the Japanese army. Close friends talked to each other of the need to fear the Soviet Union.

In early winter I found out in a letter from a friend in my hometown in Chiba Prefecture that my primary school teacher, Mr. "T," was fervently soliciting his former students to enroll in the volunteer corps. I sent a letter to Mr. "T" stating the following: "Judging from what 'S' and 'T,' who were hospitalized, told me and adding to that what I have been able to find out, should an all-out war break out between Japan and the Soviet Union, and if the Kwantung Army is defeated or collapses with great losses, the Japanese living in Manchuria will encounter an extremely tragic fate. Therefore, it is best to stop sending volunteer corps and colonization groups." Apprehensive about censorship in the military mail, I put a stamp on the envelope and dropped the letter into the postbox in the city. I heard from a friend that Mr. "T" was very angry when he read my letter.

Ishibashi Naokata,
sixty-six (m),
contract employee,
Atami

At Our Old Home in Taipei

I visited Taipei for the first time since I returned to Japan forty years ago. The city had changed so much that it was hard to find the house where I used to live. The muddy rice paddies where water buffalo slowly pulled tillers and the fields where sweet potatoes grew now sprouted many modern apartment buildings. I discovered our old house left standing alone among them. When I asked the Chinese people living there if I could visit, they cheerfully welcomed me into the garden.

Under the green lawn of the back yard my father, who was a teacher, had buried the books he valued, and his diaries from his student days. After the War's end, when he had no income, he had piled books in a handcart and had taken them to the market to sell. As we could only take back to Japan what we could carry with us, rather than burning his remaining books and turning them into ashes, my father had buried them in the yard. They must have all reverted to earth. When I thought of my father's feelings as he stood there beside me, I felt a sudden urge to dig into the earth.

Katayama Yukiko, forty-nine (f),
housewife, Koganei

Human Nature of My Father and Mother

I never once heard my father speak of his wartime experiences. Nor have I heard him sing military songs.

This is even though I was told stories many times about my father's youth and childhood and was forced to listen to his *Kuroda bushi* folk song over and over again. All I learned from my mother was that Father had gone to Manchuria as an army soldier, and that he had returned bringing with him an orphaned girl and three children of relatives who had died.

When we went on a trip, his horsemanship skills were so expert that people around were amazed. When by chance a Chinese person spoke to him, Father answered in Chinese. I wonder what Father had seen and what he had done. I have no way of asking him now. But I wonder if his refusal to accept his military pension and his repudiation of those who sang military songs were Father's way of expressing how he felt about the War.

The war that Father never spoke a word about. What Father taught me about the War was the scar from a bullet passing through his thigh and the heavy, gruesome pain residing in his heart. As a parent now, I don't want my son to have to shoulder the same heavy burden as my father. Yet I want my son to learn about this heaviness and pain. How shall I tell him, whose grandfather would have wanted to see him at least once, about the War, I wonder, as a mother who has not known war.

Kishida Mayumi, thirty-one (f),
housewife, Tatebayashi

A Dragonfly and a Mother's Grief

Autumn 1944 when the footsteps of defeat were sounding closer. As a result of what was euphemistically termed an honorable conscription, my eldest brother was laid to rest. He was callously sacrificed to the Greater Japanese Empire. The following is the way my mother, who is now past her eighty-eighth year, recalls her emotions of that time.

"In those days we were toiling hard, growing vegetables in response to the policy of increasing food production. I suddenly felt an itch on my neck. A dragonfly had perched on my shoulder, tired from the heat, making no effort to move. Even though I turned my head, it showed no signs of flying off.

"Looking closely at it, I saw that its large black eyes were staring intently at me. Those eyes were moist. They looked like they were full of tears and seemed sad. They seemed to be asking for help. They reminded me of my oldest son's eyes. To me it seemed that my son in central China had brought me news of himself by turning into a dragonfly. 'Is there something you want to say to me? My ears can hear what you have to say.' The dragonfly just kept gazing at me with a sad look of appeal."

A few months later the report of Brother's death reached us. We say that insects give us premonitions. I wonder if Brother's soul changed into a dragonfly to come and say good-bye.

"That was unmistakably my oldest son. Those eyes were pleading, 'Mother, Mother, thank you for everything for so long. I regret having to die without showing my gratitude and without being filial. Please take good care of my younger sisters and brothers.' He came to say his last farewell.

"It is cruel. It is all too horrible. If I could, I would like to go even to central China to embrace my son's body. He must have called out to me with all his heart that he didn't want to die."

The following is her composition that shows the excruciating pain of her lament:

> A Dragonfly came to me with pleading
> Is it the transformed figure of my child dead in War?
> Fallen in battle, the sad news from central China with no mercy,
> Though months go by, still grieving
> During the Festival of the Dead, merely the sight of a dragonfly,
> Is it the transformed figure of my son dead in War?

My mother's grief has still not faded.

Yoshitake Tōzō, sixty (m), former
company employee, Tosu

What I Want to Say About the *Awa-maru*

In 1945 Japan agreed to the request made through a third country that the *Awa-maru* transport relief items for the Allied prisoners of war in the South Seas locations. On the return trip the ship docked in Singapore. Guaranteed complete safety, she was loaded to capacity with nickel and other critical material in Singapore and with rubber in Saigon. In addition there were over two thousand Japanese citizens on board. Because the military was overloading her, the captain left port an hour earlier than scheduled. The *Awa-maru* sailed at a good speed, and the fact that she was some fifty kilometers ahead of schedule seems to have caused the ship to be sunk.

There was a thick fog the night of 1 April and visibility was zero. The American submarine *Queenfish* located the *Awa-maru* on its radar. Her position was fifty kilometers ahead of schedule and, because she was overloaded with cargo, her shape made her look like a cruiser. The submarine captain attacked and sank the ship. At the suggestion of an ensign in the signal corps, the submarine surfaced and made a search. They rescued a cook and realized only then that the ship was the *Awa-maru*.

Shocked, the submarine captain immediately sought the assistance of other American submarines in the vicinity for a rescue operation, but it was too late.

The American navy ordered the *Queenfish* to Guam; the captain was court-martialed and ultimately retired from the service. Citing the weather conditions that night, the United States apologized to Japan through a third country. It notified Japan that no matter the outcome of the War, the U.S. would take responsibility for compensation for those aboard the *Awa-maru,* and asked Japan to respond as to the location and date a replacement ship should be turned over. Japan gave no response.

After the War's end, the Japanese parliament waived Japan's right to compensation for the *Awa-maru* because the country was receiving food and other aid from the U.S. The Japanese government presented condolence sums to the families of 70,000 yen for one person, 120,000 yen for two people, and 150,000 yen for three people. Apparently the Americans concerned with this issue were shocked at the small amounts. My own opinion is that the American submarine did not purposely sink the *Awa-maru* because it was loaded with critical cargo.

> Takita Gaichi, seventy-two (m),
> historian, Fujisawa

Kwantung Army Families Left One Step Ahead

On 6 August 1945 I was living in Manchukuo's Mudanjiang Province, Ning'an County, Number 9 Sakashitamura settlement in Qixing, dreaming of becoming a primary school teacher. A friend and I went to Mudanjiang City to get our hair permed. My friend and I went to a photography studio and had our picture taken as a memento of our first permanent. Arranging to return on 15 August to pick up the picture, we started on our way home. From Mudanjiang station to Qixing station it took over two hours by train. When we arrived at Wuhelin station, the station attendant told us, "The train won't go any farther than this, so walk the rest of the way." We wondered what was going on. At that moment we saw Kwantung Army officers and their families headed southward on a train laden with their household belongings.

We began the twenty-kilometer trek to Qixing, walking along the rail-

road tracks. People walked on, making comments such as "Why do we walk when the military trains are running? We've paid our train fare."

I got blisters on my feet but kept following the others, not wanting to be left behind. Worried because my return was so late, my father had come to meet me at the station in a horse cart. When I told him that we had had to walk home even though the Kwantung Army train was running, my father said, "I wonder if there was a reshuffling among the Kwantung Army officers." On 9 August, the day the Soviet tanks rolled over the border, my father and other settlers were packing potatoes for delivery to the army.

On 11 August the evacuation order came to the settlement headquarters. We scurried to pile food and clothes into our horse carts to begin the evacuation march. But we came across a Soviet tank unit and returned to the settlement. The following day, 12 August, we started off again on our arduous evacuation flight. On the twenty-fourth, in the mountains, we heard about Japan's surrender. If the evacuation order had been issued on 6 August, the day the officers' families had headed south, the fate of the settlement members and the youth volunteer corps might not have been so tragic. My younger brother was among the 80,000 settlers who were left in unmarked graves.

> Mio Utako, fifty-nine (f),
> housewife, Gifu Prefecture

Be a Lovely Wife

The other day my good friend showed me the letters she had received from her husband when he was at the front, letters that became his last will and testament. In 1942, he was twenty-six years old and she was twenty-one—both in the midst of their youth. A year after their marriage, while they were still newlyweds, without seeing his child born, he was sent to the Pacific War as a member of the flight crew on a navy seaplane.

Almost all the letters were marked as sent from OO region, and the family was not informed of his whereabouts. Occasionally there was a notice that his vessel had made a port call, and she would go to visit with him. After receiving the military scrip issued by the navy, and after a stay at home of several hours or several days, he flew off again to OO region.

"I am one who extols the family, but I cannot hope for a life of ease. I can only be unswerving in my spirit of devotion and my conviction as a military man. The entire country is at stake in this war. Be a lovely wife. And be a strong mother to the child to be born. We have no choice but to fling the passions of our youth into war. It is all too dreary to call this our youth. Dear ___, ___, I only think of you, ___. You who are so far away are most beautiful. Holding close to my heart the thought of you struggling bravely day by day, I live my own today."

In 1944, just before he turned thirty, he died a heroic death in battle in the South Seas.

The letters of love sent between the two of them were tattered and hard to read after forty-one years of being read many times over. Among the forty letters sent through the military post to his wife, I was unable to see the word *love*.

> Nakagawa Miyo, sixty-four (f),
> retired, Ushiku

Father, Concerned About His Son

On 4 December 1944, I boarded the train at Komoro station for Nagano to enter into active military service. The train was full of young men from the neighboring area who were to enter into the military the following day along with me. The newspapers had articles about deaths without surrender and changes of course, indicating that defeat seemed certain. But the youths on the train were noisy and boisterous, forgetting that they were departing for their certain destruction. I happened to glance at the rear of the car and saw my father, who was standing at the boarding door looking through the glass toward me. Father's shoulders and hat were white from the snow blowing in. I hadn't realized it, but he had been riding on the same train from Komoro.

"Don't stand out there," I thought of saying, and of calling him in, but I was worried that those around me would think me a sissy, so I hesitated to go toward him. Father must have had the same feelings; he didn't try to move. Eventually the train arrived at Nagano station in the twilight, and we alighted on the platform. I saw father's small hat for an instant in the crowd, but I left without being able to speak to him.

After that, I crossed the wintry sea to China and took part in various battles. In July 1946, I was able once again to see the mountains and rivers of my homeland. One day, when I was leafing through the world atlas at my house, I came across maps with red lines drawn on them showing where I had traveled as a soldier. Nanchang, Shanghai. . . . There were many breaks in the red line because it was impossible to know exact troop locations from the news reports of the time. I spent a long time gazing at the atlas that my father had marked in a desperate attempt to ascertain his son's safety.

My father is no longer alive, and I have become older than he was at that time. And yet, every December I recall the way my father looked, standing covered with snow.

Onoyama Kiyoshi, sixty-two (m),
rehabilitation worker, Komoro

A Single Piece of Wood in the Box

In the delivery of remains from the South Seas front, they say that others' bones were put into the boxes of those whose remains were unavailable, so there would be something to hand to the surviving families. The letter from Mr. Izumi Tōru [see above, pp. 34–35] who confessed after keeping silent for so many years had a deep effect on me.

My younger brother is said to have been killed in battle in the seas surrounding Okinawa. He was a seaman and died aboard a warship, making it impossible for his remains to be found. Even so, he was returned as a light box wrapped in white cloth.

That night, I suggested in front of my father and other members of my family that we unwrap the box. That was an era in which such an action was considered a sacrilege against the souls of the war dead. Everyone hesitated for a while.

When we finally opened the box, all that was inside was a narrow sliver of wood nailed loosely to the bottom of the box. A further insult was that my brother's name on the piece of wood was written incorrectly.

The piece of wood was nailed loosely on purpose, to make it sound like there actually was a piece of the dead man's bone inside when the box was shaken. In those days it was quietly rumored that this was true.

Although he must have been resigned to this, Father caught his breath at seeing the reality of the box empty of his son's remains and sat silently in front of the family Buddhist altar, appearing to hold back his tears. Watching Father seated with his back to me, I felt with some regret that my conduct had been cruel.

My brother's date of death is unclear. Taking as his date of death the decisive day of the fierce fighting on Okinawa, I go over to the cemetery at Chidorigafuchi. Buried there are some 323,000 remains that were not delivered to the surviving families. "You sleep among them," I want to tell my brother. I don't go to the Yasukuni Shrine nearby. I can't possibly believe that my brother, who was an unruly boy, has become a "god."

Anzai Hitoshi, sixty-eight (m),
writer, Tokyo

Bidding Farewell to My Brother at Osaka Station

My second-oldest brother, Shinozaki Shunji, joined the navy from Keiō University after a rousing send-off party in the outer garden of Meiji Shrine. He became a reserve cadet in the fourteenth class. On 9 April 1945, he appeared with no advance warning at our house in Ashiya, on leave from the Suzuka Naval Air Corps unit. We were all so happy we wondered if we were dreaming. Unfortunately, Father was in Tokyo on business. (My oldest brother was at the Burma front and we had no word from him.) My second-oldest brother looked with deep emotion out at the garden from the sitting room, smoking a cigarette. No matter what I asked, he wouldn't give any decent responses to his much younger sister. He was a man of few words. Spring had come late, and in the garden the cherry blossoms bloomed.

"Will the cherries go first or will I?" he muttered. I was just in the third year of girls' school and unable to comprehend what he really meant. After two hours, he stood up. Mother, my older sister, and I went to Osaka train station to see him off. At the ticket gate, my brother said, "Well, then," stood at attention, and raised his hand in salute. Mother took out her handkerchief. My brother's large eyes glistened for an instant. "Dear brother, please come home again," my sister and I cried out. Brother nodded, turned on his heel, and, taking the stairs to the platform two at a time, disappeared.

A few days later we received a letter. "I have gone south, flying high over the skies of the Osaka-Kobe area where I played in my childhood. I had my last look at Ashiya. I dipped my wing to bid my farewell. Hisako, Michiko, please take care of Father and Mother," the short letter said. These were his last words to us.

After the War, we found out from his classmates about my brother's end. On 14 April, he departed on a mission from Kanoya base as part of a special attack team with a bomb suspended from his fighter plane. Shortly after takeoff, the suspended bomb fell and exploded. Along with my brother's body, the plane scattered in all directions. His war buddies carefully gathered up his remains and cremated them. Bits of bone rattled in the box returned to us after the War ended.

Finally the defeat. The clouds on 15 August were white. The sky was blue. It is now forty years since the War's end. My eldest brother—who barely made it back from the fierce battles in Burma—and my parents have already passed away. People can't live forever. What is important is not how long we live. It is how we live. That is what determines happiness and misery.

> Fujioka Michiko, fifty-eight (f),
> housewife, Utsunomiya

Notebook Left by My Father

My father died in battle at Kowloon on the coast opposite Hong Kong on 25 December 1941. It was when I was in the first grade. I still recall that, not knowing that my father had died, I marched in the school's flag procession to celebrate the fall of Hong Kong. Hong Kong fell shortly after Father's death.

I sometimes think that if my father had behaved more shrewdly he might not have had to die in the War. But Mother says that as an officer, Father looked after his men so well that he became a victim before the men under his command. Among the articles of his that were returned to us were bloodstained binoculars, a knapsack seared with a bullet hole, a saber, and a notebook.

When the inhumane wartime conduct of superior officers was criticized, Mother opened up a small portable safe and showed me Father's notebook. It was crammed with his memo-form notations about military life in small lettering.

One entry read, "During a march one day, I asked a passing truck to carry all my men, as they were exhausted from marching under the broiling sun. For this I was scolded by the battalion commander. But it was good that we had no stragglers."

Mother was in the habit of saying that those who are good enough to face a painful death have kindness in them, that during his time as a teacher and after he entered the military Father was beloved by everybody. Whenever I read his notebook, I cannot stop weeping.

Shimizu Hiroko, fifty-two (f),
nurse, Yokohama

Chapter 5

The War in the Pacific

Called officially the Greater East Asia War (*Daitōa Sensō*)—to emphasize Tokyo's "liberation" of the continent from the yoke of Western colonialism—the War in the Pacific (*Taiheiyō Sensō*) was in one sense the inevitable extension of the China Incident, which had begun in 1937.[*] Bogged down in China by the immensity of the country as well as by the stubborn resistance of China's government—despite a succession of Japanese military victories—the Japanese high command continued to press forward with plans for further expansion into Southeast Asia. The generals and their increasingly docile civilian supporters were irritated by American and British criticism of Japan's aggression in China. They were anxious, also, to join what seemed certain to be the winning side of the coming world war. Thus, most of the Japanese military eagerly welcomed the Tripartite Pact with Italy and Germany. It was signed in September of 1940.

This adhesion to Hitler's Axis was backed enthusiastically by war minister Tōjō Hideki and pushed by Matsuoka Yōsuke, then foreign minister, but the new alignment in itself was enough to destroy any hope that an accord could be reached with the United States. By July 1941 Japanese troops occupied French Indo-China and effectively controlled Thailand. In retaliation, the Americans, supported by the British, Dutch, and French, froze Japanese assets and put into effect an oil embargo that would have cut Japan off from access to the nearby fuel supply in the Netherlands East Indies.

Two schools of thought were then paramount in the Japanese military. The navy wanted expansion into Southeast Asia and into the Pacific, envisioning an ultimate clash with the United States fleet. The army wished to

---

[*]Interestingly enough the old term *Daitōa Sensō,* the Greater East Asia War, was revived after the War by a variety of Japanese "revisionist" historians who wanted to prove that Japan's aggression was really an act of altruistic liberation of Asia from Western colonialism.

pursue its old dream of marching northward to destroy the power of Soviet Russia in Asia—an ambition that persisted despite the sanguinary defeats inflicted on the Japanese in 1938 and 1939 by Soviet troops in border fighting at Chankufeng and Nomonhan. At the same time the militarists wished to increase their conquests in China, despite foreign disapproval. War seemed inevitable. In Tokyo's controlled press there was much talk of the dangerous "encirclement" of Japan by Western powers.

Japan's resources for prosecuting a two-front war, however, were distinctly limited. Cooler heads among the bureaucracy and the military were saying so in Tokyo. Even General Tōjō expressed his doubts about ultimate victory. (He thought a stalemate possible.) In the event, the Japanese made the incredibly rash decision to go ahead on both fronts: to attack the Americans in the Pacific to cover further moves into Southeast Asia, while continuing the spoliation of China and preparing for a showdown with the Soviet Union.*

Tōjō took over as prime minister from the enigmatic Prince Konoe on 16 October 1941. It was a sign of the times that he retained his posts as both war minister and general on the army's active list. While vocal antiwar sentiments among the public had been long suppressed, his appointment marked the end of *any* civilian opposition to the military's policies.

The Japanese military which now put the country into war had not changed its stripes. The same fire-eating infantry generals who had been running the China Incident now totally dominated the government. The navy wished to go slower. Japan possessed a great asset in the person of Admiral Yamamoto Isoroku, the navy's chief—indeed its only—modern strategist. Yamamoto devised the audacious attack on Pearl Harbor, but in his mind this was part of a wider plan. Knowing the United States as he did—he had served for some time as naval attaché in Washington— Yamamoto was well aware that Japan's comparative weakness as an industrial power would be a great disadvantage in a protracted war. He told Imperial Headquarters that, given a decisive blow at Pearl Harbor, he could "run wild" for six months or a year, allowing for a navy-led invasion of Southeast Asia. After this, however, he hoped that the Americans would agree to some kind of negotiated peace, one that would permit Japan to keep at least some of its territorial gains.

Yamamoto's remark, widely quoted in wartime America, that he would "dictate peace in the White House," was taken out of context. What he

---

*Admittedly, uncompromising opposition of the United States to Japan's China adventure had put the two countries on a collision course. It was a war for which the Americans were tactically and the Japanese strategically unprepared.

actually said was that to win a war in the Pacific, Japan would have to defeat the Americans so totally that a peace negotiated in the White House was foreseeable. He did not think this was realistic.

The attack proceeded on schedule. While Yamamoto's bombers were diving on Pearl Harbor, General Yamashita Tomoyuki smashed down the Malay Peninsula and ultimately captured Singapore, thus eliminating the British presence in the Far East. (Hong Kong had surrendered on Christmas Day, 1941.) By March 1942, the Netherlands East Indies were securely in Japanese hands. Corregidor, the last American stronghold in the Philippines, fell on 7 May. The Japanese army, having already beaten the British badly in Burma, now posed a threat to India. Indeed, the carrier force that had attacked Pearl Harbor now sailed supreme in the Indian Ocean; its aircraft had already bombed northern Australia. Japan now occupied all of Southeast Asia.

The whole country was seized with a kind of mass euphoria. The thought of defeating the United States as well as Britain and other European powers was intoxicating to a country that had been systematically working to catch up with the West ever since the Meiji Restoration of 1868. Cheering theater crowds applauded newsreel footage of Japanese victories. Radio reports of new advances were followed by constant replays of "The Warship March" and other patriotic songs. Japanese civilians willingly gave up prized possessions as donations to the war effort. Class after class of new conscripts marched off to war.

Unfortunately for Japan, the blind patriotic self-confidence of the populace was duplicated at Imperial Headquarters. Counting on the superiority of "Japanese spirit" (*Nippon seishin*) over "materialistic" and therefore weak-kneed Western powers, the Japanese generals—and most of the admirals—felt sure that their gamble had worked. They neglected to take the most elementary precautions against the possibility that Japan would have to fight a long-term war. Enemy resistance, it was assumed, would continue to be weak. Few backup plans were devised to meet possible American counterstrikes.

As it turned out, the War in the Pacific was primarily a naval and air war, in which the aircraft carrier embodied American Admiral Alfred Thayer Mahan's concept that seapower is the cornerstone of a nation's strength. The Americans recovered surprisingly well from their first shock. The Doolittle bombing raid on Tokyo in April 1942 did little damage, but it showed a surprised Imperial Headquarters that the supposedly demoralized foe was capable of long-distance retaliation. An even greater shock was the battle of Midway in June 1942, when Yamamoto's effort to establish a base just west of the Hawaiian Islands was defeated by American carriers.

In August 1942, the U.S. First Marine Division landed on Guadalcanal in the Solomon Islands and captured its airfield. In 1943 the marines attacked and occupied Tarawa, an engagement that foreshadowed other island-hopping operations of the War. While General MacArthur's forces began to inch up through New Guinea, with the Philippines the ultimate goal, the U.S. Navy advanced across the Pacific. After the battles of the Philippine Sea and Leyte Gulf in 1944, the Imperial Navy ceased to be an effective fighting force.

In April 1945, the sinking of the superbattleship *Yamato* in its unsuccessful sortie toward Okinawa marked the end of an era. The island of Okinawa itself—one of Japan's home prefectures—was secured by the United States Tenth Army afterward in a bloody three-month battle. Meanwhile, MacArthur's troops, advancing from the south, fought their way into Manila, completing the re-capture of the Philippines.

Over and beyond these obvious military successes, it was the extraordinary destructive power of American submarines that gave the Allies a stranglehold on the Japanese Empire. At the beginning of the Pacific War, Japanese navy strategists reckoned that the six million tons of merchant shipping then available was ample to maintain the links with their newly acquired possessions. U.S. submarines destroyed more than five million tons over a two-year period; Japanese industry was incapable of making up the difference. Even at the War's onset, Japan was by no means self-sufficient, with 20 percent of its rice being imported. The oil reserves of the East Indies were of little use if they could not be transported to the homeland.

Thus from 1943 onward, the War progressed on three fronts. There was the obvious step-by-step island-hopping advance of the Americans, along with the less obvious submariners' war on Japanese commerce, which ultimately made shipping unsafe even in coastal waters. Finally came the crushing and cruel impact of the B-29 firebomb raids on Japan's crowded cities.

The heady drafts of early victory had apparently deprived the Japanese military of the capacity to organize an effective resistance to the increasingly evident industrial and military power of the United States. The phenomenon is familiar. After World War II, for example, the extraordinary failure of Douglas MacArthur and his staff to acknowledge and cope with the menace of Chinese troops in North Korea was an example of similar negligence—the product of earlier success and hubris.

As the Pacific War continued, Imperial Headquarters in Tokyo proved increasingly incapable even of any reactive response to American attacks. Time and time again Japanese commanders fought their own island battles with little or no help in the form of either actual reinforcements or any kind of coordinated strategy from Tokyo. The effect on the Japanese people was one of gathering disillusionment. Despite official propaganda, the sense of cumulative loss was hard to dispel. It was probably only after the American capture of the Marianas in mid 1944, however, that the idea that Japan might lose the War began to gain currency.

Still, the decades-long indoctrination of the military continued its effects. Japanese troops blindly fought on, preferring death to surrender. They forced thousands of innocent civilians to die along with them in their island strongholds. The civilian death toll on Okinawa, over 100,000, was due more to Japanese than American action. Even after the atomic bomb had been dropped on Hiroshima, Army hard-liners tried to keep the Emperor's surrender statement from being broadcast. And by mid August, Soviet troops, belatedly entering the Pacific War, easily overran the once proud Kwantung Army in Manchuria.

The letter writers tell the story of this period. There was first the great intoxication of victory, then the gradual realization of defeat, dramatized by the heart-rending stories of individuals struggling to stay alive in the face of hunger, battle wounds, and hostile action. It is interesting that most of the letters deal with the period when it became obvious that Japan was losing. Writing one-third of a century after the War had ended, the people who were moved to describe their experiences were apparently more interested in talking about their own suffering than the suffering they had inflicted on others. Taken as a whole, their accounts of the Imperial Army's actions make one realize how terribly strong Japanese military indoctrination really was.

Starting with the recollections of early victories in China and Southeast Asia, the letters go on to describe increasing hardship and eventual disaster and defeat. Even then, some did not surrender. This section includes the extraordinary reminiscences of Lieutenant Onoda, who stayed on as a lone guerrilla fighter in the Philippines for thirty years after the War was over. He was, as the saying went, "only following orders."

The Invasion of Singapore

I was in the color guard of the 114th Infantry Regiment of the Kiku corps. In the dark of night we left Johor Baharu at the southern tip of the Malay Peninsula to land on Singapore. We crossed over a pontoon bridge amid the rumble of shelling from both sides. After landing, we wandered around the small island of Singapore for a week or so. At the front, heroic hand-to-hand combat was unfolding. First Lieutenant Ran, one year ahead of me in school, was killed. Many others were wounded or dead. I heard that Second Lieutenant Yamamoto was blown up by a bomb in a trench, a direct hit. He was a graduate of military cadet school who had entered the military the same year as I.

In the Bukit Timah highland, I dug a foxhole for myself with a shovel I carried with me. When I sat down in the foxhole, I could hear the shells from both sides hissing overhead.

Told that the enemy would use poison gas, we tensed up for a while. All infantrymen carried gas masks, but they were never used.

I could see the large shells of our new mortar weapon wobble across the sky.

On the outskirts of Singapore, the enemy was shooting at point-blank range from their stronghold. We flung ourselves on the ground, unable to make a move. I felt more dead than alive. I felt that the hair on my head would turn white overnight. After a long time, the assault ended suddenly, so I immediately retreated. Behind me was a cliff, which I crawled down. After that I went to the highland. I heard the word "banzai" here and there. It was the report of the fall of Singapore.

I shed tears of joy, but my tears were from my happiness that I was still alive, that I hadn't died. Many wounded soldiers were writhing in the rubber forests. But the battle would continue. On the battlefield, the difference between life and death is paper thin.

Wakatsuki Kikuo, seventy-one (m),
company employee, Shimonoseki

Battle of Midway

I participated in the battle of Midway as a navy seaman third class. Stationed as an antiaircraft gun messenger on the seaplane carrier *Chitose,* my nerves were concentrated on the receiver so as not to miss a single word of the battle commander's orders. With the bugle call to battle blaring out on the bridge, all the antiaircraft guns and machine guns fired at once.

The carrier first turned right rudder, then left at full speed ahead. We were sprayed by shells hitting near us. The enemy's machine-gun fire burst on the deck. Despite having prepared for the worst, my legs shook violently with my lingering desire for life and my fear of death.

Turning my eyes to the distance after the battle, I saw black smoke rising here and there, indicating the great damage suffered by our warships. The sun tilted toward the west. Planes that had lost the carrier to which they should return made emergency landings near friendly ships. One after another they sank into the sea. It seemed that my ship had received orders to retreat. We sailed northwest in a circular motion.

The following morning it was announced over the speaker that there would be a burial at sea. Leaving a few men to staff the necessary positions, the rest of us lined up at attention on the upper deck. A casket wrapped in military colors was lifted up by a crane and the music of "*Umi Yukaba*" ["Across the Sea"] was played. As the rifle shots of the honor guard rang out, the rope was cut and the casket fell into the sea. It didn't sink for quite a while, and we could see it drifting farther and farther away, in and out of the waves. That was the navy's regulations, but my heart was pained by the thought that we couldn't take it back to the base.

Miyasato Yoshihito, sixty-four
(m), printer, Chiba

Life Saved by a Metal Helmet

It was three months since we had withdrawn from Guadalcanal. Our joy at surviving was short-lived. There was no time to wait for our bodies to recover, when, thanks to our operational skill on Guadalcanal, we were reinforced by troops from Japan and reorganized into the Yano Battalion. The battalion was to meet up with the American Marine Corps once again at Munda, New Georgia Island.

Early one morning five of us from battalion headquarters had to resupply our machine-gun platoon, which had used up its ammunition. We were just about to head back when we heard the crash of a mortar barrage. It sounded a bit like air flowing out of a balloon. Four rounds impacted close to us, in an American attack which had continued from the previous day. I called out to the four soldiers, "We're going back." The machine-gun platoon leader stopped me, saying, "Wait until the shelling ends. You'll be all right in this trench." But the location of the platoon was known to the enemy from the day before. I intuitively felt that it was dangerous, but the other four men pressed themselves against the trench wall and wouldn't move.

Nearly a hundred mortar rounds exploded about a meter apart—*boom!* Finally we got a direct hit; the smell of gunpowder stung my nose. Another two hits. The dirt sides of the trench crumbled. A third hit. I felt a shock, as if my head had been bludgeoned by a big pole. I could only see darkness. Numerous stars blinked as they flashed away. Damn! My eyes got it. If I can't see, I can only die. After about a minute, I saw light shining in. I've been saved. When I looked, the trench had disappeared without a trace and nothing was left of the shelter. The shelling stopped.

Feeling something lukewarm on my cheek, I reached up and felt a lot of blood. I took my helmet off to find two holes about seven centimeters wide. I touched my head wound with my hand and tied the triangular cloth from my waist around my head as a bandage. Only then did I begin to feel the pain. Private "M" said, "Superior Private, please stop my bleeding." The flesh on his leg was torn off. I rushed to tie off his thigh. We heard the voices of American troops climbing up from the valley. They neared us, spraying machine-gun fire. It wouldn't take five minutes for them to reach us. "Please hurry and go. American soldiers are coming. I can kill myself." "M"'s eyes entreated me. "Those alive, follow me!" I called out, but no one came.

The American forces that had broken through the first line approached battalion headquarters that afternoon. We returned fire with plundered American automatic rifles.

> Miyamoto Aio, sixty-six (m),
> security service employee,
> Hamamatsu

Ghosts of Soldiers Lost on Guadalcanal

In Palau I completed the process of clipping my nails and hair and putting them in an envelope to send to my relatives. Soldiers conscripted in the same year were assigned thirty at a time to various different units. I was in the army marine transport unit. On 9 January 1943, we landed at Erventa on Bougainville Island in the Solomons. For two weeks from the following day we worked stuffing rice, powdered miso, powdered soy sauce, matches, candles, and other items into oil drums. According to the company commanders, these were provisions to send to Japanese soldiers suffering from starvation in the jungles of Guadalcanal some five hundred kilometers south-southeast.

We prepared the oil drums that we had filled, fervently hoping that one more crumb of food would get into the mouths of our starving soldiers. Tied together with cables, they were towed by submarine at night. With buoys set to mark them, they were left offshore. The soldiers who were hiding in the jungle many kilometers from the coast had to go to retrieve them before the sun rose. Our work was terminated at the end of two weeks. It seems that at first this method was effective, but by the time I got there the Japanese soldiers on Guadalcanal were so weak from malnutrition that they couldn't even go to get the supplies.

20 January 1943 was a fateful day. Strangely, on this day there was no rain, and the sea was calm. Several destroyers were anchored right in front of our eyes. It was unclear what time it was. Under the torrid tropical sun the sound of the engines of the transport corps' small iron boats grew loud as the round trips between the destroyers and the shore were repeated in a great hurry. Waiting at the shore, we gently lifted out the soldiers retreating from Guadalcanal one by one and laid them on the sand. What a sad and pitiable sight they presented.

Hardly human beings, they were just skin and bones dressed in military uniform, thin as bamboo sticks. They were so light, it was like carrying infants. Only their eyes were bright; they must have been living on their strong will alone. When I put a spoon with some lukewarm rice gruel to their mouths, large teardrops rolled down their faces, and they said thank you in tiny mosquitolike voices. I, too, felt something hot unexpectedly welling up in my eyes.

My blood roiled with anger at those who had given the orders to these men. Being low-ranking soldiers, we had no way of knowing which company this was or whether the soldiers we fed were able to return safely to Japan. The War was still to continue. We were then transferred to New Guinea.

Ishida Yahachi, seventy-five
(m), merchant, Kagoshima
Prefecture

Real Battlefield Training

On 10 March 1944, I was sent to the front in the South Pacific as a second lieutenant in the army infantry. In those days the sailing route to the South Pacific was dangerous. It took twenty-five days for us to reach Singapore after leaving Ujina Harbor, and we were under constant submarine attack. It was aboard that ship that I received the best officer training in my six years' military service.

In the mixed unit that was formed in Sakai were gathered soldiers from all parts of the country. Among them were about ten noncommissioned officers who had seven to eight years of battlefield experience from the time of the China War. They lectured me persuasively and taught me some practicalities of the battlefront—nothing like what I had been taught as a young officer.

For example: (1) Even if there should be a fierce battle, never give the order to "Charge!" Soldiers die needlessly due to orders to charge rashly given by young officers. (2) Don't make a frontal assault on powerful enemy forces in tanks or pillboxes. Avoid them rather than opposing them. It is all right to flee. (3) When taking flight it is all right to throw away bayonets and other weapons and military equipment.

Our officer leadership training company had given the strongest possible training for field operations, and its daring was known even to the enemy. I had been trained in that unit, but it was the education that I received on the ship from those noncommissioned officers that guided me in battle.

I served in the South Pacific for three and a half years, including the time I spent as a prisoner of war. I had the opportunity, but I did not kill one enemy soldier, and I didn't let anyone in my unit get killed except for three who died from illness. Even if I am criticized by those who might say that it was because of military men like me that we lost the War, I think it was better that way.

Sakata Shintarō, sixty-eight (m),
corporate officer, Yokohama

"Oh, Are You a Farmer?" the American Said

"Are you a soldier?"

The enemy soldier pointed the muzzle of his rifle at me. His eyes glared like a wolf's. He must have been on the alert for a hand grenade. Four or five days before, going from Donnii to Matansa on the island of Saipan, I had collapsed in the mountain forest, my right thigh gouged by a mortar shell fragment. My fellow soldiers carried me into the back of a hole piled with rice bales. But one evening, dreaming that my younger brothers were calling me and searching for me, I crawled out of the hole.

At night there was a hard rain. The following night, after a fierce mortar attack, American forces swarmed over the area. "Damn, you bastards have come around that side too" was the final cry of my Japanese comrade right beside me, who had been spraying machine-gun fire.

"No, I'm a farmer. I'm Chamoro," I answered spontaneously. Disguising myself as a Chamoro native, I would eventually steal a boat and make my escape from this cursed island. This was the idea that had come into my mind during the desperate battle, as we were pummeled by naval bombardment and bombing attacks.

"Oh, are you a farmer?" The heavily bearded American soldier smiled, as if this was nostalgic for him. He must have been a farmer at home. He shifted his gun away from me and pointed it toward the sky. I felt relieved. Until just a moment before, writhing and tortured with pain, I had thought I wanted to die as soon as I could. I had thrown away my trousers and loincloth drenched in blood; flies were swarming around me drawn by the stench of death, and maggots were trying to enter my body through my nose, ears, mouth, and every other hole. A person's real nature goes beyond social convention, such as fear of the death penalty if caught. What lies beneath and lurks there is the will to live.

"You look like you're hurt bad," he muttered, supporting the butt of his rifle with his foot. Lighting a cigarette, he inhaled the smoke deeply. His collar was open and I could see his chest hair, thick as a bear's. Medics carrying a stretcher came down to get me.

Kawakami Sada, sixty-nine (m),
former private, Iwaki

"There's Always a Time to Die"

I was awakened by the booming sound of an explosion. The mortar attack continued incessantly. With each shell a cloud of dust rose up. The four of us in the trench were pinned to the wall and unable to move. Almost all of those above seemed to have been hit.

Suddenly gasoline from a flamethrower was blown in. We thought that it hadn't been lit so we could be taken prisoner. "Come out." It was the voice of the American soldier speaking in broken Japanese. I had a grenade with me for committing suicide. I felt that my time to die had come, and I looked at the other three for confirmation, to prompt their resolution.

That was when the sergeant major, whose right thumb was so badly wounded it was about to fall off, piped up. "I'll take responsibility. There's always a time to die. Let's go out." He was the ranking officer. I knew full well how dishonorable being taken prisoner was, but I fell in line with the sergeant major because of my cowardly feelings. I wanted a drink of water; I wanted to live.

According to American military records, it was the Third Battalion of the Second Marine Division's Sixth Marine Regiment that attacked Maniagassa, the small warship-shaped island, some 2,400 meters in circumference off Tanapag in the coral reef surrounding the western coast of Saipan. Attacking from 11 A.M. on 13 July 1944, with 900 rounds of 105-millimeter shells and 720 rounds of 75-millimeter, they took the island in one hour. After we were captured, the sergeant major was sent to a different camp for treatment of his wound. I haven't had the opportunity to see him since then. But I wanted to thank him for making the decision to be taken prisoner—he taught me the preciousness of life. I wish I could see him one more time.

Adachi Genji, sixty-seven (m),
former corporate officer,
Aichi Prefecture

The Last of Battleship *Musashi*

"Third attack," came the warning. The damage from the second attack had been terrible. Lying on the deck were several wounded men receiving emergency treatment. I was taking a brief break. My two subordinates were on their way to the infirmary. Just at that moment, a torpedo approached with a sinister hissing sound. Shouting "Go on up!" I rushed to the upper deck. I couldn't see the two who had gone toward the infirmary.

I had to get those two. I looked down the hatch. There was already close to a meter of water flooding the ship. The infirmary was left isolated. Neither my voice nor my concern could reach that far. Was it too late? My feeling of grief ran ahead of me. Then I recalled that the exhaust vent ran through the pharmacy. I frantically threw a rope from the deck down into the exhaust pipe. But there was no response. Still I continued to call out desperately.

I regained a bit of my composure. I was crouching in the safety zone under the main gun turret. The battle gained in ferocity. I wondered what had happened to my two men. To think that a single hatch would be the difference between life and death. We had spent our days together as crew members on the battleship *Musashi*. Looking back forty-some years, I still agonize about their going to the infirmary.

After the fourth and fifth concentrated air attacks, the *Musashi,* once called unsinkable, finally sank into the Sibuyan Sea. Its bow tilted. Columns of water and flames spewed up into the sky. I heard voices of my comrades singing "Umi Yukaba" ["Across the Sea"] and other war songs amid the waves. Even now I see etched clearly onto my eyelids the faces of my two subordinates. I hear my war buddies singing as their heads bob in the waves.

Satō Kiichi, sixty-nine (m), former
blood-center staff, Yokosuka

Don't Shoot at a Sinking Enemy

As a twenty-five-year-old seaman aboard a destroyer, I participated in the sea battle off Leyte. In the midst of the battle, our destroyer was pursuing a fleeing aircraft carrier through squalls and curtains of smoke. Suddenly a single enemy destroyer headed directly for us. Attacked by the concentrated fire from our destroyer squadron, it rapidly went up in flames. As we neared the enemy ship to see its last moment, it listed to one side, with flames rising everywhere. It was about to sink. Men were floating on the water's surface or sinking beneath it, while half-naked crew members jammed themselves into lifeboats and rowed away, escaping.

We were close enough to see their unkempt beards and the tattoos on their arms. One of our machine gunners impulsively pulled his trigger. He must have been overflowing with feelings of animosity toward the enemy. But he was checked by a loud voice from the bridge saying, "Don't shoot at escaping men! Stop shooting, stop!" So he inflicted no injury on the enemy.

I read an article written after the War's end that the captain, who survived, (a descendant of the Cherokee tribe) had tears in his eyes when he recalled the scene. "A Japanese destroyer that passed by did not shoot. What is more, I cannot forget the officers on the gigantic warship who saluted us in seeming condolence for the loss of our ship." What flashed through my mind was the story of Commodore Uemura, who rescued the crew of the sinking *Yurik* during the Russo-Japanese War. *Seppū* was the name of his destroyer—known as the luckiest warship in the world.

Okuno Tadashi, sixty-eight (m),
business owner, Ōmuta

The Charity of Generous Natives

My father was aboard the light cruiser *Agano*. He died when his ship was sunk near Truk Island on 18 February 1944. Back home, my family all became weak from lack of sleep, exhaustion, and malnutrition; so we returned to the family homestead in Aizu-Wakamatsu. A year after the War's end one of my father's men came to burn incense in his memory. He brought some precious rice with him. This is what we heard from him.

Shortly after the ship had left Truk Island, it was sunk during an air strike. Told "You young men, hurry! Get away from the ship!" he jumped into the sea but then lost consciousness. When he came to, he was lying on the beach of a nearby island. He didn't even know the island's name. He had lost sensation in his arm so that he couldn't even feel pain where insects were gnawing at him. A native with white hair down his back, apparently an elder in the tribe, seemed to be ordering others to do something. The men immediately carried him to their dwelling. Warmed by their bodies, he gradually regained his senses.

He caught a whiff of a strong odor coming from their dark-skinned bodies and felt sick. He asked them to stop many times, but his words were not understood. While at the mercy of the natives, he wondered if he had the bends. As he started to feel better, due to their devoted care, he felt hungry and asked with hand gestures to be given more than the sips of coconut juice that they offered him from a coconut shell. But they said he couldn't have any more and refused. He found out later that their treatment was best for his recovery.

He was led to a place where the natives said they had dug a hole and buried some of the others who had drifted ashore but had died. He prayed for the souls of these war comrades.

As a fifteen year old I listened to this story lightheartedly as if I were hearing an adventure tale. But as the years go by I have come to wonder if for us, who live wrapped in a cloak of glittering civilization, generous human love like that shown by these natives hasn't worn thin and disappeared.

Kobayashi Mitsuko, fifty-five (f)
housewife, Aizu-Wakamatsu

Father Survived the Battle of Okinawa and Surrendered

"Receiving a top grade on my draft examination, I was selected to join the Sendai Fourth Regiment Number 2 Machine Gun Company in June 1944. From Narashino in Chiba Prefecture, I was supposed to be sent to Saipan, but the island fell, so it was on to Okinawa for me. Day after day in the fierce heat we cut down trees to construct our encampment.

"On 4 January 1945, the port of Motobu was bombed from the air. [Finally, months later,] we faced the American troops at our position in Asato. Seeing several tanks charge toward us, a fifteen- or sixteen-year-old Okinawan volunteer soldier shoved us into a foxhole and saved our lives. Thinking, 'Now we're safe,' we were just about to leave the foxhole when a fragment of a trench mortar shell hit me, wounding my armpit and right elbow. I was admitted to the field hospital. The next day I heard that a 'bamboo spear' unit of two hundred men had been annihilated. A week after entering the field dispensary I was transferred to Itokazu Hospital. Not eligible to be admitted, I commuted from our camp for treatment.

"One day, we got the news that the American forces were only one hundred meters away. We moved to our second-line positions in the middle of the night. Here we were also attacked, so we retreated farther and farther back, walking night and day. Finally we reached the seacoast at the southern edge of the island. We had no provisions and began to live in caves. When we were inside our cave, keeping silent during the day, we heard a voice from a loudspeaker saying, 'Japan has lost the War, so come out.'

"We were so afraid that we couldn't go out. At night we relied on the moonlight to forage for food left in the American positions. Then there were the sweet potato fields. I will never forget the sweetness of the thumb-size sweet potato I bit into.

"One morning a soldier who came from that locality said he was going to surrender. So I risked all too. I became a prisoner of war. Guarded by American soldiers, I did construction work for about two months. After that, at the end of 1945, I returned to my parents and wife and children, wearing the coat that the American military had given me. Of the 122 men in my company, there were 24 survivors."

The above is the gist of my father's Okinawa war experiences, as he wrote them on seven pages of stationery. I received this letter from him three years ago. Despite his two war wounds, my father is still alive and now seventy-six years old.

Nakamura Chiyoko, forty-two (f),
housewife, Sapporo

An Entire Regiment Taken Prisoner on a Hospital Ship

The hospital ship *Tachibana-maru* sailed its northwest course on a quiet night sea in the South Pacific, the red cross on its hull floating brightly over the water. *Tachibana-maru* was the same sleek, streamlined sight-seeing liner that had reigned as queen of Tokyo Bay in prewar days on the route to Ōshima. It was my reunion with *Tachibana-maru*, for I had many memories of hours spent aboard her during my student days on trips to Izu Ōshima. It was a wonder that the ship had survived in the South Seas, where annihilation and retreat were everywhere.

For over a year, the main body of our Eleventh Infantry Regiment had been left behind on a distant island, supposedly to demonstrate self-sufficiency. We had not been resupplied. In effect, we had fallen into reserve status. With the tide of war sharply worsening, we were to be transferred by hospital ship to Singapore—knowing full well that this violated international law. This transfer was to strengthen our defenses against the attempt of British forces to recapture Singapore.

Loaded with 1,562 men from the regiment's main force, along with weapons and ammunition, we left the harbor of Tual in the Kai Islands southwest of New Guinea during the beautiful sunset of 1 August 1945. Over the several days before our departure we were busy day and night packing weapons and ammunition into wooden boxes and drawing red crosses on the boxes, collecting white hospital coats, and composing false clinical reports.

As we boarded the ship, we were all told to be prepared for the order to scuttle the ship in the event of a spot check of the vessel. But we were full of the desire to escape from our situation—dreaming of a happier future—so we didn't give much heed to the warning.

Our calm crossing laden with our dreams, however, lasted only until dawn of the third day. Two American destroyers were already pursuing us. A signal was sent: "Stop ship." Already our end was approaching. Tension overcame me for an instant, and I was amazed that I was able to remain calm. It may have been due to some group psychology that made me realize that I was not alone. Decisions were delayed among the transport commander, the medical chief, and the ship's captain. The ship's engines were not yet stopped. "If the ship does not stop, we will fire"—at this second signal, the engines stopped. This was surprising, and we found it impossible to comprehend.

A large number of American soldiers boarded our ship, automatic rifles in hand. Our weapons and ammunition were discovered. "This violates international law; we are arresting all of you." This was the order, justifiably given. But looking back on this now, I think that it was because of this that my fellow soldiers and I are alive now.

> Nishihama Yūji, seventy-one (m),
> former corporate officer,
> Utsunomiya

When the Carrier *Shōkaku* Sank

It was on 19 June 1944, during the Agō operations, that the carrier *Shōkaku*, a veteran of many battles, sank. At 1120 hours that morning, three of the four torpedoes fired by the American submarine *Cavalla* hit nearly the same place on the starboard side just below the bridge. It was a jolt. I felt as if my body had jumped up thirty centimeters from the flight deck. I had boarded the *Shōkaku* when it left the base, assigned as a noncommissioned flight technician. So I was involved in all facets of the operations on the flight deck.

When the torpedoes hit, four three-centimeter wires holding the forward lift snapped, causing the lift to drop. The crash was deafening. After a while some flames appeared in the narrow space between the fallen lift and the bulkhead. Despite frantic attempts at quenching the fire, it flared up even more. Eventually the engine room was flooded and the pump stopped working, making it impossible to continue firefighting actions. At 1410 hours the *Shōkaku* sank.

When the seawater reached the ankles of those of us on the flight deck, the executive officer on the bridge ordered, "601 Squadron airmen abandon ship!" I shouted out the command, "601 Squadron airmen line up in two rows!" Almost all the men who had been fighting the fire lined up at attention. They counted off up to eighty times two. Reporting to the executive officer, "601 Squadron airmen, 161 members abandoning ship," I ordered the men, "Left turn, left. Head for the destroyer *Wakatsuki* straight ahead. All of you, do your best," and we jumped into the sea.

It was just then that four of the men surrounded me, saying "I can't swim." They were all conscripts older than I. "You don't have to swim; just stay afloat. Emergency pieces of lumber and tatami mats for judo will come drifting by. Lifeboats will come by as well, so hang on," I told them. But I didn't have the nerve to ask them if they could float.

Sugino Shusei, seventy-five (m),
retired, Nagoya

Asashimo, Which Refused Aid and Towing

According to official records, on 7 April 1945, the destroyer *Asashimo,* one of the ten ships of the Okinawa Special Attack Fleet led by the battleship *Yamato,* developed engine trouble. She was left behind by the fleet, adrift on the sea, when at 1221 she sent the transmission "Thirty-some enemy planes detected at 90 degrees." The ship was never heard from again. One hour later, however, the coast defense ship *Yashiro* sailed near the *Asashimo* on its way north toward Sasebo after being relieved of its patrol duties off the northern coast of the island of Okinawa.

The *Asashimo* reported that it had shot down four enemy planes in its antiaircraft battle. The *Yashiro* offered to aid and tow the *Asashimo,* but the destroyer declined firmly and responded that it intended to repair its engine and join the rest of the fleet. Circling around the *Asashimo,* the *Yashiro* transmitted, "We pray for your fortune in war and for your bravery in fighting." From the *Asashimo* came the response, "We thank you for your good wishes and pray for your safety on your route." The crew on deck of both ships exchanged parting salutes, waving their caps. There were shouts of encouragement—"Keep it up!"

From the *Yashiro* heading north it appeared that nothing had happened to the *Asashimo* before it disappeared over the horizon. A short while later the incessant rumble of fire from large and small guns—even machine-gun fire—was heard. Eventually a white cloud like a thundercloud was observed above the horizon, then came a deafening roar that seemed to tear the sky apart. It was the sound of the explosion of the ammunition storage on the *Yamato.* The *Asashimo* was sunk by enemy attack at the same time as the battleship *Yamato.* Its entire crew was lost.

No one is here to speak of the last of the *Asashimo.* The *Asashimo*'s refusal of aid and towing was truly an act of samurai spirit.

Miyata Hideo, fifty-nine (m),
corporate officer, Hakodate

A Draftee on the Battleship *Yamato*

I was a member of the engine room crew on the battleship *Yamato* in the sea battle off Leyte. In ordinary times the room temperature was forty degrees centigrade, but during the battle it went as high as fifty-seven degrees. Sweat poured down me like a waterfall, making a sloshing noise in my shoes. We had a continuous stream of heatstroke sufferers. One of those at my battle station was Seaman Yamamoto Shin'ichi, a machine gunner. He was from Toyooka in Hyōgo Prefecture. A thirty-seven-year-old draftee, he was the oldest and lowest-ranking sailor in my squad. Under normal conditions it was a difficult life on board, hard to bear even for us young, experienced sailors. It was inevitably even more difficult for an older man like Mr. Yamamoto.

Under orders from the squad leader, I carried him on my back up the long ladder to the temporary sick bay below the bridge.

"Damn fool, leave the spineless bastard lying there!" the medic yelled at me. Bowing my head deeply, I requested that he deal with the patient and returned to my post. Mr. Yamamoto was totally worn out, just lying in a corner of the sick bay holding a gas mask. I had no way of knowing what kind of treatment he received, but when I occasionally took him his meals, he hardly touched his food.

After the battle was lost, the fleet returned to Brunei. The next month, Yamamoto was to be admitted to the 101 Navy Hospital in Singapore. Once again, I carried him on my back, to the launch. His hands and feet were cold by then. I gasped with a gloomy premonition. The next day, our squad leader ordered us all to gather and announced the death from illness of Seaman Yamamoto, machine gunner.

The only thing I knew about him was that he and his beautiful wife had no children. The *Yamato* having been sunk, my section had the misfortune to be totally wiped out. I became the only one who knows how he died. I returned alive because I was discharged from the *Yamato* three months before it left on its final mission.

At one time I considered searching for his family and telling them of his end. Yet, concerned as to how they would take the facts, I have remained silent until now. Mr. Yamamoto, forgive me.

> Aoki Mikio, sixty-five (m), retired,
> Gifu Prefecture

Hospital Ships Targeted at Sea

I am a former nurse who worked in Red Cross relief detachments for a total of six years—I was called to duty three times, the first time in 1937. Four of those years were spent on hospital ships.

Since the start of the Pacific War, we never knew when a hospital ship might be sunk. Because so many of our transport ships had been sunk, weapons, ammunition, and soldiers were regularly loaded onto hospital ships. This was in violation of the neutrality clause in the Geneva Convention, so hospital ships were also targeted. We nurses had only one set of clothes; to our slacks we attached life vests, and from our belts hung a whistle to call patients together in the seas, a rope, and a jackknife to fight off sharks. Nurses who had children went into lifeboats while single nurses jumped into the ocean and swam.

We collected many sunburned, scrawny soldiers from the islands in the South Seas. I won't forget a young soldier in the psychiatric ward who kept crying out, "Mother, a shark!" His buttock was scarred where it had been gouged by the teeth of a shark.

We transported many student soldiers to the Philippines. Since they were told, "Books are unnecessary," they left many of their favorite books on board. Giving up works by Ishikawa Takuboku and Hermann Hesse must have felt as if they were bidding farewell to their youth. The books were heavily underlined. Images of their faces as they gallantly saluted upon disembarking are burned into my memory.

Then there were the soldiers we picked up in their white hospital clothes. After getting used to the ward, one of them would pull out a picture kept close to his heart, saying, "This is my child." Others would also show us their photos. Those children must be over forty years old by now. I wonder what happened to the fathers who had been so seriously wounded. So many young men died that it still pains this spinster's heart.

> Hanada Miki, seventy (f), former
> Aomori prefectural government
> staff, Aomori

Incredibly Shoddy Junk Transport

Changsan-got is the tip of the cape that extends into the Yellow Sea from the Korean Peninsula. I greeted the War's end there at the navy special facilities lookout. Nearby I could see the wrecks of many ships. Japanese shipping traffic had dwindled, since naval supremacy was secured by the American side, so it was curious to see large junks of over two hundred tons heading south every day with their sails set. Suspicious about these scores of junks, we went out to an anchored junk in a small craft to investigate.

The junk was part of the army supplies depot. Its dozen or so crew members included Koreans and Chinese as well as Japanese. All were drafted workers. The Japanese captain told us the following. "We carry soybeans and rock salt from Manchuria to Karatsu in Kyūshū. It takes several weeks because we can only rely on the wind. We're under orders from the authorities. Since the enemy has found out about us they have started to attack junks, and we have many casualties." He bemoaned the fact that they didn't carry any weapons.

On the day the War ended, north Korea dissolved into chaos. After disposing of our weapons, etc., we headed for Jinhae but the guard ship we boarded broke down. We began to drift. By chance we happened on the Number 282 *Antō-maru,* the same kind of junk as the one mentioned above. We moved over onto that boat. There were nineteen men aboard, including Captain Suzuki from Togawa Port, Chōshi, and four fishermen from Kyūshū. They had all escaped from Haejoo on this boat. On this junk I found out just how incredibly shoddy those vessels were and how hellish it was on board.

Half drifting for nearly twenty days, we arrived off the shore of Tsushima, where we ran into a typhoon that sank the junk. We barely survived with our lives.

Still pledging a hundred years' war, the army, under Tōjō's orders, built 750 of these junks and conscripted men to board them. After the War, Captain Suzuki returned to Togawa Port and to fishing, but he received no compensation and died a poor man.

Shimura Tomihisa, sixty-seven
(m), professor, Musashino Music
College, Asaka

Jungle Survival Necessities

Near the end of the War, I spent about four months wandering around in the jungles of Luzon—barely surviving.

What should one take along when escaping from the enemy into a mountainous jungle with no way to replenish supplies? After the War's end, I often said to young people, "There are three items that are necessities in such times. What do you think they are?" Rice, canned goods, matches, cigarettes, paper, shoes ... these were the usual replies. No one answered correctly. The three items are salt, matches, and a mess tin to cook rice in.

Rice is heavy to carry and it molds quickly, so it must be eaten soon. Canned goods, cigarettes, and paper were items of such rarity that normally officers and soldiers were unable to get their hands on them, and they are not essential to maintain life. If one's shoes should tear, another pair could be gotten from a dead soldier.

A month without salt and it becomes hard to walk. Unless you put some salt into field grasses, no matter how hungry you are, they don't taste good.

Matches are essential for boiling water and cooking field grass. If you get dysentery in the middle of the jungle, it is hopeless. Some soldiers had a lens instead of matches, but it was difficult to make a fire with the damp grass of the jungle.

The last item was the mess tin. A pot or pan would be too heavy or bulky, so a mess tin was the best. Without this, there was no way to cook or boil water. Death awaited the soldiers who lacked these three items.

> Sumeragi Mutsuo, seventy (m),
> retired, Yamato

Stabbing a Wounded Friend

I would like to write about my friend "K," now passed away. At the end of the Pacific War, he was a soldier on the Philippine battlefront. Pursued by superior American forces, his company was wandering among the jungles of Luzon. The Manila defense headquarters had already retreated deep into the mountains. Heading in that direction, his company had lost a third of its men. Many were wounded.

Passing through the jungle, exposed to the continuous rain and the barrage of gunfire from the American forces, they had to cross over a bald mountain. It was impossible to climb with the wounded. Among the wounded soldiers was "M," who was close to "K." He had been shot through the thigh, and the lower half of his body had already turned purple, like a corpse. There were many others who were unable to move and could only wait for death. Those who pleaded, "Take us with you," were told, "We'll come back to get you," and the company left, climbing the mountain under cover of night.

Toward dawn, the company finally reached a spot with trees, near the summit. There they made their headquarters. It was then that "K," along with two other soldiers, received the callous order of the company commander. They were told to go down and kill off any of the wounded who might still be alive. According to the commander, if any of the wounded were taken prisoner, they could leak information about the movements of the Japanese forces.

"K" and the others resisted these orders. Yet on being told that it was necessary to save their own lives, there was nothing they could do. Waiting for night to fall, they went back down to the place they had left the wounded. A few men were still alive. "M" was among them.

"You came back for us after all," "M" wept with gratitude. Unable to kill him, "K" engaged "M" in a rambling conversation. But the enemy could come at any time. "K" pulled his sword out in the dark and frantically stabbed "M."

"K" said that no matter how many years had passed since the War's end, he was unable to rid himself of the heavy burden on his heart.

Nakayama Juntarō, sixty-six (m),
self-employed, Tokyo

View of Life and Death Through Over Twenty Years of Isolation

"Commander! The ones who died early were the lucky ones, weren't they?" Taken by surprise at these words, I stopped in my tracks. "It's not yet certain that we're going to die," I answered. "We still have enough ammunition and we're still healthy." But the thought that flashed across my mind before I voiced these words was, "I agree completely." When I turned around, I saw that the soldier was smiling his usual smile.

Whenever the situation allowed, we charged through unexplored areas in our effort to familiarize ourselves with the geographical and natural features of the island. Upon arriving at the source of a stream in our search for water, we encountered the remains of a man who must have died when the enemy had landed. It was dusk; the sun was about to set. Typical of the area deep in the mountains, the air was highly humid, so cool as to feel chilly on the skin. It was a place unhealthy not only for humans but also for other warm-blooded animals.

Was it a joke or was it how that man really felt? I took it to be how he really felt—as well as a joke. Ten years had passed since it had become just the two of us. We hardly had any conversations that were not directly related to our current action, particularly during our movements and whenever we approached the enemy. In our daily lives we avoided being seen by the enemy and the local people. The occasions when we heard each other's voice were limited to emergencies requiring preparation for combat.

Why did he and I harbor such a feeling that could fundamentally undermine our mission after so long a time?

Since the enemy had landed, we had not received orders to cease operations; nor had we been informed of our country's defeat. The leaflets urging us to surrender were so full of errors that we could only determine that they were all traps. More than twenty years had passed since the island of Lubang had become the place where we lived.

The order that had been issued to me was "You are not allowed to take your life in battle." The order was given at the time when the plan for the decisive battle for the Philippines collapsed. Our local forces had no way of dealing with this situation other than entering into a war of attrition. This decision was based on our being compelled to expect that the enemy would land on the Japanese mainland and occupy a portion of it.

Of course, men like us, who were in the special services, could base our actions on the plans of the military commanders. We were briefed on all the information gathered by the military command intelligence section when our orders were given. On this information we based decisions as to our later course of action. Though he was not under my direct authority, this man fully understood my duties and had survived thus far along with me, one who had been ordered, "Don't die, continue to live." To hold fast to life and to abhor death is natural for humans and not at all strange. Why then, though our inclinations were such, had we, for just an instant, felt that way?

Throughout more than twenty years of isolated and unreinforced commando actions, the shadow of death always hovered in the background. The only way to wipe away that fear was to have a defiant attitude: "When it's my time to die, I'll die even on a tatami mat. When I die it means that my own judgment was wrong."

On the battlefield, if you don't kill you will be killed. A normal sense of life and death doesn't exist in a place like that. It might be called insanity, but that is the mentality on the battlefield. This may be a state of mind that is seen only in men, and temporarily at that.

It may have been because we had come to have such a casual sense of death that the change in the environment that can be felt by man's five senses had made us thoroughly forget that basic value for life.

The War for just the two of us had been a long one. Overall, what I felt was, Humans are weak beings. We ourselves are powerless people.

Onoda Hiroo,* sixty-four (m),
rancher, Brazil

---

*An army second lieutenant, Onoda received training to remain behind enemy lines as a spy and engage in guerrilla actions. Until 1974 he waged a thirty-year war in isolation in the jungles of Lubang. Now he manages a ranch in Brazil. The "he" in the text is an army private, Kozuka Kaneshichi of Hachiōji. He was shot by Philippine national police forces in October 1972.

The Last of the Manila Dispatching Office

"Here's a confidential telegram from Manila." The soldier in charge of wireless communication brought me a telegram original. I set out to translate it with the code book and the random-numbers table. I was shocked at the contents. The telegram was as follows.

"In view of the war situation, this location will burn its code book as of 1800 today. Hereafter communication with your location will be conducted by transmission from this location at the cable address below."

I immediately contacted Imperial Headquarters in Tokyo, Southern Command in Saigon, Theater Command in Rangoon, selected the best telegraph operators, and prepared for continuous monitoring. I stood by at the ready without returning to my quarters. I was in Singapore, at the Singapore army telegraph station within the Seventh Theater Command Post.

Tense hours followed. During that day and into the night, we monitored cables every few hours, as we received them.

"Fierce enemy bombings." "A unit of tank troops enter the city." "Our headquarters transferred." "Intense bombings near the telegraph station."

It was the middle of the night. Just as I had laid my tired body down on the cot in a separate room, a runner rushed in, shouting, "Incoming message from 'O.'" I immediately dashed into the communications room and put the receiver to my ear. *Pi-pi-pi, pi-pi-pi*—I could hear a clear Morse code signal. The message was "We are destroying our communications equipment and charging the enemy." This was the last message from my war comrade far away whose face I had never seen but with whom I had exchanged words every day. When I finished cabling the related agencies, I felt relief. The dawn hadn't yet broken.

Communications corpsmen are weak soldiers who are armed only with a bayonet. I wondered how they fought. A friend's fate today is our own fate tomorrow. We thought seriously about how we would fight and how we would fall.

Two months later, we were to receive the Imperial Rescript terminating the War.

Saitō Kōzō, sixty-five (m), retired,
Natori

Beliefs of a Young Manila Woman

The hospital I was ordered to move to as a patient in May 1944 was in the city of Manila. It handled only ambulatory patients. We knew that sooner or later we had to take off our white hospital gowns and head back to the front.

Each hospital room was attended by a nurse, one of the locals. They were all loyal workers. As I was the lowest-ranking soldier, I was told to help out with meal deliveries and the like.

About five days after I was admitted to the hospital, I realized that one of the nurses seemed to have taken a liking to me. We exchanged our feelings when our eyes met and held hands when my temperature was being taken. Our feelings grew stronger day by day. After about two weeks, the others were released, leaving just another seriously wounded soldier and myself. The next day new patients were to arrive. That day, during nap time, she began to talk to me without showing any reserve about others hearing. My heart leapt with joy, and I responded to her. After a while, she looked all around to see that it was all right and started to talk about conditions under the Japanese military occupation.

Freedom taken away, the lack of goods, the poverty of life, the brutality of military police, hatred toward Japanese soldiers. She concluded by asserting strongly, "MacArthur will certainly return and save us." But I was one of those hated Japanese soldiers. My blood ran backward, my lips trembled, and I glared at her. If it hadn't been firmly forbidden, I would most likely have knocked her down.

"Do you hate me as well?" I pressed her in a sharp tone. But she shook her head slowly and, with tears in her eyes, said, "Hori, you're different. You're kind. You can't kill people." I felt that I had been hit over the head. When I regained my composure, I kept this in my heart and told no one about it. Should a superior officer find out about this, it was clear that it would result in heavy punishment!

About ten days later I was released from the hospital.

Her courage, her unyielding belief, her love for her country, her strong selfless spirit. I was able to comprehend these qualities only after I saw the conduct of some of the young women in Japan after I was repatriated.

If she remained healthy, she would be about sixty-five years old now. I don't know whether the name she gave me, Nina, was her real name.

> Horiguchi Itsurō, seventy-one (m),
> retired, Sagamihara

We Lost the War in Information and Education as Well

From September 1945 I spent one year and four months in a U.S. military prisoner of war camp on the outskirts of Manila. I worked in the U.S. forces I&E (information and education) section during this time. I was surprised to find in a large warehouse piles of paperback books on conversational language for each of the Asian languages. The volume on Japanese was the *Japanese Phrase Book* (184 pages), published by the U.S. Department of the Army in February 1944.

Wartime daily conversation was printed in four columns: English, Japanese pronunciation, Japanese Romanization, Japanese characters and kana. The conversational examples and vocabulary were well selected, but what caused me to be surprised anew was that the first word listed was *help* (*tasukete*). Following that were phrases such as "I've lost my way," "I am an American," "Please take me there," "Please give me food (water)."

Another volume was *What Is a War Crime,* published in August 1944. This included illustrations and gave examples of the massacres perpetrated in by the Axis countries against their enemies during World War II in violation of the laws of war and various conventions. For example, it noted that the German military massacred a company of Polish soldiers at the front in violation of the Geneva Convention—"In particular, it is forbidden to kill or wound enemy soldiers who have thrown down their weapons and have surrendered unconditionally (*Articles of War,* Article 32)."

In contrast, the Japanese military strictly prohibited the use of an enemy language in military education. We had to use terms like "bestial devils Americans and British." We had not been informed about even the idea of "war crimes" in international law. What had been given us was a one-sided Field Service Code. "Do not live and be put to shame as a prisoner; death will not incur the sin of dishonor." That was what we were taught.

If we had received the kind of humane information and education given to the American forces, we might have avoided the human costs of 470,000 war dead in the Philippines and 365 class B and C war criminals.

> Satō Yoshinori, sixty-eight (m),
> former teacher, Philippine library
> supervisor, Ōita

The Death Struggle on Negros

On Negros Island in the Philippines. At daybreak on 29 March 1945, the main American forces landed. Our Seventy-seventh Infantry Brigade's 354th Independent Infantry Battalion held our position at 1,100 meters on Higashitarōyama (later renamed Dolan Hill by the U.S. forces).

The fierce bombardment from air and land by the main American forces had scorched the densely foliated deep jungle encampment, rendering it as a barren as a volcano. When the artillery bombardment ended, the enemy infantry approached to thirty meters and threw hand grenades in close combat. We struck nightly into the enemy encampment. One after another my war buddies went through the gates of Yasukuni Shrine. We were left with many heavily wounded soldiers. Maggots hatched in our bandages, writhing on our flesh and exuding a foul stench.

Food supplies were cut off. Having eaten up all the stalks of grasses and plants, and all the insects and reptiles, we became malnutrition cases. One's entire body swells, one's strength gives out, and it becomes impossible to control one's bodily functions. Hunger gnawed at people's spirit. There were those who ate human flesh. With the onset of the rainy season, men suffered from malaria, dengue fever, tropical ulcers, and chronic amoebic dysentery. There were those among the seriously wounded and ill soldiers who despaired so much that they killed themselves. Their gunshots echoed in the valley. Some deserted on their way to attack the enemy, or attacked the supply base, fighting against other Japanese soldiers to obtain food.

Higashitarōyama had held out for fifty-two days against a heavy siege. By 23 May, a mere dozen or so men were left under company commander Ishizuka. After ordering his men to assemble at battalion headquarters, Commander Ishizuka received a heavy gunshot wound, which perforated his stomach. I was ordered to escape alone with important documents—reports to battalion headquarters. Giving a sidelong glance at the two hundred heavily wounded and ill soldiers left behind, I made my escape. I thought of the poems "Eyes hot with tears, I see the round eyes of the infant clinging to its mother's dead body"; and "I overtake Japanese women and children carrying children on their backs, pulling children along by the hand and carrying baggage."

I reached brigade headquarters. There they had food—plenty of it. It shocked me to see the well-fed men of the headquarter units line up like ants and carry off provisions into the distance. At the front we had not been sent even a grain of unhulled rice.

> Kokubo (formerly Sakurai)
> Yumio, sixty-five (m), retired, Mito

Soldier Who Was Able to Share His Last Bit of Rice

It was in July 1945, on Negros Island in the central Philippines. Fierce battles had continued since the landing of the American forces in late March. We were out of ammunition, medicine, and provisions. Leaving many dead from battle and starvation, we marched in small groups over the jungle mountains in search of food. A first lieutenant, I had fallen behind due to a spinal cord injury. One other soldier and I finally reached the summit of the highest mountain in the dividing ridge. We were resting when a malnourished noncommissioned officer from another unit climbed up. The three of us took three days to reach the bottom of the ravine. When we prepared our breakfast in a forest of gigantic lauan trees, it turned out that the sergeant had no food or matches.

We had only a few days' worth of rice, which had been rationed to us. After finishing just one mouthful of the rice from his mess tin, my fellow soldier offered his mess tin to the sergeant, saying, "I don't feel like eating today, so please eat this." At a time when soldiers who had fallen by the roadside lay dead with their hands still pressed together begging for food, this soldier shared his food with a higher-ranking soldier who appeared not to have eaten for days. He even gave an excuse so that the sergeant could eat without reservation. Sharing the last bit of rice one has isn't something that the average person can do. This is a scene I will never be able to forget.

After that, we continued marching for a week. We walked five minutes and rested ten minutes until we caught up with our company. At the end of the War I was sent to Leyte. In 1946, by coincidence, I came across this sergeant, who was in charge of the POW mess. This time it was he who saved me with food.

Kawamura Mikio, sixty-five (m),
former company employee,
Gotenba

The Essence of Human Beings

I was drafted in 1939 at age twenty-one and discharged in 1943. The following year I was called up again and sent to a garrison in the mountains near Manila in the Philippines. It was the time when MacArthur had recaptured the Philippines. Whenever the Japanese forces made an artillery attack, there would be a response several times greater. So we couldn't make an effective artillery strike from our side. As a final measure we formed a group of shock troops to strike through the enemy line carrying explosives with us. I was enlisted in that troop.

In order to make our strike, we had to enter the enemy camp. The American troops kept up their bombardment from morning until evening. Fortunately, at night they returned to their barracks, leaving only half their soldiers on the line. We were to enter enemy territory during the night. It was slippery and hard to walk on the red clay mountain bare of grass, with trees razed by the bombardments. Any noise we made would elicit a hail of bullets. With difficulty we crossed the river and entered the enemy area, but we were found out and strafed as though by a driving rain. It was all we could do to hide in a foxhole. At last we decided to withdraw. We wandered around without having anything to eat all day. We happened to find a potato field and, waiting until it appeared that there was no enemy fire, we took as many potatoes as we could and ran back to eat them in our foxholes.

The few Japanese soldiers who survived should have helped each other out. Instead there were those who killed themselves in suicidal explosions, those who killed their fellow men for their food. Military police would take away soldiers trying to escape, accuse them of holding antiwar sentiments, and confiscate their food.

Is this the essence of human beings who are face to face with death? I believe that I was able to return alive only because of help from the gods.

Matsuu Shinji, sixty-eight (m),
retired, Yame

I Don't Want to Believe "Cannibalism"

I was appalled to read a letter about "cannibalism under extreme conditions." As one who returned alive after experiencing the extreme conditions of the battlefront on the same Luzon, I can't help but doubt the motive behind such a statement.

I believe that we were able to fight to the end prepared to die with honor in selfless devotion to our country for the very reasons that the Imperial Rescript to Soldiers and Sailors and the Field Service Code were instilled in the minds of soldiers; we had sworn with our war comrades that when we died it would be together. There was the reality that if someone disobeyed the law we would admonish each other to discharge our duty as servicemen. I did occasionally hear rumors about cannibalism in those days, but the connection among fellow soldiers was stronger than among family members. Even if it were someone from another unit, for a soldier to eat another soldier's flesh . . . I couldn't conceive of something that absurd happening, and not having the time to speculate on it I had decided these stories were groundless. If there had been such conduct, I could only think it was by someone who had wandered away from the company command, had become delirious in his emaciated state, and had lost his ability to distinguish right from wrong.

No matter how bestial human beings become, I find it impossible to think that they would eat carrion like vultures do. If it had happened, it was a crime that war itself caused a person to commit by pushing him so far. My heart is full of hatred for war.

Our unit was regarded as a crack unit among those troops in active service on Luzon. We fought with dauntless courage and achieved much. However, during battles, we followed strict military regulations and committed no atrocities.

Shimura Noboru, sixty-six (m),
produce business, Iwata

Starvation March in the Philippine Mountains

The American forces landed on Luzon. Manila and Clark Field, where we were garrisoned, fell in no time. There were no orders or instructions for movements for our unit. It had lost its function as a military force. Needless to say, there was no replenishment of weapons and ammunition; nor was there any supply of food and provisions. Wandering around the tropical forest for three months made me gaunt beyond recognition. I was so weakened that I couldn't carry anything at all heavy. I threw away my helmet, threw away my bayonet, and threw away my sword.

Finally I even threw away my mess tin. All I had fastened to my waist were my canteen, provision bag, an empty tin can, and a hand grenade with which to kill myself. When the soles of my army boots gave way, I commandeered a pair from the dead body of a fellow soldier and wore them. I foraged whatever was left to eat from the provision bags of dead comrades.

Scattered around watering holes in the jungle were bodies exuding the stench of death. Passing through the jungle, I reached a hill. As far as I could see there were dead bodies, clothed only in dirty, worn loincloths. Weapons, helmets, military uniforms, provision bags, boots—everything had been stripped off them.

Going west would lead to the coast of the South China Sea. I thought that our navy would have command of the sea. In the thicket some fellow soldiers were crawling around. Some had arms or legs cut off, some had their innards sticking out of their bodies, some had had their lower jaws shattered by gunfire. Countless wounded men writhed, getting no treatment.

When a person dies, his internal organs start to decompose first. As they breathe, flies gather, attracted by the rotten stench exhaled. Maggots hatch on the nose and mouth of soldiers still alive. Maggots of 1 or 2 millimeters crawl all over. When the maggots begin to crawl in the eyes, the men die. Spending every day among dead bodies makes one doubt whether one can know where the dividing line between life and death is. One's thoughts become hazy and disorientated.

A fellow soldier whose name I didn't know came crawling over to me. Taking off his clothes, he bared his pointed rear end. It had become dark bluish-green. "Buddy, if I die, go ahead and eat this part," he said, touching his scrawny rear end with his bony finger. I said, "Idiot, how could I eat a war buddy?" But I couldn't take my eyes off the flesh on his rear.

My recollection is unclear as to how I got out of the jungle. I passed through grassy fields and arrived at the summit of a rocky mountain. There was the time that I lined up some stones and started a fire. I found some rock salt in a bamboo tube. It must have been stored by the Igorot tribesmen.

Behind me something black sprang out. Without thinking, I gripped my knife and jumped on it. It was a medium-size dog with its ears standing up and its tail drooping. I stabbed it to death and roasted it, covered in salt. I decided to shred the meat and chop up the internal organs and take it along with me in my tin can. The salted meat may have given me energy. I thought I might be able to survive, and with my whole body I felt something like self-confidence.

No matter where I might drop dead, I didn't want my mother at home to know how pathetically I had died. So I buried my thousand-stitch belt and identification tag along with items left by a dead war buddy. Somehow I felt relieved. Waiting until sunset, I climbed down the mountain and headed for the western coast.

Nishihara Takamaro, seventy (m),
corporate executive, Fukuoka

Red Rice from the Dead

To those of us who had not had much to eat other than weeds, infantry rifles, hand grenades, and steel helmets were useless items. But because they were weapons we couldn't throw them away, even though they had become completely rusted in the rain squalls we encountered. We were in the mountains on northern Luzon Island in the Philippines. It must have been early August, just before the War's end. All those enemy aircraft that had been flying overhead had vanished. Rumors came to us that we were defeated, but some said that soon our troops would be sending reinforcements.

"I have found some rice." I had been pursuing the main body of our unit and leading thirty soldiers, all of them ill. Hearing this from one of them, whose eyes shone eerily, my body was already moving toward where he pointed. It was one among the bodies of the officers and men who had died of starvation in small groups. His rank was private second class. His backpack was at his right side, and his head was pillowed on his military boots, in which he had stored his emergency rice. His face was already decomposed, and from his mouth and nose maggots tumbled to the ground. I pressed my hands in prayer to the body and gently attempted to take his pillow. His neck jolted so that his head rolled to the side.

Out from his boots came light russet-colored rice grains, which had become so sodden in the squalls as to lose their original shape. Collecting water from our canteens, we filled a mess tin and began to cook the rice. The rubber-soled work socks that we had picked up, though sooty, burned well, and the rice was ready. It was the color of festive red rice cooked with adzuki beans.

The color was from the liquid which had flowed onto the boots from the decaying dead body and had stained the rice. For us it was our first meal of rice in a long time, and it was "festive red rice" at that. We talked about our memories about festive red rice in Japan—celebrations, track and field days, field trips. This red-colored rice was not presented by the living to the dead but rather was a life-giving, most valued rice given by the dead to the living. Having narrowly escaped death, whenever I hear about festive red rice I recall this incident.

Hara Yutaka, sixty-five (m),
farmer, Kitsuki

This Is What the Front in Burma Was Like

Every day and every hour at the front is a staring match with the enemy. Each side is always looking for an unguarded moment on the part of the other, in order to kill those on the other side. There are nothing but tools for killing on the front lines. There are no houses to live in, no toilets, no baths, no food, no clothes. In the dry season, the burning tropical sun blazed down on us in the foxholes that we dug ourselves. In the wet season there was no shelter from the rain. We would be drenched inside the muddy foxholes. If we put covers over our holes, we became immediate targets. Our bed at night was on the ground because our enemy, the Anglo-Indian troops, slept. We fell asleep gazing at the southern sky, so close it seemed we could reach up and touch the stars.

There was no way that we could have toilets under such conditions. We had to shit on the ground. There was no paper, so we used clumps of dirt or crumpled-up leaves. During the day we were unable to leave our foxholes, so we did our business inside and covered it over with dirt. During the rainy season, it was impossible to have hard shit while our bodies were soaking wet. It was all diarrhea, diarrhea, and malaria.

During the dry season there was almost no water. We had only one mess tin full of cooking and drinking water, which we risked danger in order to find. We had no way to wash our clothes or our bodies. We wore the same clothes all the time. Instead of a bath, we used our sweat as soap to rub off the dirt on our bodies. We lived together with the lice and ringworm on our bodies.

During the retreat march, I had sores on my thighs due to incessant diarrhea. My penis ached and was in the way so the only thing I could do was to pull it outside my trousers and let it see the external world. If that didn't work, then I bared the bottom half of my body and kept on retreating, hanging my trousers from a string tied to my belt. Like a snail or a tramp, we carried everything on our bodies, and when we stopped it was to prepare to camp. We searched for water and scrounged for food, and on our way we stuffed dried twigs that we found for firewood into our knapsacks. One becomes able intuitively to distinguish between what can be eaten and what is poisonous. The only thing one can rely on is oneself, as there is no information available. We didn't even know where we were going. All we could do was to follow the footsteps of the man ahead of us.

At the front life and death are side by side at each instant. Each day when night fell I thought, "I've lived through another day." That was the front.

Inaba Shigeru, sixty-four (m),
chairman, National Association of
Fuel Unions, Ibaraki Prefecture

Railroad in War Zone: Burma-Siam Line

In a recent letter there was mention of *The Bridge on the River Kwai.* I passed over this bridge in an open freight car as I was being sent to the Burma front. The following year, I passed over this bridge again in a covered freight car on my return as one of the wounded and ill. What I saw from the railroad was the reality of the abuse of prisoners of war by the Japanese forces. What follows is a part of what I wrote for a literary journal. It is impossible to describe the facts in such a short piece. This is what I felt as one Japanese military man.

The construction of the Burma-Siam Railroad between Thailand and Burma was a difficult undertaking. It was being hurried to meet the target completion date of the end of 1943, under orders from Imperial Headquarters. Fifty thousand British, Dutch, and Australian prisoners of war, 100,000 native laborers, and 15,000 Japanese soldiers—the record states that if all of these workers stretched out their arms and held hands, the human chain would be as long as the entire railroad.

It was called the "Railroad of Death." For what purpose did 30,000 natives, 10,000 prisoners of war, and 1,000 Japanese soldiers die?

I started my trip on this railroad on 11 March 1944. The train moved at a maximum of twenty kilometers an hour and stopped many times. It took three nights and four days to travel the entire 450 kilometers (equivalent to the distance between Tokyo and Sekigahara). On my return the conditions had worsened. It took six nights and seven days. We passed large numbers of prisoners of war in the jungles along the tracks. They were badly exploited. They were all naked except for a fifty-centimeter-wide loincloth. These were made from ripped-apart coarse jute bags for rice or wheat. The peachy skin of the Caucasians was soiled by streams of blood. They moved and writhed, chased by Japanese officers wielding whips. I couldn't help but doubt that this was permitted under international law. Lack of education is a fearful thing. This showed the inferiority of military education, which produced officers who were lacking in compassion and ignorant of international law.

Watanabe Hideo, sixty-four
(m), painter, essayist,
Kamakura

Nurses Who Committed Mass Suicide

I remember it as being the end of June 1944. I was attached to the shock troops heading north for Kohima in the Burma-Imphal operation. Seeing a British jeep drive around a village two miles down the valley, we were eventually forced to retreat over the Arakan mountain range in the height of the rainy season. On that path of retreat I witnessed over and over again utterly tragic scenes of hell on earth.

The road had turned into mud. When, with a group of fellow soldiers, we found our way to a river crossing and camped for the night, an eerie stench of death wafted through the air. The next morning we saw that in the grass nearby were the bodies of five women who had taken poison and died. They were dressed in dark blue uniforms, their hair was shorn like that of soldiers, and one of them wore an armband with a red cross. Perhaps they had intended it as a will, but I recall that written on a fragment of paper were words that looked like *Tokuyama corps* or *Tokushima corps.* Two or three days must have passed since their death. It was distressing to see their bodies. Ill as I was, I felt the ghastliness of the scene and couldn't help shedding tears of sympathy.

There were also such mass suicides among sick and wounded soldiers. I came across many spots where three to five soldiers had sat in a circle and had committed suicide by setting off a hand grenade.

Fujimata Masayoshi, seventy (m),
corporate officer, Yokohama

Deserters in Sumatra

There were three deserters in my company in Sumatra, the Negishi Unit (formerly the Guards Reconnaissance Regiment). We had information that they had infiltrated into the depths of the village of Kutacane in Takengon in northern Sumatra. Our unit of twenty men commanded by Captain Ōno received orders to arrest the deserters. As platoon leader, I had two of the three deserters, Private First Class Watanabe and Corporal Masuzawa, under my command. They had led the native volunteer corps in Seunagon on the coast of the Indian Ocean.

Captain Ōno had educated his men that Japanese and Indonesians should fight together against Caucasians to liberate oppressed Asians at all costs. They should be prepared to bury their bones in Sumatra. So the captain said it pained him to capture his own men. I was of the same mind as Private First Class Watanabe. I felt that I wanted to desert to the Indonesian Independence Army.

Discovering the three men who were hiding in a hut in the middle of the night, we surrounded them. They were armed as we were. About an hour passed with no words spoken. Then we heard a woman's voice inside the house. She had probably noticed the Japanese troops around the house and was informing the three men. I heard Watanabe's voice say, "What?" Unable to wait for orders from Captain Ōno, I climbed up the three rungs of a ladder made of logs and broke into the house alone, calling out, "Watanabe!" After me followed five or six men, including the company commander.

Corporal Masuzawa faced me and shouted, "Commander, please forgive me," as he grabbed a hand grenade. I pounced on him and pinned him down and pried the grenade from him. If he had dropped the grenade onto the wooden floor with a clatter before I had taken it from him, the lives of the five or six men there would have been blown away. After more than two hours of persuasion by Captain Ōno, we returned with the three men the following morning.

Tsuchikawa Masao, sixty-eight
(m), former teacher, Suwa

Timor Also Starved

The inhabitants of Timor, a colony of the Netherlands and Portugal, did not have an easy life. They were exploited, yet their daily existence was peaceful. Occupied by the Japanese forces, the inhabitants were not permitted to maintain neutrality. The Japanese forces punished those who refused to cooperate, since they were thus considered to be on the enemy's side. This was in some respects necessary to carry out the War.

Confused and bewildered, the islanders feared our punishment, so ultimately they were compelled to cooperate. It may have been that in order to put an end to the hardships of their long status as a colony, they had ideas about using the Japanese military to their advantage. They did not begrudge us their cooperation delivering goods and offering labor. But by the end of 1944 the supply of goods from Java was cut off and food provisions became severely reduced. The military considered that we could not starve before the islanders. The army had to survive even if it meant requisitioning all available goods. Water buffalo needed for cultivating the fields were bought up with unusable military scrip. We also ate hearts of palm and trunks of papaya, valuable assets to the inhabitants.

Attempts at local self-sufficiency on Timor were unproductive, as it was an area of barren soil and malaria-filled marshes. Japanese troops and is-landers alike suffered from malnutrition and fell prey to malaria. People took to saying, "Java is heaven, Timor hell."

I was anguishing over goods procurement in a unit under the command of the Reconnaissance Regiment in central Timor. The late Maeda Tōru, a poet, was then a first lieutenant in the regiment, paymaster section. His area was the Domingo kingdom under the rule of a cooperative local chief, Zukin. Zukin was in a most agonizing position, caught between the increas-ingly forceful demands of the Japanese military and the entirely im-poverished local inhabitants. After our defeat in the War, Chief Zukin, who had cooperated with the Japanese until the end, was captured and died in prison. Wretched is the only word to describe his fate.

Nakamura Yasuhide, sixty-nine
(m), former corporate officer,
Tokyo

"Value Your Lives"

As a superior private in Company Number 1 in the Eightieth Battalion of the Shōnan* Independent Guard Unit in Singapore, I heard the company commander instruct us in the following way. It was July 1945.

"We will lose the War. We don't even have enough rifles. Okinawa has been taken, and His Excellency Lieutenant General Ushijima has killed himself. The mainland is under daily bombing attack and is impossible to

---

*Shōnan was the name given to Singapore under Japanese occupation.

defend. I order you to do this: Do not allow yourself to die in the War. Alive, you can be of use to your country someday. If you do not want to endure the shame of being captured, then run away and live among the native people. It is all right if you set up house with one of the local women. Just stay alive! If we come across each other on the mainland, let's call out in greeting to each other!"

He also said, "No matter where you are, don't obey any orders to commit suicide. It's no longer the era of Kusunoki Masashige.*

There were some military men who valued human life above all, despite the foolish deeds of battle. Yet all the officers went through the same officers' training. I wonder how they parted ways in ideology, some to become crazed warmongers, others to respect human lives.

> Inoue Tsuneshichi, seventy-seven
> (m), vocational school instructor,
> Atami

---

*An illustrious warrior and an able general as well, Kusunoki supported the Emperor Go-Daigo in the bitter succession wars of the fourteenth century, committing suicide when his cause was finally lost. Inevitably, the militarists of the 1930s and 1940s held him up as a shining example to young soldiers.

The End of the Signal Unit 20

At the beginning of 1945, the general headquarters for the South Seas was shifted from Singapore to Saigon [now Ho Chi Minh City]. In May the local military headquarters in Saigon moved with its attached unit to Hanoi, leaving only a command post in Saigon. But even a small command post needs a headquarters staff who can be relied upon to give quick responses. In June, men who were working at Japanese trading firms and other companies in Saigon were drafted, forming the Signal Unit Number 20. It was about the size of a company.

All kinds of people were drafted, from men who had gone through the war in China to those who had no military experience at all. Men who had worked on an equal basis as civilians were separated by military rank. In some cases, the positions of the men in the trading company became reversed by military ranking.

The unit underwent education and training daily. People who had hired Vietnamese as servants before being drafted were now forced to clean toilets. The long marches were also quite difficult for them. During the first three weeks they were not allowed to have their families visit them.

August came. News that the Potsdam Declaration of the Allies had been accepted by Japan was published in the overseas Chinese press. It became widely known throughout Saigon. Members of the Signal Unit Number 20 were told of this by their families on visiting day. On the fifteenth, the day of the Emperor's radio address, all members of the unit gathered around the high-quality receiver in the command post. When the broadcast ended, nearly everyone shouted "Banzai!"

After the defeat, a rumor spread that all Japanese soldiers would be treated badly. Signal Unit Number 20 disbanded as if it had never been formed. All documents relating to the unit were incinerated.

Nishimura Iwao, eighty-one (m),
former university professor,
Nagoya

Japanese Military and the Storm in Vietnam

In February 1945, we officers-in-training and first-year recruits in the Hara Unit (formally, the Twenty-second Division) left Wuchang in central China. After some four months of marching southward through enemy country, we finally arrived in northern French Indo-China [now northern Vietnam]. I was assigned to the Fifty-second Mountain Artillery Regiment. The regiment's positions, when I finally caught up to it, were under daily bombing and strafing attacks from American fighter planes.

One day in June, being the paymaster, I was outside the town of Phulang Thuong procuring provisions. There was an air raid that day as well, and Grumman fighter planes attacked. I ran pell mell through rice fields. Occasionally I ducked down into dips in the ground. Behind me clouds of dust rose up, along with sharp noise.

I took cover under the eaves of a house—there was no attack on the local inhabitants' houses. I had just barely survived with my life.

At that moment I heard piano music coming from the house. These sounds, oblivious to the air raid, wafted over me. The residents were an intellectual couple in their late thirties who had married when they were students at Hanoi University.

I thanked them for giving me shelter. They even offered me some tea. Was playing the piano even during an air raid the prayer of Vietnamese who wished for peace? Or did it teach the meaninglessness of the War?

I was struck with great emotion. I felt as if I had been able to forget the War for an instant and had regained my humanity.

Thinking it over now, perhaps this incident shows the strength of the character of the Vietnamese people who refused to be beaten by America in the Vietnam War.

Watanabe Shinshirō, sixty-six (m),
corporate advisor, Tokyo

On Car Nicobar Island

Around June or July 1945, Car Nicobar Island in the Bay of Bengal was charged twice by a British attack force. After a sentry discovered a lamp signaling to shore from an enemy submarine off the island, some British who had been living there since before our occupation were arrested as spies. They were to be executed.

This was done under the utmost secrecy. A double line of sentries surrounded the execution ground. The spies were tied to trees and blindfolded. Graves were dug in front of them. First there was a single rifle shot for each, then they were stabbed with bayonets to test our soldiers' bravery. The bodies were beheaded to try out new swords. Several men carrying buckets ran over and sliced open the torsos, taking out internal organs. The army surgeon extracted the livers. I could only stare in astonishment at this coldhearted behavior.

It was said that livers cut out in this way were secretly added to the food of soldiers suffering from fever. One of the ill soldiers said he ate some food with meat in it, wondering how it had gotten there.

After the War's end a month later, the execution of the spies was considered a war crime committed by the brigade commander and his subordinates—down to the private-first-class level. These men went to the gallows in Changi, Singapore.

I was repatriated in July 1946 from this island, which had repelled enemy landings up until the War's end. Even now, due to the refusal of the Indian government to allow us in the country, we have not been able to cross over to the island to have a memorial service for those who died there.

Kondō Shin'ichi, sixty-six (m),
paper hanger, Tokyo

Chapter 6

The Home Front

From the middle of the 1930s to World War II's disastrous end in 1945, the Japanese people lived like the citizens of an enclosed hemisphere. Effectively sealed off from the outside world, they were ruled by a despotic police and army organization that existed only to root out any dissent. As the strains of a losing war increased, the grip of the security forces tightened. In a real sense, Japan had become once more a *Sakoku* [closed country]—the isolation of the seventeenth- and eighteenth-century Tokugawa Shogunate revived. And the feared Kempeitai, the military security police, proved far more destructive than the *metsuke* of Tokugawa days. Through the letters of this period runs a single strain: everyone was afraid, everyone was submissive, yet everyone participated—willy-nilly—in a mass move toward disaster.

There was no intellectual dissent to speak of in Japan. With the exception of a few independent spirits like the writer Nagai Kafū, who hated the War, there was not even a muted expression of concern. Distinguished jurists and academic liberals like Yanaihara Tadao and Minobe Tatsukichi had been dismissed from their professorships and silenced by the threat of imprisonment. With the military in total charge, all the classic Japanese social virtues—the group loyalties, the solidarity, the patience, the willingness to accept hardships in the hope of future gain—were in a sense turned inside out.

Most of the people put up with this. The country as a whole, one can say, had been swept up in the great enthusiasm of early victories. Here, as it seemed, was the Emperor's country basking in the favor of the gods. Who dared to oppose it?

As the letters reveal, many people were troubled in this time, but it was terribly dangerous to communicate your troubles or concerns even to your neighbor. The Japanese police, through the *tonari-gumi*, neighborhood groups, exercised almost total surveillance. And as we see from the letters, when normal police surveillance did not work, there was always the

Kempeitai to press home the charges of disloyalty or dissent.

Hardship was pervasive. Only a few, mostly urban, segments of the Japanese population had shared in the temporary prosperity of the 1920s and 1930s—and even their well-being had been seriously threatened by the bureaucracy's dangerous fiddling with the economy. Now the country was forced into an austerity mode. Industrial production was put under military control. Big business built empires in Manchuria based on Japan's early version of the military industrial complex.

The nation displayed a kind of solidarity behind the war effort—at least on the surface: people kept their thoughts to themselves. The letters show this. We must recall that they were written with the virtue of hindsight forty or forty-five years after the fact. People said things in 1985 that they would not have dared express forty years before, but there was little thought of popular protest, let alone revolt. Even at that, the letters offer a touching and frightening picture of what the people of Japan must have experienced under this regime of enforced conformism.

Southern Izu Villagers' Bamboo-Spear Defense

It must have been toward the end of 1943 that about twenty Americans in two boats tried to land on the beach at Motose on Cape Irō, the southernmost point of the Izu peninsula. The village was in an uproar. Eager to show off their training, the village women gathered on the beach, holding spears fashioned of bamboo. Some showed up with hoes and sickles as well. Their comments ranged from, "Come on ashore, come ashore and we'll kill you!" to "Here's revenge for my man's death—get ready for your end!"

Standing at the water's edge, they cried shrilly and waved their "weapons." Awakened to their role as defenders of the home front, these women were filled with ferocious spirit. Standing behind them, I also held two rocks in my hands. The enemy, surprised at this scene, stopped their boats far offshore and watched us but showed no signs of attacking. After a while, all the men stood up and raised their arms, saying, *"Banzai."* A piece of white cloth was tied to a pole. "All right, they've surrendered. Let's take them all prisoner." A few villagers rushed home to get some rope.

One of the men who came cautiously ashore gestured exaggeratedly, trying to tell us something. But the villagers, who had never seen a foreigner before, had no way of understanding him. They stood ready, expressions tense. Thinking that I, who worked at the weather station, might be able to get through to them, they pulled me up front. But my "this-is-a-pen" level of English was ineffective. I was able to figure out that they seemed to be speaking German. We had a nearby doctor come by. He confirmed that they were Germans whose ship had been attacked by an American submarine. They had come to our coast in lifeboats.

This meant they were our allies. The villagers' stance changed immediately. They rushed to shake hands with the foreigners. We set about preparing a party to welcome them, but they were put on a bus sent to meet them and whisked off somewhere. A dog, which must have been their pet, bounded up the steps of the bus, its tail wagging excitedly.

Shimojō Tetsu, sixty (m), freelance writer, Yokohama

Evacuees and Mean-Spirited Villagers

People who lived in the cities evacuated to our village to take refuge with their relatives and acquaintances. Some households had two and three families living together. Some of these families lived in storage sheds, woodsheds, and—to my shock as a young girl—even in a night soil shed, where large vats of human excrement were stored uncovered.

A child evacuee had undressed to take a bath at the urging of his grandmother. He was knuckled on the head by his uncle, who said, "Don't take a bath before the family does. You're just a hanger-on." On holidays, the local families did not share any of the dumplings they made with the evacuees. I am sure that many evacuees felt hurt. They must have cried at the painful and coldhearted treatment they received.

Our village had a teacher from the city. He made snide comments to his villager pupils that their parents were only good at making children, just like stupid carp. When food became scarce, he said, "My supply base is your village. Gather rice for me." The country people diligently carried food to him, but when food became abundant after the War, they didn't even get a postcard from him.

I didn't experience air raids, but seeing and hearing the kinds of things that occurred in our village pained me. I became disillusioned with the disgraceful qualities in our people. They had become a herd whose humanity had been shorn from them by war.

One of the evacuees staying in the village temple came by after the War to visit my younger brother. He was a boy about my brother's age. I was relieved when I heard that he said to my brother, "Other families just brought leftover bits of vegetables for us children staying in the temple. It was only your mother who prepared good food for us. I was so thankful for that."

This makes me recall my dear departed mother with fondness.

Aoki Kii, fifty-seven (f),
housewife, Niigata Prefecture

Sadness and Self-Reproach of an Evacuee

In March 1945, when I was in the first year of girls' high school in Tokyo, my mother, younger sister, younger brothers, and I were evacuated to my mother's hometown in Iwate Prefecture. When the new school year started in April, my brothers transferred to the local grade school. But the transfer to the prefectural school for my sister and me was not readily granted. We waited days, uncertain and fretful. We were continually rejected, told that our files had not arrived or that they were incomplete. It was the end of May by the time we were finally permitted to attend school.

After entering school, we found that a daily task was training with bamboo spears, stabbing straw dolls lined up in the schoolyard. We were mobilized to work on nearby farms. When the farmers saw that we were evacuees, they would say to us, "So, did you run away?" "Hmm, you're weaklings." We insisted that we were prepared to fight to the last person. Indeed, all our bamboo-spear–training was aimed at the day the enemy would land. No need to justify ourselves.

How injured we felt by such words coming from adults. That was an era when no one bothered to consider how children felt. Our older schoolmates and classmates shielded us without a word.

Evacuee students first had to learn the local dialect. We were to work hard for the sake of our country. That summer I was fourteen. I obeyed the principal's instructions with all my heart. I was exhausted from my first rice planting and weeding and reclaiming wasteland. Then came the defeat. I felt so reassured by the warm expressions of my teachers and classmates, who greeted me with the kind words "We're glad you're back" when I returned the following year to the makeshift school building in an area destroyed by fire.

When I heard about the day the school building burned to ashes and learned what my friends had gone through in days spent clearing the debris, my defiant spirit crumbled. I had endured my evacuation by denying that I was cowardly. Now I was assaulted by an inexpressibly guilty conscience— even when I heard the sound of the construction of the new school building, which echoed in our classroom. It was when I was no longer being criticized by anyone that I felt self-reproach.

Yamamuro Reiko, fifty-five (f),
housewife, Yokohama

Forced Evacuation to Protect the Prime Minister's Residence

After the great Tokyo air raid on 10 March 1945, orders were given for a forced evacuation of all the houses within two hundred meters of the wall around the prime minister's official residence. We were suddenly told that a week later our house would be demolished by the military. We were living in Akasaka. I was caring for a three-and-a-half-year-old child and a four-teen-month-old infant while my husband was away.

The entire neighborhood was thrown into a panic. The military had requisitioned everything. There were no trucks, no horse carts, no taxis, no transport vehicles whatsoever. We were at a loss as to what to do. It was then that Mr. "Y," a customer who always brought his petitions to be typed, told me, "If an oxcart is all right, then I can take your things to my family home in Saitama. If we run into an air raid on the way, then just consider it bad luck."

So I decided to place all my household goods in his care. It was morning when we agreed on this. By the time he went to Saitama and brought back the oxcart, it was one o'clock the next morning. It was three o'clock when we loaded up our things and the cart departed. As dawn broke the four of us—my two children, our live-in helper, and I—started on our way to Mr. "Y"'s house in Saitama. Riding on crowded streetcars and in city trains, we reached our destination in the evening. The oxcart took eighteen hours and arrived after ten o'clock at night.

Later, the rental house I found in Shinjuku was burned in the 25 May air raid, and I couldn't get hold of a ticket to get to my countryside home. Outrageous storage fees ate up our money and we lost all our belongings to burglary and rats, but I considered myself fortunate that my two little children and I were still alive.

Ordinary people were defeated by those on our own side rather than by the enemy. In order to protect the prime minister's residence, we were dispersed without any recourse.

> Yashiro Mieko, seventy-two
> (f), retired, Numazu

Facts About the Comment, "The Poor Things"

In the middle of the Pacific War, I was jointly assigned to the War Ministry press section and the Cabinet's public information section. At one regular vice ministers' meeting it was decided that each ministry would be in charge of a broadcast that would heighten the fighting spirit of the citizens.

This was communicated to the public information section, and it was ordered that the army would be the first. The job fell to me. It is easy to say, "increase the fighting spirit," but I had serious concerns as to how we could come up with an effective broadcast.

During a conversation in the press room of the War Ministry, one of the reporters told us about visiting a former minister, a viscount, at his home in Shinagawa. "As I was leaving," he said, "we saw a row of American prisoners of war pass by. The viscountess, who had seen me to the gate said, 'The poor things.* How sad to treat Americans that way.' It seems that even when we're at war with them, she still feels that Americans and British are superior."

At this I felt a flash of insight. This was it! I wrote my piece for broadcast. NHK [Japan Broadcasting System] asked for confirmation of the title "The Poor Things."

After my piece was broadcast, many newspapers and magazines reprinted it. I was surprised at the response. No other ministry made any broadcasts.

I certainly did not say that the prisoners of war should be treated cruelly. Just before that, as head of the army press section in Shanghai, I had taken American prisoners of war sent from Guam to see a baseball game. I felt that I fully understood the kind feelings of compassion of the Japanese lady who had commented, "the poor things."

But something happened in the Bataan Peninsula in the Philippines. The Americans were very familiar with the terrain, as they had used that area as a training ground. Japanese forces faced difficulties in capturing it. Two infantry battalions in landing craft landed on the right flank of the enemy, but they were cut off and came under heavy attack. One of our scouts saw American soldiers killing our wounded soldiers by rolling over them with a bulldozer.

After the War's end I spent time as a prisoner of war in the Philippines. Our meals consisted of thin gruel in which we could practically count the grains of rice. All the Japanese had their ribs sticking out like emaciated Buddhist arhats. Every day there were some fifty malaria patients who died. Those of us who fought in the War feel most steeped in its wretchedness.

Akiyama Kunio, eighty-eight
(m), retired, Chōfu

---

*There were several letters regarding the comment "The poor things," which seems to have been attributed also to other women and girls who expressed their sympathy for the enemy.

Antiwar Letters Placed in Postboxes

In the midst of World War II, in mid 1943, seditious antiwar documents began to be mailed from postboxes in the jurisdiction of the Yoshihara Police Department in Shizuoka Prefecture. They were letters addressed to Prime Minister Tōjō Hideki, his wife Katsuko, army general Hata Shunroku, the Shizuoka prefectural governor, the leader of the Greater Japan National Defense Women's Association, the leader of the Patriotic Women's Association, and other prominent figures in various fields.

"Please stop this war as soon as possible." "Japan will lose this War for certain." "Aren't you aware of how difficult the lives of the Japanese people have become?" That was the gist of the contents. Later they included threatening remarks such as "There's likely to be rioting in the country soon."

Every day we got telephone calls from the Special Higher Police section of the prefectural police headquarters insisting that we arrest the perpetrator as soon as possible. It was enough to drive us nearly crazy.

The postboxes that were used to mail the letters were different each time. Our staff staked out locations all night, but we always had to give up with no results.

The Fujinomiya military police heard about the incident. "All right," they said, "if the local police can't make an arrest, we will." So they sent several military policemen to the civic auditorium in the town of Fuji. There they summoned the local members of the Women's National Defense Association and the Patriotic Women's Association and took samples of each woman's handwriting. From the penmanship and the texts of the letters the writer was considered unmistakably to be a woman.

We were furious at the high-handed measures taken by the military police, but we had no recourse. After a desperate search during which we had to forego sleep and rest, we were finally able to bring in the suspect on 7 February 1945.

She was a widow, aged fifty-three at the time. Her husband had died quite a while before, and her only son was killed in battle in the South Pacific. Her only daughter was a girls' high school student. The widow was kept in detention for over twenty days, but she insisted she didn't know anything—quite the strong-willed heroic woman. She attempted suicide but was saved by the others in detention, who raised a fuss.

This attempted suicide made us certain that no matter how much she denied it, she was the real perpetrator. We continued our investigation. Finally, she said, "I'm sorry for what I did," and, crying, started to tell us the details of her movements.

We were able to indict her and bring the case to a successful conclusion. Yet, with the War's end on 15 August, the Special Higher Police was abolished at the end of October, and we officers were purged from public service. Having lost my job, I returned to my hometown with my family the next April. That woman, if she were still alive, would be ninety-five years old. I think of her now as an extremely impressive, heroic woman who took a worthy stand.

Ishida Sumio, eighty-two (m),
farmer, Kosai

Informed Upon and Mistreated by Military Police

This happened shortly before the War's end, when Japan's defeat was unavoidable. A military policeman suddenly came to our house. At that time, under the National General Mobilization Law promulgated during the War, my family had been forced to discontinue our hereditary textile-weaving business and convert to a machine parts factory. We were in the midst of hard times doing unaccustomed work.

After looking over our factory and finding fault with such things as the number of buckets for firefighting purposes and the lack of sandbags, the soldier said he had something to ask my father. He told him to present himself at ten o'clock the following morning at the military police substation. Then he departed.

I ran after him to ask what the summons was for, but he only said we would find out when my father got there. Apparently, on his way back he stopped by at a store near our house and asked about our family's reputation.

Father went off the next day to the military police substation. He didn't return even after nightfall. I had a sinister premonition. We telephoned, but they gave us no information. At about 9 P.M., I went alone to the substation. When I gave my reason for being there, the man who had come to the entranceway suddenly yelled at me, "We won't kill him! Go on home!" There was nowhere I could turn.

Father was finally released around midnight. According to him, someone in our neighborhood had informed on him. Father had said that Saipan had fallen to the American forces, so things were serious. He had mentioned this in conversation at a farewell party for a soldier being sent to the front. Someone in the neighborhood had reported this to the military police.

Father was questioned persistently about the source of his information about Saipan. Only after he was forced to give a written explanation was he released. After that our family was constantly under military police observation. These unpleasant days continued until the War's end. I learned from this experience that war tears apart people's hearts and leaves deep scars.

Ariyama Sachi, deceased* (m),
Kawagoe

---

*The writer died in autumn of 1984 at the age of sixty-three. He left this account, which was to be made public when the chance arose. It was sent in by his widow.

Don't You People Have Any Compassion?

Satō Toshio, who worked in Sapporo's social welfare office, was critical of the government's war policies. The day after the War between Japan and the United States started, he was arrested, ostensibly for preventive detention under the Peace Preservation Law. He was confined in Naebo Prison. This sort of thing was happening all over the country. It was the dark underside of the Japanese people's jubilant festivities at the news of the successful attack on Pearl Harbor. Under relentless torture, amid deteriorating living conditions, Toshio died in prison on 14 May 1944, at the age of thirty-four. He did not live to see the day of defeat that he had predicted would come. The blood-curdling events leading to his death are faithfully recorded in *Inside the Infirmary*. This was written after the War by Sasaki Sentarō, who was confined in the isolation cell across the corridor.

Toshio's naked body was released without a stitch of clothing on it to his wife and four-year-old daughter. His courageous wife pressed the officials, saying, "Don't you people have even the compassion to put a sheet over someone you've killed with your own hands?" They could only mumble in reply.

As a "traitorous" family, she and her daughter lived under observation by the Special Higher Police and suffered the cold stares of society. Working day and night during and after the War, Toshio's widow died exhausted.

After the War's end, the story was that the War was waged against the Emperor's will. The military men and politicians who thus went against the will of the Emperor and started the War were granted pensions, while those who died who had been in agreement with the Emperor received no compensation. Wanting to find out what crime her father was judged to have committed, Toshio's daughter, who had grown up during the difficult times after the War, requested the court to issue a copy of his trial records. The single response she received was that "the documents requested were burned up." This daughter later became my wife.

It is not necessarily the enemy's bullets that are to be feared during a war. What is frightening beyond words is the process by which a government run amok can kill its own citizens who have committed no crimes.

Yamashita Saburō, sixty-one (m),
company president, Tokyo

People Who Lost Their Lives in the Mines

I worked in a coal mine under the student mobilization order. I think that was a kind of war as well. I worked underground in the coal mine and shared with Korean workers life and death both day and night. Gas explosions, cave-ins, and other accidents were not unusual. I wonder how I was able to survive the experience. I couldn't do anything when I heard the screams of a Korean who had escaped and been caught and was beaten badly. And all I could do for someone who had contracted typhoid fever was to visit him briefly in a corner of the hospital.

The Koreans had so little to eat at breakfast that they ate up their lunch at the same time. They became too weak to work in the afternoon. We passed out bread to make them work more. Some offered me one of the two pieces they had received. I told them that I could get some separately, so they needn't worry. One time a cave-in started with a crash; I was barely able to pass below it and exit the mine.

A few years ago we were finally able to collect enough contributions to erect a memorial to 109 martyrs and bury their remains, which had been stored in a temple warehouse. Every two years we hold a memorial service. There were many forced laborers who lost their lives. Without being on the battlefield, their every day was a battle with death—not enough food to eat and no doctors or medicines.

Namekawa Matao, sixty-two (m),
Hokukōkai trustee, Akita
University Department of
Mining, Akita Prefecture

Where Did the Temple Bell Go?

The family home of a teacher whom I often visited during my student days was a temple on the outskirts of Kumamoto. I noticed that there was an impressive bell tower, but no bell. When I asked about this, I was told that the bell had been turned over to the government during the War. The temple had not yet been able to buy another one. And this was twenty-some years after the War had ended.

Just after the War, my teacher had coincidentally been walking on the beach at Yokkaichi. He saw scores of temple bells gathered from all around the country, rusting as the waves washed over them. He spoke sorrowfully of the fate of the bells, which had been in villages for generations. "I wonder what happened to them after that," he said.

These bells and other items (copper and silver furnishings, braziers, jewelry) were gathered by the government from its citizens. Were they actually used for the country?

Kōno Kiyoko, forty (f),
housewife, Kagoshima

Fighter Planes and Dustpans

We were students, but under the labor mobilization policy were working in war plants. I was an assistant in duraluminum research at a research institute. The war situation had already deteriorated. The quality of materials used for airplanes had declined to the lowest level. The collection of pots and pans was totally inadequate to meet our needs. We were working desperately to cope with the situation.

After each massive B-29 attack, we reclaimed materials from the downed planes. I had thought that since Japan was under such duress, the quality of American materials would naturally have suffered as well. But the components we analyzed met the normal standards, and the surface of the propellers shone brightly like silver. I won't forget the chill I felt at the strength of American production capabilities.

I had heard that because of poor materials, the engines of Japanese fighter planes would crack if the throttle lever were turned to full, so they could only be flown at eighty percent of power.

The duraluminum we produced after many nights working all night was not ready in time for use in the War. When I saw the duraluminum, its material label still on, used for dustpans and ladles lined up in black markets right after the War's end, I felt my energies seep from my body.

Now high-quality aluminum of much greater purity than the best of that time is used in all sorts of products. Thinking back on the past, I am reminded of how fortunate we are now.

Hashimoto Yukio, sixty-one
(m), civil servant, Tokyo

When I Made Balloon Bombs

"Students, you are allowed to go home now." All of us seated on tatami mats in the large hall fell silent at these unexpected words from the principal. In the next instant we pushed forward. The only sound was that of our work pants stiffened by arum-root paste as we slid across the tatami mats. "Did I really hear that?" said the intense expression on everyone's face.

We automatically formed a circle around the principal. When the reality that we were able to go home sank in, a shriek went up. The sound of sobs filled the room. Such was the scene at the end of February 1945, at the Kokura munitions plant where our fourth-year class in girls' high school had been mobilized to produce balloon bombs.

We glued several layers of Japanese paper together with arum-root paste, steamed them, and pressed them with steel plates. Fusing some seven hundred of these pieces of paper, we fashioned a balloon ten meters in diameter. A bomb was to be hung on the balloon. Launched on the prevailing westerly winds, these balloons floated toward the American mainland at altitudes above nine thousand meters. We worked on these through the frigid winter, and the food was very poor. We worked two twelve-hour shifts, standing the entire time. Those on the night shift were forced to take two stimulant pills to stay awake. It was a constant struggle against drowsiness. Our dormitory, which slept twelve to a ten-tatami-mat room, was a place where we went only to flop down to sleep.

In these vile conditions almost everyone got athlete's foot and frostbite. Nearly one-tenth of our number died soon after graduation. Many suffered from tuberculosis, neuralgia, rickets, and overexhaustion. Our response to the news that we were able to go home symbolized the severity of our lives and the sadness that we had endured as mobilized students.

Takamizawa Sachiko, fifty-seven
(f), housewife, Chiba

Ex-Officer Principal Worked to Liberalize School

On the eighth of each month schools and workplaces held ceremonies to promote fighting spirit in commemoration of the start of the Greater East Asia War on 8 December 1941. The elderly principal of my middle school suffered from poor eyesight. He had left out one section of the Imperial Declaration of War when he read it aloud at the assembly. This principal, who had dedicated a half century to education, left our school without any words of farewell.

His successor was a former army lieutenant general who had had a distinguished record on the north China front. We young boys had imagined that a brave general in command of all the forces would be an imposing figure, but the person who appeared before us was a small, stooped, elderly man who seemed courteous and gentle. As soon as he assumed his post, he forbade the private disciplining of younger students by older students. He prohibited corporal punishment by teachers, removed the ban on movie viewing, and did other such things aimed at "liberalizing the school."

Unlike in other schools, the pressuring of students to apply for military preparatory schools or army or navy officers' training stopped. When I wanted to volunteer to become a youth soldier, the principal admonished me for this, the hot-blooded rashness of a militant youth. "Dying on the battlefield," he told me, "is not the only way to show loyalty. Why not use your young energy in the service of constructing a new Asia?"

I had heard that the unit the principal belonged to had massacred many prisoners of war in China and had burned them with kerosene. When I think it over now, his actions among us must have been quite deliberate. He must have been concerned about the evil practice of the Imperial forces that exploded into inhumane, barbaric treatment of prisoners and local inhabitants, who were unable to retaliate against soldiers who had themselves been beaten by older soldiers. He feared that such conduct might spread to educational institutions.

Last year I visited the principal's oldest daughter. She said that he often said, "I don't like being a military man. I want to quit." He copied Buddhist sutras at home. This warm-hearted principal, Lieutenant General Kunizaki Noboru, worked to assist the families of military men who died in the War. In 1960, the year of the protests against the renewal of the U.S.–Japan Security Treaty, he died at the age of seventy-four.

Ume Yasuzō, fifty-nine (m),
Wadatsumikai trustee, Kashiwa

Forbidden Books Read in Secret at Night

Here is my bookworm's-eye view of the forbidden books in the library of the famous technical school (now a university) where I spent a year and a half during the War.

Separated from the general books, which could be read in the reading room or charged out, there was a large group of forbidden books. Their cards had been pulled out of the card catalogue, although the books themselves were left in the stacks. They were divided into three main categories. Group A were works critical of fascism by liberal professors like Minobe Tatsukichi, Tsuda Sōkichi, and Yanaihara Tadao. These were sealed and locked up in the glass-doored rare-books shelves on the top floor of the library. There must have been about thirty volumes in all. Group B included over 1,000 volumes of works with socialist and communist leanings. There were so many of them that they were left around in full view, scattered in several places within the stacks. Group C comprised documents edited and issued by the bureaus of various ministries, such as the War, Home Affairs, and Education ministries. They were all stamped "Classified" or "Top Secret" in red. These had been sent to the student affairs department, which kept surveillance over student ideological tendencies. Due to lack of space, they were deposited in the library.

Two months after I started my job in April of the year after the Pacific War began, I was assigned alone on alternate days to the afternoon shift (from 1 P.M. to 9 P.M.). As I had hoped, it became possible for me to read the forbidden books. In the midst of the War, this was an experience filled with fear.

It was the fear that someone might come in just as I was using the key and taking out one of the books on the top floor. I would place the book inside my desk drawer to read, so that I could hide it quickly. If someone came by, I closed the drawer and looked at the book on top of my desk or worked on the library-use figures for the day. At the end of my shift I returned the book to its shelf. Then, pocketing a Marxist book from group B or a document from group C, I went home, where I read these until two or three o'clock in the morning. Occasionally I got hold of the *Special Higher Police Monthly Review* and was able to read about numerous cases of irreverent speech and conduct toward the Emperor, communist movements, antimilitary and antiwar movements, professions of faith and criticisms of Yasukuni Shrine by Christians, and anti-Japanese actions by Koreans. The Special Higher Police detective came twice a month to take notes on the readership. There was also a notebook in which we were to write down the names of all the students who requested a book by any author who had written even one forbidden work, even if the book asked for wasn't forbidden.

As a result of reading so many works which the Imperial government forbade or hid, I nearly became schizophrenic. I was one of the worst soldiers in the army. Not a few friends and acquaintances of my generation died and became "fallen heroes," even as they suspected that something was being hidden behind the beauty of the "national polity." Even during the War I couldn't make myself believe that they were sanctified in Yasukuni Shrine. The bureaucrats of the former Home Ministry, practicing a policy of political and educational suppression, impounded many writings, regarding citizens as insignificant worms, unfit to know about classified documents in a bureaucrats' country. It can be said that this policy is alive even today.

Abe Hōichi, sixty-two (m), former
prefectural library librarian,
Yamaguchi

A Seventeen Year Old's Long Day

I will never forget 2 January 1944, the day I received a summons to "report to military police headquarters tomorrow." I was seventeen years old and a student at a Christian mission school in Hiroshima. My parents and I were astonished at the sudden summons. I could think of no conduct on my part that would cause me to be investigated by the Special Higher Police. I didn't sleep well that night.

When I arrived at the headquarters the following day, I saw that a classmate of mine had also been summoned. We were taken into separate rooms. I was made to sit across a desk from two officers. It was just like the interrogation rooms one now sees in television detective dramas. My heart beat rapidly and I felt quite oppressed.

The subject of the questions was the conduct of my school teachers. "Didn't teacher 'A' speak about this during class?" "Didn't teacher 'B' say this sort of thing?" "What did teacher 'C' say?" "Reply truthfully to our questions." They surmised that there were some Christian teachers at the mission school who may have spoken words of criticism against the War to the students. I denied any such thing.

I was confined in that room all day long. My responses were recorded, and in the end I was made to sign and put my thumbprint on the document. Finally at dusk I was released. It was a long day for me.

Komatsu Mineko, fifty-nine (f),
retired, Yokohama

Teacher's Sobs Made Us Realize

In 1944, those of us who were students at the Miyazaki teachers training school had been mobilized to a farming village short of hands. There we spent our days far away from our studies, working solely on increasing the yield of produce.

Mr. Noguchi was a thirty-seven- or thirty-eight-year-old teacher. Along with his students, he tended the compost pile, turned the earth, planted seeds, and found the time to teach us steadily about theories of soil makeup, vegetation, and physical properties. A thickset man, we nicknamed him "Mr. Dirt Ox."

For some reason he never scolded students who tried to slack off out of hunger. We were drawn instinctively to him as he worked in the dirt, and we admired the spark of learning that illuminated the tasks he gave us. Our unspoken response was to work silently and steadily.

Near the end of that year Mr. Noguchi was served with his draft notice. For several years we had heard heroic words of parting spoken to us from the podium by one young teacher after another. That day we lined up as usual to await our teacher.

Mr. Noguchi bobbed his head in a single bow. No words followed. Finally, the thick eyebrows of the teacher we had nicknamed Mr. Dirt Ox began to tremble. We heard his stifled sobs, and tears flowed unceasingly from his large eyes. This was the first time I had seen a man's tears. I caught my breath. Like a child, Mr. Noguchi raised his arm to cover his eyes and wailed aloud. Sobbing with hiccups as a child does, he left the podium without a word.

A mere three months later, just before our graduation, we received word that our teacher had died of illness at the front. That teacher who had been as strong as an ox. . . . Even now my heart aches at the memory of our teacher's sobs. They made us feel the reality of the War.

Tsuji Hisayo, fifty-nine (f), elementary school teacher, Nobeoka

Pupils' War Experience Noted in My Diary

We were victims. We fought believing in certain victory, and so did the country's children. In 1945, at the age of eighteen, I was in charge of the sixth grade as a substitute. I took the place of a teacher drafted into the military, in an elementary school on the upper reaches of the Ōi River in Shizuoka Prefecture. During daily air raid warnings I took notes in my desk calendar. Reading over my notes now, I feel that we should never again allow children such experiences. Here are excerpts from my 1945 calendar.

12 April. Air raid alert at 2 P.M. Twenty-five P-51s and 250 B-29s fly overhead. Pupils dismissed and dispersed to return home.

26 April. Students go to assist in picking plants: third grade and younger pick club moss; fourth grade and older pick bracken. Upon their return to school, they write letters of encouragement to soldiers.

29 April. All pupils attend ceremony in honor of the Emperor's birthday. The principal gives admonitory lecture on all the efforts being made for victory's sake.

6 May. Due to students having to return home so often during air raid alerts, classes held on Sunday mornings. Arithmetic, geography.

12 May. Diarrhea due to soybean meal as the main food ration.

29 May. While students were picking tea leaves for a family who had lost a serviceman at the front, one of our fighter planes slammed into a B-29 overhead. Pupils cried out "Banzai!" Gave them an assignment to write a composition about their emotions.

1 June. In preparation for a possible incendiary bomb attack, training to open the shrine which houses deity. We must protect the Imperial portrait and the Imperial Rescript on Education, no matter what.

7 June. Heavy fighting in the battle of Okinawa. Went to the train station to send a student's father off to front. Gave students an assignment to write letters of encouragement.

8 June. Anniversary of receipt of Imperial Rescript at the start of the Pacific War. Early morning prayers for victory at shrine with students; practice bamboo-spear attacks on shrine grounds.

11 June. Cultivate school grounds and plant sweet potatoes and pumpkins. In the afternoon, transport military supplies to next village with students; a student who asked about the contents was scolded by the officer.

23 June. In between air raid alerts, cut wheat on the riverbank. After this, practiced bamboo spearing and stone throwing in the event of enemy land invasion.

18 July. Distribution of dried squid, which helps out greatly. No rice for over ten days. I feel dizzy from hunger while teaching class. It is amazing that I am still alive. At night, bayonet fencing drill with youth association.

19 July. Attacks by carrier-based planes increase. Carried charcoal from deep in the mountains five miles away, drenched by evening shower. Spurred on crying pupils by saying it was all for victory's sake.

20 July. Mr. Suzuki in charge of the third grade was called up; he is forty-two years old. The only other male members of the teaching staff are the principal and me. To be ready whenever I am drafted, I organize my service bag and pledge selfless devotion to my country.

23 July. To accelerate production, the following are quotas given to sixth-graders. Ramie: 50 pounds; wisteria bark: 100 pounds; bamboo bark: 165

pounds. Staff does bamboo-spear drills. Called a student who had stolen a lunch into the teachers' room and gave a stern reprimand.

9 August. Called in for training and returned to my hometown. Military training for three days at my alma mater.

15 August. The radio at school is broken, so I heard the Emperor's voice announcing the surrender at the home of a student whose family had evacuated to our village. Unable to make sense of it all, I cried on my return to school.

Shimizu Mitsuo, fifty-nine (m),
former teacher, Kashiwa

"Teacher, Don't You Dare Die!"

An eleven-year-old pupil suddenly shouted out in a strong voice so that everyone could hear, "Teacher, don't you dare die!"

It was 22 February of the year before the start of the Pacific War. I had gathered my class on the hill in back of the school grounds for a farewell meeting before my induction on 1 March. This happened while I was advising the students what had to be done before they graduated.

"Teacher is joining the military forces. He will go to the front and fight in battles; he may be killed in action. We want him to stay alive and come back to our school no matter what." It was his wholehearted childish feeling that this boy expressed. In those days such words were taboo. I could only reply, "Thank you for being so brave to say that." I couldn't tell him, "I won't die."

Not to die for one's country in war is the utmost of traitorous acts. It was shameful of me, but as an educator I was not allowed to have the courage to assert, "You bet I won't die."

Kamisaka Shigemitsu, sixty-six
(m), former elementary school
teacher, Iwai

"Bow Deeply to Enemy Flag"

Those of us born in 1934 who were in the first class to enter the restructured national elementary schools in 1941 seemed like a group of god-favored children bent on war. The news organizations daily reported glorious military achievements. No one anticipated the tragic results that would follow. One day during morning assembly, when all students were lined up at attention, the principal asked, "Let's say that an American flag is placed here. You are all walking toward it. What would you do?"

Everyone shouted in concert, "Trample on it as we pass by." This was an era when everywhere we looked we saw the demonic caricatures of Churchill and Roosevelt. Among the fifteen hundred pupils, just one, Arita Suzuko, a girl in my class, replied, "Bow deeply as I pass by." A thunderous roar of denunciation flooded the schoolyard. Word spread as quickly as a swift wind from one child to another. Her mother was immediately called to the principal's office and cautioned severely about what should be taught at home. Suzuko was a tomboy with many siblings, whose father was a doctor. I often admired the originality of her way of thinking and her way of responding. I bow with admiration for the courage required in that period for her mother to instill a sense of respect for a national flag, even the enemy's. It was a symbol of that nation, and should be bowed to. And I also admire the courage that it took for Suzuko to be the only one to raise her hand and say what she did.

A girl who liked to study, she must now be making her mark somewhere as a doctor.

Nakamura Kyōko, fifty-two (f),
housewife, Ube

Labeled Sixth Rank for Being Bad

I was in the fourth grade of elementary school in 1943. There were two classes of fourth-grade boys, and we were taught by two male teachers, "Y" and "S." In "S" 's class, all pupils other than the class president and vice president were divided into eight ranks. Those in the lower ranks had to salute those in the higher ranks. If they neglected to do so, they were denounced in faultfinding sessions that were called "review meetings," and sentenced to a demotion in rank. Initiated by "S" to make class administration more efficient, this was "playing soldier." It was unclear what the standards were for ranking the students. They were probably arbitrarily determined by "S."

Eventually the system was introduced into "Y" 's class as well. I was placed in the sixth rank. The review meetings made friendships entirely meaningless.

Primary school was a training ground for future strong soldiers. Students who were physically weak and uncoordinated were destined to fall through the cracks. Even if we studied hard and got good grades on grammar and arithmetic tests, bad grades in moral teaching would lower our overall grade average. These grades in moral teachings were a reflection of the teacher's subjective evaluations.

It was 15 August 1945, when I saw the light at the end of the long, dark tunnel of my misery. When I entered middle school the following year, I realized that the War had finally ended for me.

Satō Rokurō, fifty-two (m),
convalescent, Beppu

Don't Enlist

I was swimming in the river with a few friends in the summer of 1942 when a soldier rowed a boat toward us. He was an army corporal, about thirty years old. We became friends right away. When we asked him which branch of the service he was in, he replied the air corps. He worked on the ground crew for a squadron flying the *Hayabusa,* an object of admiration to us children.

"Hey, that's great! When I get out of school I'm going to enlist in the air corps and fly in the *Hayabusa,* too," we shouted. The corporal's eyes flashed sharply. "Don't say such a foolish thing. Don't ever become a soldier." We were taken aback at his sharp tone of voice. "Listen here, don't think of enlisting in the youth corps." "But, you're a soldier yourself." "In my case it's different. According to our country's law, those who have reached adulthood have a duty to serve in the armed forces. I didn't want to go into the military. When you reach that age and you become soldiers, then you can do your best to serve our country."

Which was correct: what he said or what our teacher said, that we were traitors not to enlist? Our older schoolmates and classmates eventually went off with a flourish to military training school and the youth air corps. But none of my friends who went swimming together that day enlisted. Even as children we felt the truth in the stern words the soldier had spoken to us.

Ozawa Hiroshi, fifty-seven (m),
company employee, Kashiwa

Hungry Maiden with an Appetite

Defeat looked more and more certain. An oppressive air hung over villages and towns, and everyone seemed to become silent. Even so, we girls' school students dug an air raid shelter in the corner of the playground and hoed the fields behind our school. One after another the younger teachers left for the battlefield. Only the female and elderly teachers remained. Without textbooks or notebooks our classes were not conducted adequately. I was in a small city in the mountains where there were no air raids, but every now and then we could see a B-29 flashing as it flew through the high clouds. Energetic students in the upper grades yelled at the skies, "Bastards!"

On 7 August, we were collected in the auditorium under orders for an emergency assembly. With a pained look on his face, the white-haired principal told us, "A special type of bomb has been dropped on Hiroshima." The rest was silence. We could tell from the tense atmosphere that something terribly out of the ordinary had occurred.

Day after day we ate watery gruel in the cottage of the farmhouse to which we had evacuated. Things got even worse and our daily chore was to gather field grasses. One day, I came across a book of Western cooking among the few remaining books on the bookshelf. I turned the pages to shiny photographs of roast beef, Spanish omelet, Scotch egg. It became my secret pastime to stare at the beautifully taken photos and read the book over and over. I didn't care what the outcome of the War might be. I swore in my heart that when the War was over I would eat all these dishes. Looking back on that time now, I smile ruefully that I was a hungry maiden with a big appetite.

Hashimoto Kumiko, fifty-eight (f),
housewife, Tokyo

Miso Soup Thief

Having sent my family to my hometown, I was staying at a friend's house a bit beyond Rikkyō University. This house was burned completely in an air raid on the night of 24 May, and I lost everything. With no other place to go, I stayed with a colleague who lived alone nearby. Food rationing was so strict then that we had no salt or soy sauce, and only about a thumbnail-size dollop of miso paste per person each day. For vegetables we were lucky to be able to eat the leaves grown in a vacant lot.

These were my materials to cook with—since I was the hanger-on. I soon used up the small amount of firewood that we had. After trying to think of a good alternative, we decided to tear up and use the old magazines stored in the house. Ripping out twenty pages or so and burning them made the flame rise up too quickly. So we had to watch the fire constantly. Twisting the pages together made it last a little longer. With a three-hundred-page magazine I could cook a cup and a half of rice. But it took one and a half magazines to cook miso soup.

This amount of rice and miso soup was what the two of us ate for our three meals. For lunch we took a small sushi-size ball of rice and a bit of miso wrapped in paper. I was so hungry that it was a chore to climb the stairs. At night we stuck it out by eating cold leftovers. One day when we returned home, we found that even though we had locked the house tightly, a thief had entered. Nothing was missing except our small amount of rice and miso soup. We looked dumbfounded at each other, amazed that someone was worse off than we. It was impossible for me to sleep that night.

Kumagaya Motokazu,
seventy-seven (m), self-employed,
Kiyose

"Show Me a Road Without a Police Box"

In the spring of 1944 with food increasingly scarce, strict controls were placed on staple foods. One evening a boy at the side of the road called out to me. He had a name tag on his chest that showed he was in fourth grade. I could tell that he had come from a city to buy food. He seemed very tired and pleaded, "Auntie, please show me a road without a police box."

"Where are you from?" "I'm from Osaka. I came day before yesterday. Everyone at home is waiting for me." Shocked, I stared at his cute face. He had come from Osaka all the way to Izu, taking one train after another through the paralyzed transportation system. He must have traced his way to this mountain village, hearing that it produced sweet potatoes. His backpack looked like it was filled with five or six kilograms of potatoes.

Wiping away his tears he said, "I came because my mother said that if I was caught they would let me go because I'm a kid. But I want to go home on a road without a police station." I quickly made a ball out of rice and millet and gave it to him wrapped in paper, along with a roasted sweet potato. I took him to the village train station and watched as he went off. I'm sure that the boy lived through the Osaka air raid and has now become a respectable grownup.

Aihara Yū, seventy (f), farmer,
Shizuoka Prefecture

A Boy's Lonely Death on a Broiling Street

It was a sweltering hot day a month before the War's end. A crowd of people had gathered on the street about a hundred meters from my house. I rushed over and saw that a boy had collapsed.

"Where are you from? Where are your mother and father?"

He had no strength left to reply to questions from the people around him. All he could do was nod or shake his head, keeping his eyes closed.

He was thirteen years old. His family had all died in the major March air raid over Tokyo, and he was all alone. Attempting to go to relatives in the countryside, he had come as far as the town of Fukuroi in Shizuoka Prefecture. He had not eaten for days, so his body was emaciated, and he had no energy left to walk or open his eyes. Thinking they had to get him to eat something, several women ran home and brought back stewed pumpkin and roasted soybeans and put them in his hand. The boy opened his eyes slightly, and seeming to say "Thank you," he gazed at the people around him. He brought his hand toward his mouth to try to eat the food, but he missed and it fell to the ground.

Two hours later, the boy no longer moved. He died of hunger at age thirteen in an unknown town on a street with a hard surface. We all cried and pressed our hands together in prayer. A man from the neighborhood found a straw mat somewhere and covered the body. The broiling summer sun beat down on the matting.

Ozawa Namiyo, fifty-three (f),
housewife, Shimizu

Worked on Mail Censorship

On 13 December 1944, the Mitsubishi generator factory in Nagoya was bombed during the day. For the three days following, mail was censored. Those sections that touched on military secrets or mentioned the damage were deleted: blacked out with ink on postcards and cut out from letters. We put a tag on the mail asking the recipient to warn the sender not to write such things in the future.

On the first day of censorship, members of the military police and Special Higher Police appeared. The military policemen left right away, and the Special Higher Police staff left by noon. Reading other people's mail was a new experience for us. When we came across an interesting passage we read it aloud and laughed about it, but soon we tired of this. It became a nuisance, so we didn't read the postcards. It was the clerical staff that was assigned to censorship duty, and other employees were exempted. Soon no one wanted to do this work. Those of us who were in general affairs and accounting were mobilized. I opened registered letters as well and was surprised to find an envelope containing precious metals. In the end, it was only for three days that the censorship was implemented.

Thinking it over now, I wonder why they did such a ridiculous thing. If it had been a single bombing incident, I could see the reason for hiding the extent of the damage from the citizens. But the following January, the entire city was bombed, and news of the extent of the damage was spread by word of mouth. There was no way to prevent this. I don't know which agency issued the orders for censorship, but I can only think that those in control had gone overboard.

Sakurai Shizuo, sixty-nine (m),
former postal worker, Nagoya

The Craziness of Censorship: An Example

"Unit commander Kanō died in battle grasping ____." This was a news item from the Shanghai front in the Sino-Japanese War in October 1937. I wonder what you readers think the unit commander was grasping when he died in battle. At the time I was posted in Tokyo as the Tokyo office's deputy-chief-cum-investigator for an import company subsidiary of the South Manchuria Railway Company. I assisted in importing—buying products from eastern Japan and gathering information for the navy, so I realized right away that this was the doing of the army newspaper censorship officer. I telephoned my acquaintance at *Asahi Shinbun*, Mr. Nomura Hideo, and was appalled when I heard that the reporter had written, "Unit commander Kanō was severely wounded by enemy fire. Just before his death he asked that he be allowed to hold his unit's flag. As he grasped the flag, he smiled and died." When this item was submitted to the censor, a correction was demanded. "Because the unit flag would indicate the regiment, so change it to ____." During the time I was on the telephone, the young staff members in my office had been joking about what the ____ was that he had been grasping. I still recall that when I told them, "Keep this to yourselves," and gave them the facts, they shamefacedly grew silent.

The Sino-Japanese Incident expanded into the Pacific War and led to the defeat that caused the nation's citizens to suffer such distress. One reason for this was the effect of laws and regulations that prohibited any impartial reporting by the newspapers. These included the Military Secrets Protection Law; the National Defense Secrets Law; the Public Peace Police Law; the Peace Preservation Law; the Emergency Law for Control of Seditious Literature; the National General Mobilization Law; the Military Resources Secrets Protection Law; the Press Law; the Publications Law; the Emergency Law for Control of Speech, Publication, Association, and Assembly; edicts issued by the army, navy, and foreign ministries; and orders prohibiting the printing of articles. Newspapers that ought to have published impartial reports had their hands tied and ended up printing information full of fallacies. Not only did the newspapers forfeit their own authority, they confused the citizens and made them lose their ability to judge right from wrong. In other words, these laws reduced newspapers and citizens to mere shells of themselves.

To prevent future wars, I think it essential that journalists unite together and risk their lives to obstruct the revision of the Constitution and the passage of a state secrets act. I wonder how others feel about this.

Kii Shūichirō, eighty-six (m),
war history scholar, Tokyo

"Pour Water on the Traitor's House"

In the evening of 18 April 1942, I headed home from my workplace in Nihonbashi and got off the train at Shin-Ōkubo. When I turned from the main street into the side street, I saw that the street's surface was wet. A fire truck was stopped there. From a distance of some three hundred meters, I could see that most of the neighbors' houses had burned to the ground and were smoldering, while my house and the houses beyond it were still standing. It was the first of the Doolittle air raids on Japan. The extensive Toyamagahara Army firing range on the north side of my house was closed to the general public after the air raid, and anti–air raid drills became more rigorous.

One Sunday, neighbors gathered, one member from each household, carrying buckets, fire dowsers, and ladders for the neighborhood anti–air raid drill. On that day rows of several tens of people marched under the orders of a reserve soldier. We passed through Nishi-Ōkubo, Higashi-Ōkubo and entered Ushigome district. To march under the broiling sun clad in cotton-padded anti–air raid hoods and work pants was arduous; it exhausted us almost to the point of collapse. Our questions as to why we were made to walk so far, to another district, were squelched by the scoldings of the reserve soldier and the block association officers.

Our group stopped in front of a private house, and we were pushed into the yard from a back gate that was pried open. Summer flowers bloomed riotously in the flower bed. Two quilts were being aired on the second-floor railing.

"Today we're going to practice extinguishing a fire by actually using water," our superior said. "This house is burning after being hit by an incendiary bomb. Your target is the quilt on the second-floor railing. Charge!"

We were made to fill buckets with water taken from the pond. The corridors and windows were open, so the homeowner must have been inside. We looked at one another's faces and hung back.

"Apparently the owner of the house is a diplomat." "They say he doesn't cooperate with the neighbors or the block association." "I hear he's a traitor." "Right, he's a traitor." These comments were whispered around. The women scooped water up from the pond and formed a bucket line; the men leaned ladders against the eaves and splashed water into the second-floor room. Although concerned as to what the homeowners were feeling—wherever they were—the throng wreaked havoc and continued until there was no more water in the pond.

"You've done a good job." With the reserve soldier's words of praise, the drill ended. The second-floor room and the quilts were drenched. The flower bed and plantings were trampled. Leaving a muddy lawn and fish gasping in the pond, we withdrew, our footsteps heavy. Agitation and pangs of remorse shut our mouths. There was not one glimpse of anyone at that house the whole time we were there.

Iwasaki Taiko, sixty-two (f),
housewife, Aizu-Wakamatsu

A Small-Scale Perpetrator

I was an editor at a small publishing house in the Kanda district when war broke out between Japan and the United States. We were unable to publish a single book without permission from the Imperial Headquarters of the army and navy. After submitting our manuscript to them, we would go to Imperial Headquarters a half dozen times. Behind the scenes, we had to invite the officer in charge to a restaurant in the Shiba district two or three times. His mistress was the waitress there. After two months or so, we finally received permission to publish the book.

The president of my company told me to visit and write a report on the hometowns and places related to the nine war heroes who died in submarine torpedo boats at Pearl Harbor. I secretly took along my wife, whom I had just married. We made a month-long grand tour of Gumma and Mie Prefectures, western Japan, and Kyūshū costing 1,200 yen. After this trip I submitted a three-hundred-page manuscript. Because I had included anecdotes of the "war heroes" brawling and whoring, permission was not granted to publish it, and I was fired.

At the small publisher's in Kagurazaka that I next worked for, I was a member of the project team to establish a subsidiary in Manchuria, and so I went to Xinjing. As I had expected, it was a land full of rapacious people. I spent about two months passing money out to obtain permits to establish the subsidiary company. During that time I avidly sent home in packages secondhand suits, the kind that were already unavailable in Japan, and clothes for my wife that I bought from a Russian dressmaker.

I was asked to become chief editor on my return, but I refused and entered *Nihon Sangyō Keizai* (the current *Nihon Keizai*) newspaper company. This was because I had heard that newspaper employees did not get draft notices. For a year I was not drafted. At the news of the fall of Saipan, I saw that air raids by B-29s would be inevitable and evacuated with my wife and mother to my wife's family home in Hokkaidō.

If we exclude the courageous men of religion and members of the Communist Party, I am one of the perpetrators with the least contact with the War, and I think I was a victim as well. This was due to my being educated during the height of Taishō liberalism. Education is a frightening thing.

> Tomoda Shōjirō, eighty-one (m),
> retired, Tokyo

Contents of Comfort Bags and Their Cost

The Sino-Japanese War started when I was in girls' middle school. We made comfort bags, which were sent by truck to the army relief department. Recently when I was cleaning out my closet, I discovered a small notebook made of cheap paper. It was mine from my girls' school days. I had written down what we had put in the comfort bags and how much the items had cost:

Comedy sketches 10 sen; popular songs 10 sen; dried-plum candy 20 sen; cup-and-ball game 10 sen; *shōgi* chess 20 sen; fan 10 sen; doll 10 sen; notebook 20 sen; set of soap, ear cleaner, razor 20 sen; loincloth 20 sen; tissue paper 25 sen; stationery 25 sen; needle and thread 30 sen; fava beans, mashed and dried sea bream 60 sen. Total: 2 yen 90 sen.

I had also noted that honey and bean-jam sweets cost 15 sen and buckwheat noodles were 15 sen. The first day of each month was a day in the service of the development of Asia, and our lunches were always sesame-seed-and-salt-flavored rice or rice like the Japanese flag, with one dried plum placed in the middle of the box. There was nothing else in the lunchbox. The comfort bags were also collected by block associations, and we always included a letter of encouragement. After we entered into World War II, the scarcity of goods made it more and more difficult to make comfort bags.

Tsubaki Yoshiko, sixty-three (f),
housewife, Tokyo

Wartime Stories Seem Unreal

During the War there were many things that would probably impel today's young people to say, "That's not true. No way." I was a substitute teacher after graduating from a regular girls' high school.

When I planted some flower seeds left over from the flower garden at school alongside our house, my father, an architect, scolded me. "We're at war now. You should be planting beans and pumpkins." My father had until a few years before taken us along on evening walks to tulip fields and peony gardens, and he taught us the names of stars on the banks of the Shinano River. I felt sad at hearing him scold me in such a way.

When the air raid alert was sounded, even in the dead of night I rushed to the school where I worked. This took an hour and a half on foot. There were no buses, trains, or private cars, and we couldn't ride bicycles. It was dawn by the time I returned home after the all-clear sounded. Mother stayed awake waiting for me. I can understand well a mother's worry about the dangers her daughter faced on the way home. After a brief sleep, I would go off to school again. This was physically hard on my parents and on me.

Being burned out of one's home caused an inevitable life of hardship. Here are some recollections by my friend's mother. "My five children were in grade school and girls' high school. I didn't have anything decent for them to wear. I undid a kimono that I received from relatives and sewed a standard uniform set for girls' school and a pair of work pants. I used the black lining of the sleeves as a hand towel. With that one hand towel we all wiped our faces, and we took turns using it in the bath."

In 1944 public baths were limited to operating twice per week, and there was a time limit. So we could actually only take about two baths a month. Soap was a valuable commodity, and of course there was no shampoo.

One of my friends at girls' high school was told by her parents, "There's more food in the mountains than in town," and she was sent to marry a doctor in the mountains of the next town.

There was nothing to be sold in confectioneries, rice cake shops, or vegetable shops. The colors disappeared from towns. Lovely lyrical paintings by artists like Nakahara Jun'ichi were forbidden. Fragile and delicate things became objects to be crushed.

The teachers who had been popular with the students left school. I heard later that it was because they could not agree with the educational policy of the new vice principal, who was one of the first to wear enthusiastically the national uniform for civilians. On the day that these teachers departed, the train station was so crowded with students, parents, and graduates sending them off that the police arrived to maintain order. The only other time this had happened was when the city's middle-school students had departed to work in military supply factories.

My physical endurance was at its limit. There was nothing to eat. When I was on the verge of malnutrition I heard voices talking about a "hundred-years war." No fighting spirit welled up in me. I was worn out. All I felt was despair.

A policeman went repeatedly to the house of the wife of a serviceman at the front under the pretext of patrolling the area. He forced himself on her, saying, "Do as I say." Geisha and waitresses were drafted to provide services to workers in munitions factories. The workers reveled in the fragrance of cosmetics for the first time in their lives.

The records in the town offices were burned up in air raids, causing lawlessness in the area. Land rights in the burned-out areas became unclear. The cunning roped off places on the street leading to the station, sold food piled up on boards, settled on empty lots of land, and, clawing their way up, expanded their shops.

" . . . I'll stop getting my hair permed; I'll no longer wear tall shoes; I'll wear wooden clogs. . . ." (This was a verse from "The Girl in Manchuria," which was sung then.) The other day my seventy-year-old sister-in-law and I were reminiscing and sang the song together, and we burst out laughing. If they had said "high heels" someone would have warned them not to use the enemy's language, so they had to say "tall shoes."

When I recall those days, it seems that the outrageous was considered normal. I wondered why this could have been so. I arrived at the term "time of crisis." So that was it. The routine, the everyday things were all denied, and the opposite went unchallenged. Now I understand. It was a time when we were forced to go against the natural feelings that we had about family love, beauty, truth, and goodness.

I urge you young people to read many books. The horror of war is written about in unexpected places.

Watanabe Fukumi, sixty (f),
retired, Nagaoka

Chapter 7

The Bombing of Japan

Many of the letters in this book have described a variety of atrocities perpetrated by Japanese soldiery on the other peoples of East Asia, as well as on the prisoners of war who fell into their hands, from the beginning of the so-called China Incident to the end of World War II. A second major theme has been life for Japanese people under the restrictions of government dominated by the military, one that single-mindedly mobilized the country to fight a continuing and disastrous war. But there are other horrors that the letters reveal. In the following section, the writers tell of their own suffering and that of others in the mass bombings of Japanese cities carried out by the U.S. Air Force and with navy airpower. These, of course, culminated in the atomic bombs dropped on Hiroshima and Nagasaki in August 1945. The last six of the letters, selected from many others, seem to sum up the suffering of the victims of the A-bomb, as well as their incomprehension at what was being done to them.

Yet the A-bombs were merely the final chapter in a campaign of fire-bombing against civilian targets almost without precedent in modern history. The bombing of Dresden, Germany, is often cited as a classic example of the wanton destruction of a city and its people in the guise of military assault. But Japan had many Dresdens. Tokyo was systematically razed by the B-29 bombings, which began in late 1944 and continued until the end of the War. Other cities were equally harshly dealt with. When I visited Nagoya for the first time in October of 1945, what had once been a flourishing city was literally a desert of rubble and smashed houses. The same was true of much of Osaka and other Japanese cities.

Little effort was made by American bombers to concentrate on military targets. Rather, mass firebombings of Japanese cities was part of the systematic campaign to destroy the will to fight of an entire nation. Perhaps one can understand why this was done in the closing years of a war that had been fought on both sides with savagery and on the Japanese side with almost unbelievable cruelty. We must nonetheless wonder at the ghastly totality of these attacks. The bombers left nothing behind in their zeal to obliterate every trace of the country they were attacking. Some civilians were even machine-gunned by low-flying navy aircraft. The worst damage, of course, came from the carpet firebombing of the B-29s, silver forms flying securely beyond the range of Japanese antiaircraft, oddly beautiful in the moonlight before they rained down destruction on the land below. The devastation was indiscriminate. Families were literally roasted alive in their homes in attacks from which there was no escape.

This book is a record of the War as experienced by the Japanese. It would be improper for an editor to impose his own commentary on these accounts other than to set the context for a new generation. Yet, as one of the early occupiers of Japan and one who thus visited Hiroshima, Nagasaki, Tokyo, Nagoya, Osaka, and other bombed-out cities, I retain an abiding horror of the terrible havoc and slaughter wrought by my fellow Americans, secure in their mastery of the air.

The letters reveal, even at the distance of four decades, that there was relatively little personal resentment among the Japanese. The firebombing and even the dropping of the A-bombs were regarded almost as natural calamities. There was perhaps an almost unspoken consciousness of the fact that Japan's own army had perpetrated unspeakable horrors on others to provoke this vengeance. Yet the suffering and the horror brought on Japan in 1944 and 1945 cannot be erased with the passage of time.

The First Doolittle Air Raid

In 1942 I was a staff member of the overseas posting contact office of the general affairs subsection located on the rooftop of the Yokosuka navy arsenal. I was conducting business by navy telephone with the staff of the Sasebo naval arsenal shortly after noon on 18 April 1942.

Suddenly, the air raid alert sounded. Soon loud booms shook the entire building. This attack on Tokyo was the first time the Japanese mainland had been bombed by the American army's Major General Doolittle. In my surprise I looked out the window and saw a ferocious cloud of black smoke rising rapidly from the Number-1 dock directly in front of my building. I went out on the roof and peered down to see that the warship *Daiho,* then in dry dock, had been hit. Large numbers of wounded were being carried on stretchers to the infirmary next to the docks.

As I gazed stupefied at the scene, I heard a voice behind me say, "The enemy is quite something." I turned around to see a short flag officer smiling ruefully. It was the arsenal chief Naval Vice Admiral Tsuzuki Ishichi. Recovering my bearings, I saluted. He said, "All right," and disappeared into the passageway specially designated for the arsenal chief.

The sky was full of the unfamiliar low-flying squat black American military aircraft. Antiaircraft fire exploded in the sky high above them. Japanese fighter planes were flying up to meet the attack. For me as a nineteen year old it was the occurrence of a moment. But when I recall it now, I realize that I had happened upon an important historic event.

> Koiwa Kazuei, sixty-four (m),
> corporate officer, Mizusawa

Corpses in a Pool, Park Turned Into a Graveyard

The night of 9 March 1945, we listened intently to the radio report of yet another air raid on Tokyo. My husband and I went outside at the explosive noise of aircraft, which seemed to press down on our house. We were riveted to the spot. The area surrounding us was bright in a sea of fire. As the airplanes spread their large wings in the sky, antiaircraft fire shot upward from Sumida Park. "Let's hurry and get ready to escape." I roused myself at my husband's words, but we had nothing to take with us. Pouring some water into a large bottle and putting the remainder of our rationed soybean curds into a bag, my husband took our child's hand and I took my mother-in-law's. We left our house.

A soldier ran by, shouting, "Sumida Park is no good; go to some other place." We went to the area behind the gas company near Shirahige Bridge. Incendiary bombs fell like rain. The town was a blazing hell, lit by the swirling and roiling flames. At dawn Asakusa was filled with so much smoke it was hard to keep one's eyes open. Everyone was dazed and could only gaze dumbly at one another.

We saw my older brother, who lived in Asakusa, but fearing that my older sister's family of seven might have died—they were in Senzoku, where the damage was severe—we searched among the corpses. We saw blackened bodies, half-burned bodies, people who expired even as they called out "Water! Water!" and firemen dead on fire trucks. The swimming pool at the school was a mountain of corpses. The Sumida River was full of the bodies of people who must have been trying to escape the fires. Sumida Park had become a graveyard with lumps of earth piled up in rows. People dug large pits and poured kerosene on corpses to incinerate them.

"It's no use thinking about what's going to happen, so you go to Atami." I caught my breath at my husband's suggestion. We had evacuated our second-grade daughter there. Determined that if I was going to die, I wanted to die with my children, I waited in line for two days at the station to buy a train ticket and went to Atami. But what awaited us there was the hardship of food shortages worse than we'd known in Tokyo.

> Ogawa Sumi, seventy (f),
> retired, Saitama Prefecture

---

10 March, Capital in Flames

We were among those surrounded by flames on 10 March 1945. My mother, older sister, and I tried to make our escape. Wherever I went, a wave of fire rushed toward me. Finally I made it to Oshiage station. There were thousands of people there. It was so hot and suffocating that I pressed my cheek to the ground. The air was cool and clean down there. I saw the legs of all sorts of people in front of me. Occasionally on my way a man I didn't know would splash ditch water from a bucket on us and urge us on, saying it was just a little further. Behind me a man sat covered with a large quilt. My back pressed against his, I waited for day to break, fearful and worried about the heat.

With the coming of the pale dawn, people started heading for home. Several military trucks came by around that time. Thinking they had come to help us, I stood up, and the man behind me toppled over. I shook him, but he was dead. They said he died from smoke and the heat of the flames.

On the way home, I thought I saw some black work gloves. When I took a closer look, they were hands that had been torn off. Many red fire trucks were burned out on the major road next to the streetcar tracks, with firemen dead on their vehicles. The dead were blackened and had shrunk to the size of children. It was impossible to tell if they were men or women.

I finally made it back to the charred remains of our house. My mother and sister were there. We hugged each other, weeping. We dug up the crockery, furniture, and food that we had buried in our yard. The rice that had been washed and in our pot was now charred, but we ate it. The tin cans of food that had been stored in the basement of the school building, which had been spared, had burst open due to the tremendous heat of the surrounding fires. I had two younger brothers in first and second grade, but they had been evacuated and were not in Tokyo, so they were safe.

Shinoda Tomoko, fifty-seven (f),
housewife, Yaita

Memories of Youth Turned to Ashes

It was 25 May 1945. We had no relatives to whom we could evacuate. My father, older sister, and I, lying on our cold futons, were exhausted from lack of sleep due to nightly air raids. At the sound of the air raid alert we went outside into the garden and saw things falling from the sky. Here and there in the garden were small fires caused by incendiary bombs. We walked over the tatami mats in our shoes many times to get water.

The fires only grew in force. My father shouted, "We can't stay here any longer! Let's get out!" We ran along streets that were a sea of flames and escaped into Shinjuku Gyoen gardens. Live trees burned up with a crackling noise, and the smoke was suffocating. Suddenly, the wind changed direction. At the same time, all my strength left me, and until dawn I could only sit on the ground. When I stood up in the smoldering wasteland, what hit my eyes was a single standing building, the train station at Harajuku. In one night the flames of war had eradicated not only my home but also the memories of my youth.

The entire traffic system had been cut to shreds by repeated bombings. In the midwinter twilight I had walked with an empty stomach for two hours and somehow reached home from school. With no fire to warm myself, wearing the clothes I had on, I crawled under my quilt. Those were the days in which the wretchedness that is war turned to ashes what should have been a brightly colored time of youth. I still cannot recall how I returned home from the factory where I worked on the day that the War ended.

Hiratani Yasuko, fifty-eight (f),
housewife, Musashino

"Doesn't Seem Too Bad"

It was spring of 1945. I was a sixth-grade member of the rising generation living in Hiroshima. An order was issued to evacuate children from the city, so I was on the evacuation train heading east with my father, bound for northeastern Japan, where we had relatives. At that time, Hiroshima had food shortages, but it had not been directly bombed. As a youngster, I was not yet fully aware of the misery of war. I was actually excited about escaping from my daily routine and going on a long trip.

As the train progressed eastward and we neared Akashi, we saw more and more houses that were leaning or had collapsed. My jaunty spirits gradually turned to apprehension. And when we saw the narrow city of Kobe stretching out interminably as a complete wasteland, I caught my breath at the extent of the disaster. Yet what were the first words that I uttered? Contrary to the violent shock I felt, I unthinkingly blurted out, "It doesn't seem too bad."

The kindly middle-aged man sitting next to me inquired quietly, "You don't think this is horrible?" I was stuck for an answer, but pointing to some houses left standing in the Rokkō Mountains, I insisted, "See, there are still some houses left." The gentleman responded, "You do have a point there," and our interchange concluded. Flustered by the gentleman's question, I clearly felt uncomfortable in his presence. The thought flashed across my mind, "I wonder if he is a spy."

This was what might be called my first experience of the War. War is what made a young boy say "It doesn't seem too bad" when he saw a city turned into a scorched wasteland, and it is what made me suspect as a spy a man who had the courage to look at the wasteland and to state in public, "This is horrible." Without this kind of abnormal psychology, war cannot be prosecuted. Once into a war, many people reach this kind of psychological state. The war leaders of the time justified this crazed psychology by calling it "courageous." As a young boy I fully believed this.

Shirai Naruo, fifty-two (m),
civil servant, Nagoya

Hand Like a Maple Leaf

This is the first time for me to write about a sad wartime memory.

When I was in the fourth year of girls' school, I left Tokyo and went to Fukui Prefecture to produce aircraft parts in a war plant as a member of the volunteer corps. This had once been an impressive silk-weaving factory, but with the worsening of war conditions it had been converted to a war plant. It took grim resolution for us young maidens to toil through our lives full of hunger and smeared with grease. Having just arrived, I wasn't familiar with the area, and I felt forlorn hearing the sound of explosions, shrieks, and wails.

A four- or five-year-old girl must have gotten separated from her parents, and she clutched my hand, saying "Take me with you." Feeling a bit relieved, I told her, "Let's get away from here together." Holding hands tightly, we ran for our lives. Flames rose everywhere. The little girl's face was black from sweat and dirt, and her eyes shone bright with relief.

Just then I saw a firebomb dropping toward us, spewing flames and making a shrill noise. In that instant, I dropped the little girl's hand and ducked into a nearby vacant house. Then, "Oh no, the girl!" I cried. I turned around to see behind me several people engulfed in a ball of flame, their screams rising up with the flames. A fragment of the little girl's padded hood drifted high into the sky.

The little girl died because I had let go of her hand for just an instant. I didn't even know the name of the cute little girl. I have never been able to forget the feeling of her soft, little hand, like a maple leaf, in mine. My heart still aches even after the passage of forty years.

Ōkubo Michiko, fifty-eight (f),
housewife, Iwaki

"A Keepsake of My Daughter" Amid the Wasteland

The massive air raid on Tsuruga on 12 July, close to the War's end, made an unforgettably powerful impression on me. The enemy's large formation of aircraft dropped incendiary bombs as if they were dumping water on the city. The shore breeze fanned the flames rising from various places in the blacked-out, silent city, turning it instantly into a living hell.

I was then stationed as a communications officer in the Central Area Detachment (136th Unit). I set out before dawn the following morning on a scouting mission to assess the damage to the demolished communications lines and prepare for recovery. Amid the stench of death emanating from the still burning bodies of many victims, I urged my reluctant horse forward and rushed about the city. I was shocked to see a firebomb sitting like a porcupine on the white gravel on the grounds of Kibi Shrine.

As day broke, I saw a burned-out wasteland almost devoid of people. In the distance a lone elderly woman in kimono and wooden clogs repeatedly leaned over to pick up pieces of something with chopsticks. She put the pieces on a plate. I approached her and asked what she was doing. With a stately and unflinching demeanor, she replied, "I've lost everything, and now my daughter has turned into this. I want to have a keepsake of my daughter so that I can pray for her soul." So saying she continued to pick up and place on the dish pieces of brain from her daughter's burnt skull.

I had seen many scenes of the wretchedness of war, but this scene of a mother's love for her child impressed on me the cruelty of war, which causes such pain for innocent citizens. This scene was so brutal that I have kept it to myself, but I decided to send this in after reading the column.

Ōtsubo Hiroaki, sixty-four (m),
retired, Kamio

Fireflies in the Red Sky

On the night of 1 August 1945, and into the predawn of 2 August, there was an air attack on Nagaoka. My younger brother and I clung to each other as we shivered in a rice paddy where the rice was starting to ripen. It was during the time women and children were forced to evacuate from Niigata, and we had gone to my father's parents' home in a town four stops toward Niigata from Nagaoka. By that time Niigata had prepared some defenses against fires caused by air raids. As a result, roads were widened regardless of homeowners' individual rights. We particularly feared the low-flying carrier-based aircraft. There were many days when we took everything out of the closet and hid inside, with our bedding piled up by the opening. Many was the night we rubbed our sleepy eyes and entered the bomb shelter my father had built.

After we were evacuated, we had no such fears. Occasionally we would go into vegetable fields and swipe eggplants or tomatoes. The air raid on peaceful Nagaoka was particularly frightening. Red dots lined up with precision. Floating down on the wind were large objects the size of several door-sized screens tied together.

The whole area became as bright as day. Pillars of fire rose, and I could clearly see objects scattering. It seemed that I could also hear people's screams carried on the wind. I lost sight of my uncle, with whom we had run out. My brother and I were left alone. The rice plants waved in the wind, and in a sky stained red were the blue-white glints of fireflies. I felt so lonely, miserable, and forlorn.

Mitomi Hideko, fifty-two (f),
housewife, Niigata

An Angelic Smile

I enlisted as a communications specialist. After my training, I was stationed at the Hiroshima communications office and later at the Ujina maritime headquarters. My final posting was to the headquarters of the Second Military Force located behind Hiroshima station. I was there at the time of the atomic bombing.

Our three-story building collapsed and burned to ashes in an intense fire. A tin-roofed shed on a slope on the Higashi drill grounds was spread with straw mats, and an emergency hospital was set up there. Those who were taken to this makeshift hospital were the fortunate ones. One of my war buddies was hospitalized with a severe wound, and I took him food and water between my shifts. The expanse of the drill ground was so full of corpses that it was hard to find room to walk. When I stumbled on some bodies, they groaned in frail voices.

A bare-breasted middle-aged woman lay in a ditch. I thought she must be dead. Her infant daughter grasped the woman's nipple and smiled at me. She was as cute as a doll, a single flower blooming in the wasteland. Touched by the little girl's smile, I waved at her.

After I hurried to deliver water and food to my friend, I felt concerned about the little girl. I went back to see what had become of her. But already there was no sign of her or her mother, who had probably died. I told myself that the little girl must have been taken to a safe place, and went on home. I still clearly recall her angelic, smiling face.

Yamaguchi Fumio, sixty (m),
barber, Gumma Prefecture

Skin That Slipped Off

Around 6 o'clock in the evening I was having supper with my squad after returning from fatigue duty digging dugouts on Kanawa Island in Ujina Harbor. There were fewer men than usual. From morning through afternoon my fellow soldiers had been called out to help the people in Hiroshima. As I was chewing each grain of sorghum, which at first glance looked like festive rice with red beans, the squad leader suddenly rushed into the room. "All men, stop eating," he said. "Assemble at the pier with stretchers immediately."

What on earth had happened? We had no idea, but in the military, questions are prohibited. We dropped our chopsticks and, glancing regretfully at our unfinished meal, rushed out. At the midpoint of the pier stood four military doctors, two on either side, with stethoscopes at their ears. "Hurry it up!" came an agitated shout at our backs. We moved forward.

At the end of the pier were many large boats covered with heavy planks.

And what were the things lying jammed together on brand new straw mats? They were women, children, and the elderly, who looked more like mud dolls than anything else. It was midsummer. Hardly any of them were wearing any clothes. From head to toe they were coated with a white, doughlike ointment that shone light gray.

They moaned, asking for help and for water in weak voices. When a buddy lifted one person's head and I the legs, the burned skin slipped off in my hands.

The doctors spent less than a minute examining each Hiroshima resident as one after another they were unloaded from the boats. I was ordered to carry those that were pronounced dead to a raft and cover them with straw mats. When the raft filled up with corpses, it was towed to Ninoshima, where the bodies were cremated.

> Harada Tsutomu, sixty-two (m),
> former company employee,
> Yokohama

Like Pink Wax Dolls

Seven or eight military cadets from Mito on our way to assignment in Korea, we were forced to get off the train at Kaita station due to interrupted rail service. We started walking toward Hiroshima. As far as we could see, houses were smashed down, tiles still on the roofs. There was no evidence of bomb blasts, nor were there any fires. Peering into the air raid shelters made of sandbags piled along the road, we saw bodies, clothed and showing no wounds, piled up in a row. This was twenty-four hours after the atomic bomb was dropped.

I realize now that I was walking through areas strongly contaminated by radiation. The center of the city was still burning bright red, like live charcoal. Roof tiles were popping. We passed by numerous war dead who had been carbonized. At one point we came across dozens of soldiers who had fallen down without any wounds. They were all naked, but we could tell they were soldiers from their army boots. Their bodies were yellowed but with no trace of injury. They lay like dolls in a circle, their arms reaching up toward the sky. We could say nothing. We stood transfixed at this wretched sight. A kilometer further we found five or six half-burned, roofless streetcars. Inside were piles of corpses smoldering under white smoke.

Amid the horrific scenes we saw a strange sight that made us doubt our eyes. In the space of about a hundred square meters, the pink-colored bodies of some forty men, women, and children without a stitch on were scattered. A young mother lay face down, her baby tucked under her breast. They looked more like pink wax dolls than human beings. For a moment, I saw beyond the horror and they looked beautiful. Hiroshima was a city full of death with no one walking about. We must have been the last witnesses of these early scenes. We were there the second day under the hot summer sun. The bodies must have discolored and deteriorated soon afterward.

The sour stench pervading the city; the figure of a lone girl, a student mobilized to work in a factory, crying as she walked toward the city; the poisonously bright yellow of the squash flowers blooming on the riverbank. These are things that I have kept secret in my heart for close to half a century.

> Nozaki Kiyoshi, sixty-four (m),
> former teacher, Kitakyūshū

Hair Frizzy Like a Permanent

My younger brother, who was mobilized as a student, had been at the clothing depot in Hiroshima. He hadn't yet come home by the morning of 7 August. My father and I went to the city to look for him. The city had been laid waste by fire. No landmarks were left, so it was impossible to get our bearings.

What I saw then were chocolate-colored, shiny corpses that looked like mannequins of indeterminate gender. Firemen were silently prodding the bodies and rolling them with their fire axes to pile them up in one place.

An ox had fallen down, its body bloated to the bursting point. A mother, tightly holding her baby, had died in a water tank. The mother and child had no visible wounds, and their clothes were not burned. They must have fled from somewhere and, unable to stand the heat, jumped into the water.

My brother, fortunately, had been behind a building and had not been exposed to direct radiation. He soon came home. It was later that we suffered from bleeding gums, hair loss, diarrhea, lack of energy. My brother's straight hair frizzed up as if he had gotten a permanent.

Komatsu Mineko, sixty (f),
retired, Yokohama

Bomb Flash: Discomfort Pierced My Brain

Sasaki Kazuji, my father, was a Japanese grammar instructor at the army paymasters' school. He had gone to Hiroshima to proctor examinations for student applicants. He was there during the atomic bombing on 6 August 1945, and it was 12 August when he returned to his childhood home in the town of Sōryō, Hiroshima Prefecture, where our family was staying. On 18 August, twelve days after the bomb was dropped, he died.

The following is an excerpt from the draft of his report to the head of the paymasters' school. He dictated it to my mother just before he died.

Just after 7:30 A.M. on 6 August, an air raid warning was issued, but this did not turn into an air raid alert and was canceled at about 8:10 A.M. Therefore, we began to put on our uniforms to assume our duties. Major Takasaki was standing on the veranda of the eight-mat tatami room on the second floor. Professor Sasaki (myself) was inside the room putting on his underwear and shirt. Officer Trainee Sawaki was taking off his nightshirt in the next room. At that moment, there was a strike, a white flash accompanied by an explosive blast.

Major Takasaki on the veranda screamed, "Ah! ah!" At the same time the building collapsed instantaneously, and I was pinned beneath it. At the instant of the attack, I felt an indescribable discomfort pierce my brain. In total darkness underneath the collapsed house, I called out Major Takasaki's name, but there was no response. So I pulled all my strength together and decided to dig myself out. After removing with some effort the pillars, beams, walls, and other obstacles, I was able to crawl out onto the roof some ten minutes later.

I called for Major Takasaki again, but there was no response. Next, I called out for Officer Trainee Sawaki and heard a faint response from under the rubble. He reported that it was impossible for him to get out. Therefore I worked to remove the rubble, pillars, and beams in the area he seemed to be. Finally I was able to confirm his location and pulled him out through a narrow gap among the obstacles.

By that time the collapsed house had caught fire. The flames grew fierce all around our location. Compelled to forego a search for documents and to abandon the attempt to ensure Major Takasaki's safety, I assisted wounded Officer Trainee Sawaki and decided to retreat from the site to avoid the fire. It was a heartrending decision for me.

The collapse of the house felt like a blow directly from above, not like up-and-down and side-to-side shaking as in an earthquake.

My physical symptoms were localized pain, intense headache, high fever, frequent vomiting, complete lack of appetite.

Although I exerted every effort, I allowed all the documents to be ultimately destroyed by fire. I deplore exceedingly the vast difficulties in the admission of new students induced by this outcome. I am deeply aware of the gravity of my responsibility and find no way that I can excuse myself.

I recall my mother writing down these sentences as she wept.

Wada Michiyo, fifty-two (f),
housewife, Abiko

Chapter 8

"We Are All Prisoners"

When the reedy voice of Emperor Hirohito came over the radio on 15 August 1945, Japan underwent a sea change. Thousands of people wept. Shock mingled with disbelief, not merely at the thought of the imperial nation being beaten, but the fact that the God-Emperor himself announced the bad news. (Since the Emperor, incidentally, spoke in the stilted phraseology traditionally restricted for the imperial *persona,* the average Japanese had trouble understanding what he was saying; many had to ask their neighbors for a colloquial translation.) But there was no mistaking the words "We must endure the unendurable and bear the unbearable." This was the end.

Transfixed, the nation nervously awaited the new conquerors. As things turned out, the American Occupation brought relief rather than the murder and rapine which Japanese soldiery had visited on so much of Asia. Some unpleasant incidents occurred. There were cases where American troops stole from, raped, and cheated Japanese civilians. But for the most part, their behavior was good, if a bit uninhibited. The emotional release of the Japanese turned into something akin to gratitude, as the Occupation took over the work of feeding what was then a starving country.

The losses of the War had been extraordinary. About 1,500,000 Japanese soldiers were killed in action, according to final reports, and roughly 500,000 Imperial Navy sailors. More shocking was the death toll of civilians: probably 600,000 lost their lives in the War. This was due not only to the atomic bombings of Hiroshima and Nagasaki and the wholesale firebombings of Tokyo, Nagoya, and other cities, but to the hardships and atrocities perpetrated on Japanese civilians in Korea, China, and Okinawa. Thousands of families were left broken and destitute in the collapse of Japan's colonial empire.

Soldiers taken prisoner did not have an easy time of it. The Chinese Communists, in many cases, were quite lenient with their captives, preferring to indoctrinate them as they later "turned" many Nationalist prisoners during China's civil war. The Soviet Army was not so lenient. Most of the Kwantung Army was taken prisoner in the Russian advance. Soviet tanks swept through the broken remnants of that once proud army, whose best troops had already been dispatched to fight the losing battles in the Pacific islands and the Philippines. Thousands of Japanese troops spent the next four or five years in Soviet forced-labor camps, mostly in Siberia. Out of 1.3 million taken prisoner, an estimated 300,000 died of starvation, beatings, or worse. Much of their ill-treatment, as these letters indicate, was the result of their own superiors' efforts to curry favor with their new Soviet masters. For with the ultimate surrender, the bonds of military discipline and the sense of loyalty to the Emperor's army gradually evaporated.

The prisoners of war from the Pacific islands and Korea were the first to be repatriated, in 1945 and 1946, but it took four years before any repatriates were sent back from the Soviet Union. Coming home in 1949 indoctrinated into Soviet ways, they created a minor shock wave. But their communist solidarity vanished when they rejoined their families—at last out of reach of their captors. Some of the Japanese prisoners in Allied hands did not fare much better than those in Siberia. Quite understandably, British and Americans, French and Chinese were not backward in visiting on them some of the harsh treatment which had been given to their own people. It was not a very happy fate, for example, for a Japanese to be taken prisoner in Burma, where the memory of the "death railway" was fresh—or for that matter in the Philippines, where the Japanese soldiery and Special Naval Landing Forces had gone down in an orgy of atrocities against civilians, torching Manila before their ultimate defeat. On the whole, however, the Western Allies managed the repatriation smoothly.

The stigma of having been taken prisoner remained in some ways, but mostly among the old-line military. In a very real sense, Japanese felt that "we are all prisoners." Most bore their lot quite stoically and gradually began to write about it. A whole literature emerged about those taken prisoner by the Americans, and later, by the Chinese and Russians.

The soldiers, in one respect, had an advantage: they at least were grouped in their own formations. The civilians—almost 350,000 in Manchuria alone—were left to the mercy of Chinese civilians, many of whom, not surprisingly, wanted revenge after years of spoliation by the Japanese. The same thing was true when Koreans had a chance to turn the tables on their imperialist masters.

The letters recalling this time show a mixture of shock and reflection. Many are full of anger, as men and women recall the horrors that were visited upon them in captivity. Yet some felt at that time that they deserved to be punished. Many people wanted revenge on the men who had led them into a disastrous war. This consciousness of retribution was quite strong in the late forties and fifties, but it eventually waned, as later generations of Japanese bureaucrats tried, with varying degrees of success, to pretend that the War was merely a remote bit of history—something so distant that it almost seemed never to have happened.

Many Japanese were all but shattered by their experiences as conquered prisoners. Few survived the experience unscathed. Women as well as men wrote letters about the suffering they or their kinfolk endured. Yet even in that troubled time, a traditional sense of solidarity rescued many people from despair. These letters are among the most moving of the entire series.

Even the Horses Were Prisoners

At 7:00 A.M. we departed from our campground in Siberia. It was still pitch dark as we headed for the train station. We prisoners of war trudged along, each keeping his eyes on the backpack of the soldier walking ahead. Due to cold, hunger, and fatigue, we felt no emotion. All we could do was continue plodding ahead. At about 11:00 A.M. the sky finally grew light. In the distance was a range of low mountains covered in snow. At its base a pine forest stretched for tens of kilometers. A snow-covered plain spread from the forest to our formation.

By chance we noticed what looked like a herd of dark animals on the far reaches of the plain. A closer look revealed that they were horses. As soon as one lifted its head and glanced at us, it galloped toward us at top speed. Then a second and a third followed. Finally scores of horses ran toward us all together. We could see that they were Japanese horses, and military horses at that. They were so emaciated that their ribs stuck out like the ridges on a washboard. Atop their thin necks were large skull-like heads.

They seemed to be jumping for joy at seeing the familiar uniform of Japanese soldiers. They must have recalled the days when they had been military horses. They no doubt were reminded of the soldiers who had cared for them without rest, who had given them water and fodder and brushed their coats. Compared to those times, their present condition must have been unbearable—they were overworked, undernourished, and had to sleep standing in the snow. Cutting into our ranks, they tried to put their noses into our pockets. Soldiers wept, thinking of the horses' feelings. It was pitiful to see the horses neighing with pleasure at having their noses patted. We soldiers were also prisoners of war, the same as the horses. There was nothing we could do for them. We could only express how sorry we felt by rubbing our faces against theirs and embracing them.

When a coldhearted Soviet guard shooed the horses away, their eyes filled with sorrow. In their home villages, each horse must have been treated just like a member of the family.

To the souls of the many military horses whose dead carcasses no doubt lay exposed to the elements, we ask forgiveness.

Miyazaki Kiichi, sixty-eight (m),
former teacher, Kumamoto

A Soviet Soldier Carried Our Load

The winter after the surrender, our company was marching toward the depths of Siberia from our campground in north Korea. As sunset neared on our mountainous trek, powdery snowflakes floated down and the temperature dropped to –30° centigrade. On both sides of us stretched Siberian pine trees, no matter how far we traveled. Packs of wolves appeared among the trees. We had to advance, unable to extend a helping hand to the exhausted old soldiers who squatted or lay down beside the road. The words of the Soviet commander upon our departure weighed heavily on our hearts— "Stragglers will unfortunately have to be shot."

Behind us automatic rifle shots occasionally echoed off the surrounding trees. We trudged silently ahead, thinking, "Ah, another one is done for."

By six in the evening it was pitch dark. We reached what appeared to be a public hall at a collective farm. Fifty of us were put into a room about fifteen feet by twelve feet. Unable to lay our exhausted bodies down, we slept sitting and leaning against each other's shoulders. Suddenly, the doors opened. In came a young Soviet soldier. We were startled to find he carried the backpacks of four Japanese prisoners. He pulled along four old soldiers, two clinging to each arm.

The rifle shots must have been aimed toward the sky to threaten the men. Seeing the old soldiers too weak to walk on, this young Soviet soldier must not have been able to leave them behind. The room stirred with our words of thanks. We were amazed to find such a kind person among Soviet soldiers who seemed like devils to us.

The young Soviet soldier doffed his thermal hat. Steam puffed up from his close-cropped head. Saying nothing, he saluted shyly and disappeared into the dark. Following his back was our chorus of "Spasibo," expressing our thanks.

> Miyazaki Kiichi, sixty-eight (m),
> former teacher, Kumamoto

Atrocity in POW Camp

For a long time the Emperor still reigned as absolute ruler inside this Siberian internment camp. Every morning our company commander insisted that we all bow in the direction of the Imperial Palace and recite the Imperial Rescript to Soldiers and Sailors. He demanded absolute obedience. The officers feared the company commander, yet some of them used violence against their own subordinates.

Some searched out petty offenses and punished them by forbidding the men food. They then proceeded to eat the meals themselves. Some, saying they were taking men's watches for safekeeping, sold them off.

At mealtimes they would persistently demand seconds, when none was allowed for prisoners. The mess corporal loyally performed his duty and refused the demand. He was beaten half to death. One soldier stole pig feed and was caught by the Soviets. Told to punish him, the commander and other officers took him to the bath and stripped him. Putting lumps of snow into a tub of cold water and calling it ice cream, they rubbed the man's body with the slush and placed him in a concrete cell. The temperature was below −30° centigrade. He died a few days later. His best buddy, who tended him at the end, still is not able to tell the facts surrounding his death to his surviving family.

These were occurrences in the internment camp where I was imprisoned forty years ago. I was the mess corporal who was beaten half to death. I absolutely cannot abide any efforts to make justifications for that dark age.

Katō Yoshio, sixty-two (m),
farmer, Nishio

Battalion With No Privates

"Army Private Second Class XX has been promoted to Army Private First Class as of this date, 8 December 1946. I respectfully so report." It was the anniversary of the start of the Pacific War in the year following the defeat. The predawn in the Siberian internment camp was a frigid several tens of degrees below zero. The earth was frozen solid. The first-year soldiers all lined up abreast and faced toward the Imperial Palace.

Taking a couple of steps forward, they each shouted out the words, their breaths white puffs in the cold air. Accepting each report was the battalion commander, a recently promoted captain without a badge of rank, who returned the salutes by raising his arm and then dropping it like a puppet on a string. This promotion ceremony was only for the first-year soldiers. Thus we formed an army without any privates second class. We were under the orders from the Soviet side to have a certain number of officers, noncommissioned officers, and privates. There was no way to change our status, other than by death or transfer. Food supplies were based on these units. The reshuffling of soldiers' ranks was done at this time no doubt to mitigate at least some of the dissatisfaction among the lowest-ranking soldiers, to make them vie with each other for higher rank, and to maintain the military system, which requires that higher-ranked soldiers be popular in order for them to get good evaluations.

It appeared that the Soviet side had a hands-off policy regarding the POW camp's internal management. We had autonomy, at least on the surface. Here lay the chief cause of the unfair distribution and pocketing of food and luxury goods. There were also antimilitary struggles and kangaroo courts. The Japanese officers, obsequious in the face of Soviet authority, maneuvered shrewdly for their own gain.

Yamazaki Yukio, sixty (m),
pension operator, Suzaka

POW Camp in the Tundra

Our internment camp was built on Siberian tundra. It was said that the internees there numbered a thousand or fifteen hundred men. They say that over one winter five hundred men died of illness or starvation. They were apparently called "the be-deviled wrecked battalion" by others who had been in Siberia.

Meals were gruel served in the lids of the men's mess tins. With only this to eat the men worked on building the roadbed for the railroad or on logging operations. The old Japanese military system was kept as it was, with its generous treatment of higher-ranking officers and poor treatment of lower-ranking, younger soldiers. This meant that the younger soldiers were the first to die.

The dead bodies were piled up in the empty barracks in the camp. When the men died, they were stripped of their clothes, and their bodies froze stiff as logs. Graves couldn't be dug fast enough to keep up with the deaths because the earth in Siberia was frozen. Large bonfires were lit on the frozen tundra to melt the surface. With steel pikes, the earth was dug one and two millimeters at a time. After a certain depth was reached, a number of bodies were thrown into the pit together. Because they were frozen, the bones broke and shattered. This went on day and night. I will never forget the bonfires lighting up the night sky for as long as I live.

Taken to task for the large number of deaths, the Soviet military officer in charge of the POW camp was transferred to a prison camp. With the arrival of his successor, a civilian, the treatment of the POWs improved.

Two or three years after I was transferred to another internment camp, I went to take a look at the remains of the first camp. The tundra was half covered over with water and turning into a wet marsh. Weeds had overgrown everything. There was no sign of the grave pits nor the crosses made of white birch that had marked them. The reddish-brown Siberian dirt was all that I could see.

> Kagawa Haruyoshi, sixty-three
> (m), former company employee,
> Chiba Prefecture

Homesick Feelings Carved in a Pillar

As a member of the former Kwantung Army, I spent a month being transported in a freight car from Siberia, finally arriving at the Lada Number 118 Internment Camp near the city of Tambov, four hundred kilometers southeast of Moscow, in early January 1946. There I lived in a dugout shack until August of that year. The rows of shanties whose roofs were all that could be seen above ground had been built years before. The pillars inside were black with handprints.

In one of these shacks stood a pillar carved with Japanese words from years before we entered the camp. It was said that these carvings were left by homesick Japanese soldiers who were taken prisoners of war in the Nomonhan battle.*

I heard that in the city of Tambov lived a former Japanese soldier. After the Nomonhan Incident, he had given up on returning to Japan and became a Soviet citizen. He was supporting a family there. It seems that a consider-

---

*In May 1939, a border clash between Japanese and Soviet troops at Nomonhan, an outpost on the frontier between Manchukuo and Outer Mongolia, led to a full-scale battle, which lasted until September of that year. One Japanese division was almost destroyed by the Soviet tanks and mechanized infantry, led by then General Georgiy Zhukov.

able number of Japanese soldiers were taken deep into the Soviet Union as prisoners of war after the Nomonhan Incident.

At the Lada internment camp in addition to us Japanese there were not only German prisoners, but also Dutch, Hungarians, Australians, and others who had been POWs of the Germans. In the early summer of 1946, we held the "Lada Olympics," a camp track and field meet.

Shimizu Yoshio, sixty-four (m),
corporate officer, Hōfu

In Mongolia

I was a member of an airfield battalion when the War ended. I had managed to get from Chifeng to Jin County on the Gulf of Liaodong and was sleeping in the hangar on the airfield when I was herded onto a freight train and sent to Siberia. Just before we reached Lake Baikal we headed south into the Mongolian People's Republic. To us Japanese, this was an unknown country. Prodded by the bayonets of Mongolian soldiers, we were loaded onto trucks and sent to Ulan Bator, the capital of this fairyland.

There, thirteen thousand Japanese prisoners of war spent two years doing various types of forced labor. More than one-tenth of them, sixteen hundred men, died there. My main work was construction of the University of Ulan Bator. The number 5 internment camp was across the main square from the university in a former wool factory. Each morning and evening we passed through the main square in formation. At first it was just a huge square with a rough surface and nothing there. With the labor of Japanese prisoners of war, the surface was smoothed over, and a statue of the young revolutionary Sukhbaatar on horseback was erected in the center of the square. Japanese prisoners built the square, the university, the central government offices, the foreign ministry, the opera house, a movie theater, a hotel, and apartments, buildings that surround the square and form the center of Ulan Bator.

I do not want people to forget that these Japanese prisoners of war left behind their contribution to elevate the culture of Ulan Bator.

Ebe Tadao, seventy-one (m),
former high school teacher,
Tsuruoka

I Think of Siberia as I Rub My Backside

Listening to the rain outside the window and spending some time relaxing as I sweat in a hot bath, I happen to rub my backside. Thinking my body has wasted so much due to the passage of time, my entire body recalls the time I spent forty years ago beyond Irkutsk, near Lake Baikal in Siberia.

At our monthly physical exams we were lined up in four rows, naked, summer and winter, our cocks shrunken in the shivering cold. A solidly built female Soviet army doctor examined us by pulling at the skin of each man's backside. Beneath our skin was bone. Our skin was as rough as sandpaper, and we learned that this is what gooseflesh looked like. Thin and emaciated, with no way to remedy our vitamin deficiency, the cold stung us like needles.

We were classified into three ranks according to how fleshy we were. We prayed to be classified in the third rank, those who did light labor, so we might preserve our lives one day longer. The fleshiest were put into the first rank. They may have felt reassured, comparing themselves to their scrawny froglike buddies next to them, but when they thought of the hardship and heavy labor awaiting them the following day, their elation was mixed with disappointment.

I am amazed that I managed to return home alive. I think of the old army slogans we often heard in those times—"Win and fasten your helmet strap," for example. We thought we had won, but our straps weren't long enough. Rather than "I won't desire it until we have won," we might say "I won't desire it even though we haven't won." "Extravagance is the adversary," went the old slogan. On the contrary, "extravagance is wonderful." [The Japanese word-play is on "adversary" (*teki*) and "wonderful" (*suteki*).]

I close my eyes as I soak in the bath and think of how quickly the seasons have passed. In the back of my mind looms the long Siberian winter when everything froze. I recall the preciousness of the single basin of warm water with which I deftly washed from head to toe once a month in the steam room. The hot water gushing from my faucet now makes me realize how appreciative I am to be alive. How my heart aches, how sorry I am that so many of my wartime buddies died.

As my feelings about the blizzardy north country and the warmth of the bath intersect, I gently rub my backside. As I have aged, the gooseflesh of the past has been revived in the wrinkles brought on by the years.

Yamamoto Yoshimaru, sixty-five (m), printing company owner, Beppu

The Military Police Sang the Red Flag

This occurred around February 1947 at the Number 19 Internment Camp in Siberia. The storm of the Red Army's "democratization" education gathered around us ten thousand POWs.

All of us wholeheartedly wished to return to our homeland. We were filled with fear and trembling that any opposition to the "democratization" movement would result in a delay of our return to Japan or a transfer to an internment camp deeper into the Soviet Union.

In this camp there were quite a few former military police [*Kempeitai*], former Special Servicemen [*Tokumu Kikan*], and former Special Higher Police [*Tokkōtai*]. These were the very officers who had harshly suppressed the Communist Party in prewar times. Naturally, they were on unfavorable ground.

A work group called the "Democratization Shock Troop" was formed. The shock troops were numbered from one to ten. Labor conditions were tough, but I heard that the compensation was good. The former military police officers joined this shock troop. They raised their voices high chorusing "The Song of the Red Flag" and "The International" during their morning departures and evening returns to the camp. These were the men who had repressed antiwar theorists, scholars, and writers under the authority of the Peace Preservation Law and the National Mobilization Law. I was dumbfounded at their about-face.

One night we had a meeting to discuss the actual facts regarding the military police. According to the confessions of a former military policeman, if a military man went out and raped a married woman, the punishment would be light for an officer, while it might even be imprisonment for a mere soldier.

Hirao Hitoshi, sixty-one (m),
farmer, Yokkaichi

In Singapore

Work camps were set up in various locations on the island of Singapore. First interned in Sumatra, where we had been captured, we were housed in several warehouses near the piers. We numbered two thousand men. We slept piled against each other on straw mats spread on the concrete floor. Wake-up call was at 5 A.M. Breakfast was half a mess tin of a thin gruel of corn and rice mixed with six or seven parts water.

We did all kinds of work. It varied from day to day. At the jetty we unloaded freight from ships. In the city we transported cargo in and out of warehouses. Whether it was rice or rock salt, we carried one-hundred-kilogram bales on our backs. The rock salt burned into our naked backs. On our way to the workplace the angry shouts of British soldiers riding in jeeps flew over our heads. Our twelve hours of labor began at 7 A.M. Lunch was two pieces of hard biscuit about eight centimeters square. We had twenty minutes to rest.

The worst indignity was cleaning the sewers of the town where Chinese, Indians, and Malays lived together. We were told to dredge by hand the dead rats and human excrement that flowed down. Or we had to stand up to our chests in excrement to scoop it out. In the cement warehouse, we were forced to run repeatedly through cement powder up to our knees, carrying two sacks of cement. And we weren't allowed to assist anyone who keeled over.

We had no days off, and if we disobeyed our captors at all we were beaten with rifles and kicked. The date of our repatriation was not specified. There were those who went crazy and those who died from malnutrition. I endured two years of harsh treatment at the hands of the Allied forces, buoyed by my single desire to return to my homeland alive. People still talk about the abusive behavior of the Japanese military during the War. But this kind of behavior existed without regard to race or nationality. I am not excusing the conduct of the Japanese. War makes all of us lose our humanity.

> Shikimachi Gentarō, sixty-five
> (m), barber, Fukuoka

"Hee!"—His Wife Fainted

The supply ship heading for Car Nicobar Island was sunk. Senior Lieutenant Yoshinari Sadao, the commander—from the ninety-second class of the Tokyo Merchant Marine, where he had played before me on the school baseball team—and his men, thirteen in all, were rescued from the sea and taken prisoner by the enemy. It was winter of 1944 when they were sent to the internment camp in Karachi after being treated at the British army hospital in Ceylon. This camp was in the desert three hundred miles from town. It held nearly a thousand Japanese army soldiers. The head of the POWs was a prominent regular officer from the crack *Hayabusa* air corps. His death in battle had been reported with great fanfare, but he himself did not know that. There were officers of higher rank in the camp, but as he was the only career officer, he was designated the head of the POWs by the British officer in charge.

When Senior Lieutenant Yoshinari arrived, the officer was transferred, and Senior Lieutenant Yoshinari became the POW head. The camp commandant, a lieutenant colonel in the British Army Reserve, was a courteous gentleman knowledgeable about Japan. He often invited Lieutenant Yoshinari to his room for conversations on a wide range of topics. The commander had a high estimate of Yoshinari's decency, and treated the prisoners with great care. He urged us on many occasions to write home, but that was one thing that all of us refused throughout. It was impossible for the British to understand how we prisoners felt.

We were able to return to our homes the winter after the War's end. Senior Lieutenant Yoshinari's home was in a small city just beyond Morioka. Overwhelmed with emotion, he telephoned his house from the train station. How many years had it been? It was his dear wife, whom he had dreamed about for so long, who answered the telephone. But he wouldn't give his name at first. "Who is this? Who?" The conversation was incoherent. The lieutenant became uncharacteristically impatient and said, "It's me. Have you forgotten your husband's voice?" At that, there was a shriek—"Hee!"—and the line went dead. His wife had fainted on the spot. That was the very day of Yoshinari's formal funeral.

Asaoka Izumi, eighty (m), retired,
Funabashi

Japanese Sake in a Burmese POW Camp

At the end of the War the Japanese troops in Burma were transferred to internment camps in various locations, where they labored under the direction of Allied troops. Our Kiku[*] army unit was in a camp at Rangoon. A thicket was cleared and the four sides were surrounded by barbed-wire fencing. On sentry duty were Gurkha soldiers carrying bayonets. We pitched tents supplied by the British forces, and lived together in platoons and squads. We were poorly supplied and received only a fixed amount of rice and dried vegetables. Of course we had no cigarettes. Japanese soldiers would smoke what they rolled up from the cigarette butts they scavenged when they went into town on work detail.

One day we were surprised to find that each platoon had been supplied with a mess-tin-cover's worth of sake. The flavor, bouquet, and color were all unmistakably those of pure Japanese sake. We soldiers were flabbergasted. We took one sip each and passed it around. Some teared up at the scent of their homeland that they had dreamed of so much. How was it possible that sake could be distributed in a POW camp isolated from the world?

Just as there is a trick to magic, the secret to the appearance of the Japanese sake lay in the astonishing resourcefulness and knowledge of one soldier. Our meals were prepared all together. This soldier suggested that he wanted to make sake. He had been a sake brewer by training. Under his direction, some rice was taken out of our supply each day and stored. When he was drafted, he had taken along a small amount of rice-malt yeast in an airtight can. He had carried this with him through battles in the Burma front, never letting go of it, even when the Japanese forces were in retreat, and had brought it with him to the internment camp. This bit of yeast had turned up as the mellow fragrance in front of us. He must have faced much hardship during that time. I admired his tenacity and spirit.

The Japanese sake was delivered to the British forces camp commander. He was so surprised he wondered if there was a magician among the Japanese troops. Since then the brewer continued to brew sake in small amounts, and we soldiers were comforted by drinking sake a few times a month. This sake brewer was Leading Private Tanaka Shigeo of Ōkawa. Unfortunately he passed away a few years ago from illness.

Miura Tokuhei, sixty-nine (m),
former innkeeper, Fukuoka

---

[*]For security reasons, military units were often known by their official code names, for example, *Kiku* [chrysanthemum] or *Hayabusa* [falcon].

Japanese POWs in the U.S.

I was at Kennedy internment camp in southern Texas when the War ended. Actually, I was in the U.S. forces and lived with Japanese prisoners of war as an interpreter. I learned of the War's end right away, but after discussion with the highest-ranking Japanese POW, Navy Captain Yamaga, we decided to avoid upsetting the POWs and have him make an official announcement at a suitable time. A couple of days later he gathered all the men and, telling them to listen carefully, announced Japan's defeat. The disturbance that we had feared did not occur. The prisoners did not put it into so many words, but from their own experiences and from news reports they seemed to have already anticipated defeat. Most of them were officers and noncommissioned officers who had been transferred to Kennedy from McCoy Barracks in Wisconsin in June of that year.

At the huge McCoy camp the noncommisssioned officers and lower-ranking soldiers were interned separately from the officers. I had initially been with the noncommissioned officers and soldiers, but later there were rumors of unrest in the officers' camp, and I was sent there to monitor the situation. In the camp of the lower-ranking soldiers there had been occasional troubles, such as attempted escapes. In the officers' camp there were no incidents after I got there. Two months before the War's end everyone was moved to Texas, and I accompanied them. At McCoy the POWs had been treated more like "restricted distinguished guests" than prisoners. They were given Japanese food much finer than what we American troops ate. We second-generation Japanese-Americans were often invited to dine in the prisoners' canteen. They were supplied with beer and cigarettes and treated unbelievably well compared to prisoners in other countries. This all changed at Kennedy, where the American military authorities dealt harshly with the prisoners. If there was the slightest violation of regulations, the prisoner was locked naked in a holding cell.

In December of the year the War ended, they were all shipped to Uraga, and I accompanied them.

Hiraide Katsutoshi, sixty-five (m),
journalist, Tokyo

War's End in Luzon

I was a private first class, an older draftee. My unit had been completely scattered after several battles and guerrilla attacks. On 4 July, about the tenth day I had been wandering alone in the mountains of central Luzon Island like a ghost, I was discovered by a local native and interned at the POW camp. At the end of July, the newspaper extra on the Potsdam Declaration was distributed to us prisoners in the camp. When I heard about the atom bomb dropped on Hiroshima on the seventh or eighth of August, I felt despair, seeing defeat ahead. Then there was the news of the Soviet declaration of war and their crossing the border into Manchuria. Now all was over. I could imagine the chaotic situation in Japan.

I think it was 13 August that we heard the rumor that Japan would surrender today or tomorrow. They said that the Allied forces were urging Japan to surrender. With Manchuria gone to the Soviets, the Japanese islands were totally isolated. It would be impossible for Japan to continue fighting.

It was 15 August. It must have been just after sunrise, about six o'clock. American soldiers loaded onto a truck made the V sign with their fingers and shouted "Victory! Victory!" as they passed by our tent. So, finally what was to be had come about.

At around eight o'clock Japan's surrender was formally announced. Inside our tent we all faced the north and bowed in silence. I couldn't stop my flowing tears. As we began to recover from our initial emotions, here and there voices were heard saying that since the entire nation had surrendered, we should be happy that we could go home with pride. An MP came and told us that we were going home. He seemed genuinely happy for us that we were able to return home. That day we had no work and talked excitedly about our homeland.

But I felt that I couldn't be entirely happy. I wondered what would happen to Japan after surrender. What would happen to the state polity and to the lives of the people? Would the country be ruled under partition? All day I was deep in thought. This was fate, it was destiny. I decided that there was no way for me to live in the future but to do my best under the guidance of the gods.

Shimodaira Tadao, seventy-seven
(m), retired professor, Chiba
University, Chiba

Don't Be Ashamed, You Are Heroes

The warship I served on was sunk in the Battle of Leyte Gulf and I became a prisoner of war of the American forces. I was interned in the Leyte POW camp for one year. There were about twelve hundred Japanese POWs in this camp. All of us were ashamed that we were clinging greedily to life and forced to be idle in the midst of the enemy. Occasionally we felt that we wanted to die.

As the days wore on, we realized that the attitude of the American troops toward us was different from what we were accustomed to. The MPs who guarded us, the military doctors, and the medics were all kind without exception. And we were supplied with clothing, food, and even PX items like candy and cigarettes on the same basis as the American soldiers. On the bulletin board was a sign saying POWs were allowed to write letters to their families and have necessary items sent to them. This was the way we first found out about the existence of the Geneva Convention article on the treatment of prisoners of war.

One day, the camp commander, a first lieutenant, gathered us dejected POWs and told us, "You men fought bravely until the end without fleeing, so you have no reason to think that you are lacking in courage. You men are heroes." Having been indoctrinated for years that we must die with honor rather than surrender, these words were shocking to us. We had thought ourselves to be dishonored prisoners of war. But the Americans not only dealt with us humanely, they also treated us as warriors who had fought courageously until the end and fallen into enemy hands.

Sekiyama Eiji, sixty-four (m),
company employee, Abiko

Order to "Kill All Those Under Thirteen"

The War ended when we were on Cebu. We were taken prisoner by the American forces. We were moved to Palo POW Camp near Tacloban on Leyte. I had been raised in America until I was seventeen, so I could speak

English well and was able to act as interpreter. In general, the treatment of the POWs was good. The consideration given Japanese women and children was particularly warm. The children sang songs and danced under the direction of a female American officer. It looked like they were in kindergarten.

We found out that before the War's end, when the Japanese forces were under attack by American troops, an order had been issued by the Japanese military that resident Japanese children under the age of thirteen would be an encumbrance and should be killed. It was thought that this order had been implemented. The American forces ordered two young officers to make a thorough investigation. I took part as their interpreter. The high-ranking officer who had given the order had died in battle, so the facts could not be confirmed. A first lieutenant named Aoki and a sergeant were questioned. Under tough interrogation, the two men acknowledged that they had received the order but strongly denied that they had carried it out. In the end, this matter was considered to be an internal Japanese military matter, and the investigation was terminated with no firm results.

Ironically, this incident contrasted the actual nature of the American forces, who had been called "fiendish," and that of the Japanese forces, who had been entrusted with protecting Japan's citizens and its territories. I remember the desolate expression on the faces of a middle-aged couple whose child had been taken from them.

George Fukui, sixty-five (m),
retired, Yokohama

POW Sergeant Major Johnson's Thanks

The summer before the surrender, as a soldier in the reconnaissance regiment, I was assigned to guard a temporary POW camp in the highlands in central Taiwan. The prisoners were American troops from Corregidor.

Sunday was a day of rest. The prisoners gathered under the trees and sang hymns and prayed. I had occasion to chat with Sergeant Major Johnson. He was a short man with a fearless face. His expression earnest, he said to me with tears in his eyes, "I have nothing to offer in exchange, but I'd like to let my men smoke. Won't you give me some cigarettes?"

Escaping prisoners were shot. But there was also the danger of being killed by the prisoners, and it was risky to be easily swayed. I promptly refused, saying no. Cigarettes were valuable items, and I myself was not smoking mine but saving them up. But I also had men under me, and I understood how much he cared for his men. I lost out to his spirit and gave him a few packs of cigarettes behind the latrine. He looked overjoyed. Quickly hiding them in his shirt, he said, "Thank you very much," in a low voice, and dashed back to his barracks.

One evening several days later, all of the POWs departed for transfer to mainland Japan. I saw them off along with my subordinates. After three units had gone by, there was a sudden order given in faltering Japanese: "March to attention! Eyes right!" It was Sergeant Major Johnson's salute thanking me. The gaze of the American POWs was upon me as they marched to attention in an orderly manner. I took this as his parting gift, as he had had "nothing to offer." The stirring military tune whistled by the POWs drifted in the night air as they disappeared into the darkness. This incident was a saving grace during my dismal youth.

> Ōshimo Shigeji, sixty-seven (m),
> former company employee, Hikari

POWs Who Worked in the Mines

It was autumn of 1943 that about eight hundred American, British, and Dutch prisoners of war were sent from the Philippines and other fronts to Ōmuta in Kyūshū. They were put in mines, refineries, electrochemical plants, etc., and given hard labor, to help increase Japanese production. In those days I was working at the Mikawa Mine of the Miike Coal Mines, known for its huge coal dust explosion. Later I was in charge of the roll call when the POWs entered the mine, and I became friendly with them.

When they first arrived, the POWs walked energetically with long strides. Hard labor and acclimatization were difficult. With rice and pickles as their main foods, many contracted diarrhea. The mine stank from their condition. But it was not easy for them to get off work due to sickness. On sentry duty were men from an infantry platoon. The first POW camp commander was a young army second lieutenant. With him there was a military civilian, who had lost his left arm in battle and who always wore a Japanese sword at his side, and an interpreter who was born in Hawaii.

If, as they entered the pit, a POW showed any sign of resistance, he was forced to sit, legs folded under him, on two mine pillars laid side by side. If he moved his body, he was beaten with the butt end of a rifle. Double-slapped in the face if he didn't obey, he was sanctioned severely.

The conditions deteriorated and the meals for the POWs were worse. They became emaciated. As they walked from their camp to the mine, they would fight each other to catch frogs or snakes to eat. Taking pity on them, we gave them some tangerines that were rationed to us. They wept as they gulped them down. I wonder how many of the POWs died. Many died in work-related accidents and from illness. Those who were able to return to their countries alive were the fortunate ones.

It was this young army second lieutenant who was the first of the war criminals convicted of POW abuse in the war crimes trials and sentenced to be executed by hanging at Sugamo Prison. The two military civilians also received the death penalty.

> Kawano Tokuo, sixty-seven (m),
> agricultural association official,
> Ōmuta

A Field Hospital at the War's End

The air in the hospital room was oppressive with gloom. Sergeant Major "S," in the bed next to mine, looked over at me. "I envy you," he said, "since you're well educated. Once you get home, you'll be able to work anywhere. My only experience is in the army. That isn't going to mean much out in the real world. What am I going to do?"

It was the afternoon of 15 August 1945, in the post-op ward of Tianning field hospital. "S" was the third son of a farmer and couldn't count on any land being set aside at home for him to work. After years of active duty, he had signed up to become a noncommissioned officer. He dreamed of being promoted in the future. Now, with over ten years in the service, he was just about to become a warrant officer.

"I wonder what will happen," I responded. "Now that our country has collapsed, it's hard to tell whether there will be the same kinds of jobs as before. There probably won't be any more munitions companies, and only light industry is likely to be left."

"Still, if you have specialized training, you can count on it. I may act important in the military, but I'll be like a monkey that has fallen out of his tree." His expression was pained, and his voice despondent.

Sergeant "W," in the bed across from mine, was an unpleasant sort who always bragged about the raping and pillaging he did on the Chinese front. But today he believed that under American occupation Japanese men would all be castrated and enslaved and the women would be offered up for the Americans' pleasure. He was trembling in fear, worried about his wife and daughter at home.

After supper, I was outside gazing at the stars when army doctor "I" came toward me. He said in a happy tone, "Takada, this means farewell to the military. I'm finally free and can get back to doing my research."

But it took another three and a half years before we were able to go home. We were taken prisoner by the occupying Soviet troops. We were given no compensation at all for that time. That was the final stage of the War for me.

It was only after I returned home that I found out about Article 9 of the Potsdam Declaration: "The Japanese military forces, after being completely disarmed, shall be permitted to return to their homes. . . ."

> Takada Yahiko, sixty-nine (m),
> retired, Hakodate

We're the Same Color, Let's Join Hands

A month after the War's end, my squad was sent to assist in maintaining security at the field warehouse at Shayangzhen, Hubei Province, which had already been commandeered by the Chinese forces. Our main force had been sent far south to the internment camp at Tianmen.

About two weeks after we had started our security operations, one of our soldiers came down sick. His fever wouldn't subside, and he had no appetite. Each day he grew weaker. With no military doctor or medicine and no way to contact our main unit, we became increasingly discouraged. One day a Chinese soldier on guard duty brought in a Chinese army doctor. He was a major and only about thirty years old, tall, with a light complexion. From that day on he came to treat our soldier each afternoon. The patient regained his health and was able to return to his duties a week later.

At first I had unfounded doubts and deprecated this army doctor's knowledge and skill as a physician. And yet the soldier recovered his health. This was entirely thanks to the Chinese doctor. As a token of my appreciation, I attempted to give him a new uniform from the warehouse. But he casually refused it and left with a light step. Watching his departing figure, I felt reverence and gratitude toward him welling up inside my heart. I couldn't let him go like this. I rushed spontaneously toward him, the uniform in hand. Chasing after him for about a hundred meters, I called out to him and held out the uniform, my emotions overflowing.

Turning around, he gazed fixedly into my eyes. Perhaps having understood my intent, he squatted down and began to write some words on the ground. I was thankful that even though we couldn't understand each other's speech, we could understand each other's written words. I was able to comprehend what he meant. To summarize what he wrote: "We have suffered for many years under the white man's oppression. Chinese and Japanese people share the same color. Let's join together and cooperate for Asia's good from now on."

I repeated the only Chinese words I knew: "*Xie, xie,*" ["Thank you"], and extended my hand to shake his.

It is now forty-one years since then. If he is still alive, he should be over seventy years old. I wonder if he remembers the words he wrote as a young man on the pathway on the Hanshui riverbank in Hubei Province.

Ōsako Masaaki, sixty-five (m),
retired, Kitakyūshū

The Kwantung Army's Final Broadcast

With the invasion of the Soviet troops, our military police detachment withdrew from the Tumen River and roamed from place to place in northern Korea. It must have been on 16 or 17 August when, in the mountains of Musan we came across the Nanam divisional signal corps unit. They were listening to something on the wireless. Getting closer, we could tell that it was a broadcast by the Kwantung Army's war information chief.

" . . . We bear full responsibility for the situation having come to this state. There is no way that we can express our apologies. An autumn wind is blowing desolately in Xinjing. We intend to entrust everything to the Soviet troops soon to enter the city. Praying for the day when we can meet

you in good health in Japan, we end this broadcast. Farewell, farewell."
This was the first that we learned of Japan's defeat.

> Tanaka Sayu, seventy-seven (m),
> merchant, Niigata Prefecture

Violent Soldiers Snuffed Out

I was in Datong in north China at the War's end. As soon as we were stripped of our weapons, anger at having been oppressed by rank and age exploded among a segment of our soldiers. With a few superior privates as their leaders, these soldiers ganged up to threaten the unit commander, our company commander, and other officers. The other noncommissioned officers and soldiers could do nothing, out of fear of this violent gang. In the spirit of "let sleeping dogs lie," they were loath to provoke the gang members. The gang rode around in the unit commander's car and took off with the unit's food provisions. They went off base and fooled around. When they returned to the unit, they bossed around the other soldiers.

Their conduct was so excessive that some of the noncommissioned officers met in secret and planned to punish them as a group, in order to bring some order to the unit. They sought the approval of the officers and other soldiers and received their agreement. One evening, when the gang came back through the gate in the car, the soldiers rushed as one body at the gang members with a great yell and beat them with sticks. With several hundred men beating them up, it was a deadly attack.

The lives of three gang members were snuffed out just before they were to be repatriated. If they had had more patience, they would have been able to go home to their families. But they were killed by their own comrades.

> Iwata Isao, sixty-six (m),
> company employee, Tokyo

Saved by My Buddies' Bets

Our company, which was in Xinglong, Rehe Province, at the War's end, started on our withdrawal march from Manchuria toward north China on

1 September. I was not well. From the first day of this withdrawal march I was short of breath and suffered physical pain. My war buddies carried my rifle and called out words of encouragement to me to prevent me from dropping behind. Even more than physically, I was weak mentally, and I came to stop caring what happened to me. I began to believe it was just a matter of time before I was left behind.

Seeing me in this state, my buddies placed bets on whether I would stay alive. When I found out about these bets, an electric shock ran through my body. They were able to make their bets because the outcome was unknown. Not even a fool bets on the losing side. My buddies hadn't yet given up on me. I thought that I had to live for the ones who had bet that I would stay alive. I became filled with a will to live.

This will to live galvanized my limp body, and I finally made it to a secure area. I am deeply thankful to my buddies for their priceless compassion. I owe them a lot for saving me from falling behind with this bet, a highly original trump card. It is due to them that I have been able to live past the felicitous seventy-seventh year of age.

Suzuki Tatsuzō, seventy-eight (m), retired, Fujisawa

My Last Sweet Potato and an Old Woman's Gold Watch

Northern Luzon after the surrender. The days of fear had finally ended, after the incredibly fierce bombings, the oil cans dropping from the sky and the incessant bombardment from the area around National Route 11, one valley away. We soldiers were thankful for the peace, now that we could make a fire anywhere, anytime. And yet, the pitiless rain continued to fall. The soldiers who survived the hellishly fierce battles of Balete Pass, Salacsac, and Baguio had no more provisions. We had eaten up the sweet potatoes in the few fields of the Igorot tribe as a last resort. The soldiers chased into Amin, Tokukan, and the area surrounding Mount Pulog were like ghosts. On the narrow mountain paths muddied with human excrement in Amin and Tokukan, maggot-infested dead bodies lay less than ten meters apart. Around 20 September, my wandering group finally contacted headquarters. We were told to gather at Kiangan to surrender to the enemy.

During our retreat we weren't able to forage for food. The four or five potatoes that I collected with difficulty before departure were all I had to sustain life during the four days it took. Late on the afternoon of the third day, our band of three arrived at an Igorot hamlet of five or six huts and collapsed, still carrying our weapons and equipment. My ears were ringing. I seemed to have lost consciousness. I came to when I heard my war buddy saying, "Hey, tomorrow we can eat American military rations. Let's finish off the rest of our potatoes." Pulling out my last potato from my mess tin, I began to eat it.

It was then that an old woman wearing a Japanese kimono came out of an Igorot hut and slowly approached my buddy. "Mr. Soldier, I haven't eaten for days. Would you please give me that potato?" she said in a faint voice, and held out a dazzling gold watch. My buddy shoved the rest of his half-eaten potato into his mouth, took a swig from his canteen, and rolled over on his side. The old woman, having been unsuccessful, shuffled over to me, and wordlessly held out the gold watch. I was at a loss as to what to do, but my hand grew rigid and wouldn't pull the potato away from my mouth.

I thought that if I gave this to someone, I was sure to fall dead on the way tomorrow. Should I choose my own death or another's death? Unable to look her squarely in the face, I dragged my tired body away and went to sleep. The next day only ten of what should have been thirty men made it to the camp where we were to gather.

Nowadays in these times of plenty, whenever I see sweet potatoes at the vegetable store, the figure of the delicate old woman in her kimono in the mountains of Luzon looms in front of my eyes. My heart is filled with self-reproach.

> Kawamura Toshio,
> sixty-two (m), former company
> employee, Tokyo

Skillful Handling by American Forces

At the War's end our independent railway battalion was stationed in Pusan when it became an unpoliced city. In contrast to the Japanese, who were downcast in defeat, the Koreans appeared energized by their sense of liberation. Open-air shops sprouted everywhere, and people bustled about. The atmosphere of unrest grew day by day as people who were rumored to be "released political prisoners" rode around in automobiles, calling for independence and liberation.

All sorts of wild rumors flew, claims such as that "Japanese troops with swords bared caused havoc at an independence meeting attended by Koreans"—something that might have occurred, although I would have hoped not. Since the Japanese military was still armed, concerns grew that any serious disturbance could develop into a major riot involving the general Korean population and Japanese civilian residents.

It was then that a large number of leaflets was dropped onto the city from American military aircraft. The portions written in Japanese stated, "The War has ended, so the citizens (including military troops) should behave calmly and avoid unnecessary disorder. Those who engage in subversive acts will be severely investigated and punished after the American forces occupy the city, regardless of who they are." This was thoroughly effective, and the city immediately regained its calm. Under the administration of the American forces, who occupied Pusan at the end of September, the Japanese troop withdrawal was begun without incident.

The American troops were strictly disciplined to a man. There was no victors' arrogance. With their splendid intelligence capacity and their skillful handling they prevented the worst-case situation from developing.

Hayakawa Fukutarō, sixty-five
(m), self-employed, Chiba

Aircraft "Happy" Flew Until the Last

A few days after the surrender, the captain attached to the flight unit of Third Air Army Headquarters and his crew, five men in all, received orders to fly their Type 97 heavy bomber to Southern Theater Headquarters in Saigon. There we would receive instructions. From Saigon we flew to various areas to make contact. Unrest was everywhere. Unable to use the wireless, we couldn't get weather reports. It was hard even to get sufficient fuel. In Bangkok we were able to beg some fuel. Told that an Allied forces order banned all flights—which meant that we might be shot down—we flew off. Bangkok was overflowing with soldiers who had come in from

Burma. They were in very bad shape. When we landed in Saigon a few days later, we were assigned to Air Corps Area Headquarters. Thus we were unable to return to the Third Air Army.

Soon British forces occupied Saigon and began seizing our weapons. Since our beloved 97 heavy bomber was still flight worthy, it was taken over for a special air unit. It was painted green with a white cross on the fuselage where the red sun used to be; unit markings on its rudder were erased. The airplane was to be used for British transport operations. The bulk of its duties was transporting vegetables, fruit, eggs, and provisions from Phnom Penh to Saigon. I inferred that the British must be nearly unable to replace their own aircraft.

A young British second lieutenant wrote the word *Happy* on the nose of the plane in pencil and instructed that it be painted in white. After that, the plane was called *Happy*. It seemed that other former Japanese military aircraft in the special air unit were being used for similar duties. With no contact among us, it was impossible to know under which unit's command the other planes had been.

Nearby, the liberated French forces and the Vietnamese independence forces were fighting each other. Stray bullets came our way. I became friends with the British soldier who was a maintenance man for the Spitfires. Then the Japanese troops were interned in a camp to wait for a repatriation ship. But *Happy* continued to fly in the southern skies, avoiding the stormy squalls. I don't recall how many months *Happy* flew, but it must have been the last Japanese plane flying at the time.

Ueki Yashichi, sixty-nine (m),
former fire chief, Matsumoto

Captured by the Eighth Route Army

On the rainy night of 26 August 1945, having hurt my leg in the battle of retreat from Zhangjiakou and fallen behind, I spent the night in a woodshed. In the morning I had my rice cooked in my mess tin at the house near the shed. The old peasant whom I asked did so willingly. As I started to eat, my arms were grabbed from behind by a man in plain clothes. It happened in an instant. Outside, a dozen or so Eighth Route Army soldiers, all wielding weapons, were ready to attack. Realizing that I was doomed, I blurted out,

"My father and mother are dead. Please go ahead and kill me." Whether my Chinese got through to them, they dropped their aggressive posture and locked me up in a nearby shed.

The next day, I was sent to their headquarters on a horse, traveling up the same Badaling peak I had descended with difficulty two days earlier. I had no lunch. All I ate were two doll-shaped cakes made of hardened rice flour that my escort bought for me at the roadside. We finally reached their headquarters in the evening. After eating a fried millet dish with the Eighth Route Army soldier who was escorting me, I was confined in a house. A young Korean interpreter was kind to me. He brought me meals twice a day and carried me on his back to the medical corpsmen to get treatment for my leg. Three days later there were four of us prisoners. On the thirty-first, the Eighth Route Army acceded to our request. We were told that we would be returned to the Japanese forces the following day. That night they gave us a farewell party with plenty of good food.

Now that we were free, we left on 1 September, but we went in the wrong direction, heading for the Silk Road. An Eighth Route Army soldier came after us on horseback and shoved his pistol at us. We were taken back. This time we were all put on horseback and climbed down Badaling, finally reaching a village. Until the tenth we took a roundabout route, passing through farming villages that had regained their vitality now that peace had returned. The Eighth Route Army soldiers escorted us to a location where we could see the Japanese military encampment and then went back. We were all full of confused feelings at seeing the Japanese troops. Just then a man with fluent Japanese said to us, "I am a driver for North China Transportation. I'll take you to the unit." He was a savior in our hell.

After we were investigated by the military police, we were given supper. My tears flowed as I took a big bite out of the pure white rice ball and pickles.

Ōta Masaru, seventy-one (m),
retired, Yokkaichi

The Potassium Cyanide Packet

I turned ten years old the year the War ended. I had been living in Xinjing [now Changshun] in Manchuria, but when my father was drafted I was evacuated to Jungjoo, a town in north Korea. The classrooms of a grade school for Japanese in this countryside town were allotted as a shelter for evacuees. The third day after we arrived was 15 August. Our group of women and children gathered in one room that evening to listen to our group leader. "There has been an imperial broadcast and the War has ended. We surrendered unconditionally. I would like you to behave like virtuous Japanese women and not invite dishonor. There will probably be some unrest among the Koreans tonight."

The sun set and lights were turned on. My mother, younger sister, and I changed into clean underwear and trousers and sat with our legs tucked under us on a blanket spread on the floor. Mother pressed a white paper packet into my hand. These packets had been distributed to all by the group leader. "When the time comes, swallow this," she said.

Near us a woman who was a former nurse was preparing many syringes, slipping on the needles and busily pressing out spurts of liquid. Not even the babies cried, and all was silent. The medicine was potassium cyanide. Though a small child, I knew that one packet would easily kill me off. I wanted to live; I wanted to survive. I didn't want to die in a place like this. I wanted to escape. I screamed inside myself with my whole body. Forty years later I still haven't been able to erase the fear of imminent death.

Later, the Japanese principal of the grade school said he would take all responsibility for us. He was taken away by some youths who came to raid the school. I heard a rumor that he was later imprisoned. I also heard that he died from being tortured. The figure of the elderly principal, clad only in his cotton kimono, the man who sacrificed himself to protect us, is seared into my memory, along with his lighthearted manner.

When I complain about the difficulties I face as an adult, my mother tells me, "Just do your best, since they aren't saying they'll take your life." Compared to that night of 15 August, the problems I face now seem like nothing, and I soon feel better.

> Miyamoto Kazuyo, fifty-one (f),
> administrative recorder, Yokkaichi

The Escape From Tonghua

Our family of five left Tonghua on a refugee train: my husband, a doctor for the South Manchuria Railway, my oldest son, in the third grade, my second son, who was suffering from a high fever, and my third son, who was a baby.

The announcement to "gather at Tonghua station in thirty minutes" came all of a sudden. I thought I had prepared for this eventuality, but my feelings raced ahead of my actions. I was in such a rush that, although it was August, I made the children wear layers of clothes topped by their winter coats. I grabbed all the diapers and powdered milk I could carry and put the baby on my back in his cotton-padded coverlet. Leaving the stew simmering on the clay charcoal stove, we ran toward the station and made it just in time for the train's departure.

On board I saw a train conductor shoot and kill a Japanese who had been in the patrol unit, then throw him off the train. The windows were all shut and blacked out. The August weather was indescribably hot inside the train for those of us wearing winter clothes. As children died, they were thrown off, one after another. At each stop, the passengers' baggage was looted, so our belongings kept diminishing. I had enclosed some paper currency inside the baby's diaper cover, but the constant wetness from the diaper caused the ink to run, rendering the money useless.

We were allowed to stay in the singles' dormitory of the South Manchuria Railway for one week in Siping, but women and children were not allowed outside. Unable to wash any diapers, I could only dry the dirty diapers and reuse them even though they were stiff and foul-smelling.

Months later we reached Mukden with nothing left. We were called the first refugees. We stayed in empty South Manchuria Railway employee housing. Winter had come and there was no heat. We used borrowed bedding that we left out all day. It was there that we slept, huddled together for warmth. Several times in Mukden I saw women selling their children, trying to bid up their price.

This was where my sick son died. We broke apart the wooden bookcase in the house, chopped up railroad ties, and cremated his body near the tracks. We had been unable to bathe during the seven months since leaving Tonghua. Our bodies were full of lice and we smelled like beggars.

> Murakami Ayame, seventy-six (f),
> housewife, Fukuoka

A Goddess Who Came Down to Earth

I was in Jinzhou, in Manchuria, just after the War's end. My husband was discharged from military duty in eastern Manchuria. I had protected our house from attacks by rioting civilians who came through the wire fence surrounding the compound. When he arrived, he was very pleased and told me, "Say, this is first class." The bank and post office had been attacked by rioters, and we had no way of withdrawing our funds. With no cash on hand, we were forced to set up a straw mat on the street and sell our household goods. Japanese and Chinese were intermingled as they set up shop.

Four or five Chinese poked around looking at our things. One man stretched out his hand, took a wristwatch, and tried to run off. I should have remained silent, but I inadvertently shouted out, "I've been robbed!" Four or five men standing around dragged my husband off and began to beat him up.

Thinking that he would be killed, I screamed, "Someone help!" but none of the Japanese men came over to help. I could understand that they valued their lives. They were doing all they could to be able to return with their families to Japan. They couldn't involve themselves in other people's problems.

Then someone yelled out in a loud voice. It was so sudden, I couldn't tell what was said, but the men who had surrounded my husband disappeared into the crowd.

An old woman in a navy blue Chinese outfit was looking at me, smiling. She had white hair, bound feet, and a smattering of yellow teeth. She was the one who had saved us. All I could do was to kneel in front of this old woman and say, "*Xie, xie*" ["Thank you"].

I wonder who that old woman was. I think of her as a dust-covered goddess who descended from heaven to save us.

Ishitaki Keiko, sixty-nine (f),
housewife, Fukuoka Prefecture

Women Who Couldn't Cry Out

Immediately after the surrender, we Japanese were detained in the South Manchuria Railway singles' dormitory in Dehui. The district commander of the occupying Soviet forces ordered us to hand over a list of the names of the Japanese women between the ages of twenty and forty. Shocked, we were distressed as to how to respond. The chairman of the Japanese association made up his mind and asked the purpose of this demand. The commander said that he wanted the women to take turns cleaning his offices and serving tea. We thought that this was a disguised excuse, and that what they were really after was women they could make accede to their whims under the cover of legality. After the leaders of the resident Japanese civilians met, they decided to send one woman as a representative.

The mothers, in tears, went to persuade a single woman in her twenties to take on this duty. The woman sobbed, saying, "Please kill me instead. I can't possibly do it." Both sides were in tears as she agonized, but finally she answered resolutely, "I'll go." The leaders and mothers brought over a kimono and dressed her up like a glorious bride. The Japanese association chairman and other community leaders escorted this victim to the Soviet commander.

She had already cried her eyes dry, but our tears flowed as we looked after her retreating figure with our prayers of thanks. I have no way of finding out what happened to her.

> Yanami Yoshimi, seventy (f),
> retired, Kitakyūshū

Double Suicide, a Japanese Woman and a Soviet Soldier

The Soviet troops remained stationed in Manchuria until December 1945. At night a moon curved like a razor hung in the chilled sky, and stray dogs wailed in the distance in Jinzhou. Only the Soviet barracks in Jinhua district were brightly lit.

One night in early December when the withdrawal of the Soviet troops was announced, two pistol shots rang out in the Soviet barracks. The bodies of the double suicide were those of a young Soviet soldier and a Japanese woman who had volunteered to go to the barracks. The woman was Mrs. "K," a beauty who had just turned thirty. Her husband had been drafted when they were living in northern Manchuria. After she received word that he had died in battle in Okinawa, she wandered to Jinzhou. With no one to take her in, she volunteered to work as a serving maid.

Mrs. "K" had volunteered on her own to go to the Soviet barracks. Some people who had evacuated from northern Manchuria with her said they urged her many times to reconsider, saying "You still have a chance to go home to Japan." But Mrs. "K," her mind made up, would have none of it. The young nineteen-year-old Soviet soldier first shot Mrs. "K," and then shot himself in the head. He had the pistol in his hand when he died.

I think the incident resulted from the runaway feelings of a young man who, drawn by his love for the first Japanese woman he had known, couldn't bear to part with her. I suspect, though, that in Mrs. "K"'s mind were only feelings of love for her departed husband. Just a handful of Japanese knew about this murder-suicide that occurred under the brutal Soviet occupation.

In those days, at the request of the Japanese residents' association, I was desperately working to gather serving maids demanded by the Soviet troops. There was a limit to the number of professional women of the night. Conditions were such that the safety of ordinary woman and girls could not be protected. I returned to Hakata in May 1946, but even now I recall Mrs. "K"'s death.

Makino Hideo, seventy-four (m),
company employee, Tokyo

I Couldn't Despise These Intruders

One autumn day shortly after the defeat, a Soviet soldier broke open my front door and marched into my house in Jinzhou in Manchuria. He had a rifle in one hand and a long narrow package wrapped in a newspaper tucked under his left arm. Dropping the package at his feet with a thud, he demanded, "Give me your watch." He didn't want the wall clock or mantel clock. I had no choice but to give him the woman's wristwatch that I had been hiding. Putting it to his ear, he said, "The sound is bad. It's too quiet." He then asked, "Do you have another?" "No." After a few more exchanges of words he swung his gaze all around, still standing in his boots in the middle of the room. He seemed to give up, and pointing at the package, he gestured that he was leaving it and departed.

It was then that I realized I was shaking, but he appeared to have braced himself for the confrontation as well. I opened the package to find a roll of cotton fabric. I was able to make good use of it later.

The following February, in 1946, someone knocked on my window and shouted for me to open the door. I peered out to see two Communist soldiers with fist-size rocks in their raised hands. I let them inside, and they looked around my house with great curiosity, touching the furniture and opening drawers. After a while, they sat down heavily in my chairs and started talking to me.

"We've come from far away, fighting battles. It's cold here, and we want to go home soon. Won't you be my wife? I'll take you with me." "I have a child, so I can't." "I'll make the child mine, so it'll be all right." "No, I can't." They asked to see some pictures, so I showed them my photo albums. Whenever they came across a photo of me, they pointed and said, "That's you." They talked to each other and laughed. After spending quite a while, they said, "We'll take these." Then they left, taking an album each.

I was probably lucky. But I want to believe that soldiers like these, commoners who hadn't lost their sense of right and wrong, were the inconspicuous majority in each nation's military forces.

Yamashita Fumiko, sixty-four (f),
retired, Nagoya

General Marshall and I

When I was working as a conductor on board the military transport train between Mukden and Kaiyuan in the spring of 1946, a field observation team came on board to mediate the civil war between the Chinese Nationalists and the Chinese Communists. The team consisted of General George Marshall from the U.S., Lin Biao of the Chinese Communists, and Chiang Ch'un of the Chinese Nationalists. Shortly after the train left Mukden, I was called in by General Marshall.

He asked me about the living conditions of the colonization groups that had withdrawn from northern Manchuria. I was surprised at his knowledge of the wretched conditions the colonists endured. He also asked me what the Japanese currently living in Manchuria most desired. The resident Japanese were especially concerned that they might no longer be able to use their Japanese currency. If the currency held by the Japanese became valueless, it was clear that the foundation of their livelihood would crumble. They would become homeless. When I told General Marshall that the continued use of Japanese currency was the greatest wish of the Japanese, he said that he was well aware of that.

This general is known for the Marshall Plan for Europe's recovery, for which he received the Nobel Peace Prize. His amiable countenance, rare for a military man, hasn't faded from my memory.

Kawano Toshio, seventy-two (m),
retired, Yamaguchi

Merely a Quarrel Between Brothers

At the time of the surrender, I was a second-year student at Huwei girls' high school in Tainan County, Taiwan. Some of the local people called us Japanese dogs. "We're first-class citizens," they said, "Japanese are fourth-class citizens." The attitude of my classmates changed completely; they spoke loudly in Chinese on their way to and from school. The curriculum changed to Chinese education, and we were told to give our greetings strictly in Chinese. Children threw stones at us on our way home from school, so we walked in silence. I learned the phrases "What do you think you're doing? Are you serious?" in the local dialect from a friend so that I could put them in their place. When a group of children were lying in wait for me, I ducked into the fields and ran away as fast as I could.

Soon soldiers from China landed on Taiwan. A welcoming arch was built in the town and the eyes of the dragon were lit up. From the top of this gate cherry bombs were thrown down. The town turned lively at the arrival of high-level government officials. Soldiers crowded the streets. A flag procession was held, and we waved the sun-in-the-blue-sky flags, shouted three rounds of "Cheers for the Republic of China!" and sang a welcome song.

One sunny day, I waved the sun-in-the-blue-sky flag almost until it shredded. We lined up in the school yard to welcome the military leaders. An officer made a speech. I held my breath, wondering what would be said. It was a short speech, but each word was forceful.

"The War has ended now, and we have returned to being brothers as before. China and Japan had nothing more than a quarrel between brothers. We must now go forward hand in hand with Japan." Our Chinese-language instructor interpreted these words with care.

Our classmates' behavior improved after this. I will never forget what happened that day. The following year we returned to Japan. I still correspond with the friends I made in Taiwan.

> Bazura Yoshiko, fifty-four (f),
> shopkeeper/housewife, Fukui
> Prefecture

A Family Protected Amid Verbal Assaults

Immediately after the defeat, an eerie atmosphere of unrest increased day by day deep in Yántonggou, Tonghua, in Manchuria. This unrest exploded in the early morning of 21 September when a mob swarmed into the company housing of the Yantonggou development technicians' training center. Carrying clubs, sickles, and shovels, they let out yells as they smashed the glass windows. Someone shouted out, "Take refuge in the dormitory!" After the mob had booted out the Japanese, they looted the housing area until dusk. On my way to take refuge, I called on the house of Mr. Takemoto, a worker at the center. There I saw an unbelievable scene.

Seven or eight Chinese men with clubs stood surrounding Mr. Takemoto's house to protect it, determined to keep the rioters away. Mr. Takemoto's ill mother was over seventy and bedridden. When the pillaging abated, these Chinese men carried the mother to the dormitory on a door plank. But the mob surged toward the dormitory as well, throwing rocks as they yelled and shoved the Japanese out. We rushed desperately to the warehouse to take refuge there. When they had finished plundering the dormitory, the rioters pushed toward the warehouse and threatened us, saying, "Give us your money or we'll kill you."

Barely emerging from this crisis, we waited until dawn and retreated to the ransacked company housing. After we spent two months of refugee "life" there, a rescue train was arranged for us. All of us formed a long line to walk the six kilometers to Linjiang station. At the end of the line were the Chinese men carrying Mr. Takemoto's frail mother on the door plank. Impressed as I was by Mr. Takemoto's reputation, I was even more touched by the sight of these Chinese men. Tears welled up in my eyes. During our time living as refugees, there were instances of Japanese persecuting other

Japanese. And yet, here were Chinese who were calmly carrying an old Japanese woman in the face of verbal assaults by their comrades.

Nagashima Shigetoshi,
seventy-eight (m), self-employed,
Fukuoka Prefecture

Were Poison Gas Bombs Abandoned?

From late April 1945 until the surrender, third-year students of the Beijing Japanese middle school, three years below me, were led by their teacher and mobilized as laborers at the munitions depot of the troops posted in north China. This was located in Sanjiatian on the outskirts of Beijing. It was rumored among the students that what were called red bombs, blue bombs, and yellow bombs stored there might actually be poison gas. When that became known, a first lieutenant explained with trembling lips at the morning roll call, "The Japanese military does not use poison gas. They are merely called red bombs or blue bombs for the color of the smoke when they explode."

The day after the surrender, the army started to carry away these bombs. Once in the morning and once in the afternoon, a total of five times until the morning of the eighteenth, a ten-to-fifteen-car freight train pulled into a railway siding. The students were forced to do the work of carrying the twenty-to-forty-kilogram boxes of bombs and loading them onto the freight cars. They were thought to be gas bombs from the munitions depot tunneled into the mountainside. They loaded solid explosives with fuses packed in wooden crates. (They were used for anti-tank mines.) Two Japanese soldiers rode on each car. They were prepared to be blown up, freight cars and all, along the way. When some students asked the soldiers what happened to the trains, they replied that the rails led to the bottom of the sea and that the bombs would be abandoned under the sea off Tanggu.

The students, however, did not hear accurate information as to where the bombs were transported and how they were disposed of. One of the mobilized students recalls that the munitions depot company was called the North China Post Army First Class 1810 Unit Takehana Company.

Azuma Kōichirō, sixty (m), high
school teacher, Urawa

A Boy, Fleas, and the War's End

I was ten years old when in March 1945 I was evacuated from Kamakura to Tsuchikata, Shizuoka Prefecture. It was thought that this peaceful village, with its fields of tea plants, wouldn't be attacked by Grummans and Curtisses. The local boys showed me how to fish, and I traipsed about the rivers carrying my homemade fishing pole. It took me thirty minutes to walk to school in my straw thongs, looking up at the Takatenjin Castle keep.

One day we were taken by our mothers and other adults to the seashore for salt making. Around noon, a black cluster rose up from the water's surface way off on the horizon, surprising the adults. It was a large formation of B-29s heading for Mount Fuji. We all crouched under the pine trees, rattled. It was then that I found out that the earth is round.

From the storehouse window that night I saw the eastern sky burning bright red. It was the air raid on Shizuoka. The western sky was also scorched. That was the air raid on Hamamatsu. We ran under the bridge during this night of booming bomb explosions and flashes of light.

It was rumored that the American forces would land on the coast. But we boys didn't neglect our play, and when summer came we held a swim meet in the pond. Tired after all that swimming, we were walking home naked when a grownup came running toward us. "The War is over. Japan has been defeated." We boys didn't feel much emotion hearing this. When we went to our school, the school yard was full of soldiers. It was the dismissal ceremony for the company posted at Cape Omae. Entering the classroom, we were attacked by fleas. I ran out of the room at top speed. The new era for us boys began with days of combating the fleas left by the departing soldiers. In autumn of that year the Takatenjin Castle keep was struck by lightning and went up in flames.

Nakagawa Akihiro, fifty (m),
forester, Gifu

Lamplight and a Dress

As an elementary school teacher in southern Nagoya, I evacuated a group of fifty third-grade boys to a temple in Minami Kasuya on the Chita Peninsula in August 1944. At night I had to deal with children crying that they wanted to go home. Others wet their beds. It took about a month for them to get used to group living.

Just as we were heading into winter, when it was easier to become depressed, our days of fear began with air raids and a strong earthquake in the region. We had little to eat and were not able to bathe very often. Small pink spots appeared on the boys' skin, which was filthy with grime. It was a skin infection called scabies.

By 15 August we were nearly at the limit of our endurance. We had no idea when the War would end. It was a hot day. I heard the Imperial Rescript on the War's end on a scratchy radio broadcast. I told myself that the War had ended, but I had no real sense of it. That day I went to a meeting. By the time I was on the way back to the temple, the sun had set, and I was ambling along the country road with a few other teachers, dragging my heavy legs. Suddenly a lamp was turned on in the second floor of a large house ahead of us.

"Hey, that's bright. I guess the War really has ended." The person lit by the light wasn't wearing the familiar work pants, but was an older woman who wore a dress. There was no blackout covering on the lamp, and it shone brightly through the open window. We chorused as one, "The War has really ended. We can take a bath. Now we can go home."

My steps grew light. We sang our usual song of the mountain cedar at a faster tempo and with a lighter beat than usual. Smiles flitted across our faces.

Hayashi Masayuki, sixty-three
(m), high school teacher, Nagoya

What About the Emperor's Lunch?

That day, as on other days, I went as my schoolteacher ordered to catch frogs along with my friends and fellow lodgers.

A little over a month before, my family had been burned out of our house by B-29 firebombs in the 12 July Utsunomiya air raid. Along with my father's acquaintances, some ten families were living together in the call office of a geisha establishment. I was a sixth-grader. Following my teacher's instructions to "catch frogs and dry them for food in preparation for the decisive battle on the mainland," I had already spent nearly a week diligently catching frogs every day.

In the morning, before eating breakfast (actually, there was nothing to eat), three other children who were my buddies and I walked through the burned-out wasteland of the town and went to the rice paddies on the town's outskirts. The hot sun glared down even in the morning, but we weren't very successful at catching frogs. The four of us were able to catch only six. Our stomachs empty, we decided to go home as noon approached. The view was clear because all the buildings in the area had collapsed. The asphalt road felt hot under our bare feet. As the phrase goes, "The going is easy but the return is tough." No one talked as we walked along. We were thirsty and hungry.

We saw the call house from over a hundred meters away. What was unusual was that there were people milling about the entrance. Wondering if something had happened, we quickened our steps. When we arrived, we saw scores of people in the large entryway. Some were quietly sitting on the dirt floor, others were crouching or leaning against the wall. They were listening to the radio. It was the Emperor's broadcast. Perhaps because I started listening partway through, it was hard for me to hear his voice. To be truthful, his voice sounded as weak as I felt. I wondered if the Emperor, like us, hadn't yet eaten his lunch. This thought made me realize how hungry I was, and it made me want to eat pumpkins, potatoes, and sweet-potato-flour cakes all the more.

Takezawa Shōji, fifty-two (m),
company employee, Kawagoe

I Attempted to Commit Suicide by Slitting My Belly

I had switched from being an official in the Ministry of Communications to the field of education. After a bout of pleurisy, I pushed my weakened body and, believing in Japan as the divine land and in Japan's victory, honored the Imperial proclamations with all my might and obeyed the government's orders.

Before dawn one night immediately after the War's end, as proof of the sincerity of my apologies to the students in whom I had inculcated militaristic values, I attempted to commit suicide by seppuku with a sword in the night watchman's room at the school. At that time I was twenty-one years old and an assistant teacher in the grade school. Suddenly I heard a clamor in the hallway. The old caretaker, Nishiwaki Chime, cried out, "Teacher, teacher!"

With this shriek her face turned pale. "Teacher, hold on a minute." Tears in her eyes, she was desperate to restrain me. "Just give this old woman the sword," she cried out hoarsely. I came to my senses with a start. The old woman was pressing her hands together in prayer and muttering, "*Namu Amida Butsu*." Placing the bloody blade in front of the praying caretaker, I toppled forward. I still have the scar from my wound.

What I, a substitute teacher for just over a year and not yet a full-fledged teacher, had questioned myself about was the grave concept of responsibility for the War. The issue at the core of postwar history lies in responsibility. The responsibility of the Emperor, politicians, and bureaucrats; and of military men, businessmen, public leaders, intellectuals, scholars, teachers, mass media, etc. Rather than simply passing off responsibility for the War onto others, haven't each of us who were adults at that time neglected to come to grips with our own guilt for the prosecution of the War? For as long as I live I will never forget that I was resuscitated by the warmth expressed in Buddhist prayer.

> Kaga Seiichi, sixty-two (m),
> education history researcher,
> Nagaoka

My Uncle Was Knocked Down on the Day the War Ended

On 15 August, when I was sixteen, it was a day like this. Even after the sun set in the west, the Amami Islands were sweltering. No matter how often we wiped away our perspiration, it poured down our bodies. I was bathing my little sister in a stream near our village. Two soldiers came rushing up to us on the mountain road and asked, "Where is the postmaster's house?"

About to answer, "My uncle is the postmaster. We live in the same house," I held my tongue. Had my uncle done something wrong? My body shook.

Running up to my uncle, the soldiers claimed, "You're a traitor. You have spread an outrageous rumor. We can't let you live. Can't you tell that the radio broadcast was an enemy plot?"

Slap! slap! They hit my uncle's face so hard he fell down. Clinging to one of the soldier's legs, I wailed, "I'm sorry, I'm sorry. Forgive my uncle, forgive him please."

Lying face down, my uncle didn't say a word. I pounded on his back with both fists and shouted, "Uncle, did you really hear that the War has ended on the radio? Aren't we supposed to fight until the day of victory? I hate you, Uncle, I hate you."

"We'll take you in tomorrow. Consider yourself dead." With that the soldiers left. That night no one in the village talked about the War's end. My uncle kept his silence. He didn't answer no matter what he was asked. Pressing his hand against his swollen cheeks, he straightened out the post office documents and his own belongings. All night long I prayed that my uncle wouldn't be taken away.

> Sachimoto Kyōko, fifty-seven (f),
> housewife, Kagoshima

"Traitor—For Saying You Want to Go Home"

On 3 July 1945, 260 pupils of Tateishi National Grade School in Nishinomiya departed in group evacuations. I was among seventy-four boys in the fourth and fifth grade who went to live in the judo gymnasium of a vocational school in Kagato, Okayama Prefecture. The Emperor's broadcast on 15 August was so full of static it was impossible to understand. After supper, I went to a nearby house to take a bath. They treated me to special Obon festival food and gave me some fruit. I returned happy.

Our teacher came to our quarters and told us about Japan's defeat in the War. Tearfully he explained to us that American forces would occupy Japan and were expected to use all sorts of measures to crush the Japanese spirit [*Yamato damashii*]. Although surrender was unavoidable, we must resolve to gather strength for a renewed attack. We listened to his words, our faces red from crying.

One sensitive fifth-grader realized that defeat in the War meant the end of our lonesome life as evacuees.

After the teacher left, he muttered, "Now that the War is over, we'll be able to go home." One boy near him, who was indignant about the defeat, shouted, "This guy is happy that he can go home because we lost the War." Several boys pounced on him and angrily beat him up, saying, "You traitor!" and "We swore we would do all we could here until the day of victory."

"I'm sorry, I was wrong!" he cried out, in tears. No one went to stop the attackers. The boy finally stopped crying long after the beating had ended, and we went to sleep in the silence.

Iwamoto Akira, fifty-two (m),
company employee, Yamato

So Naive and Ignorant

I was an eighteen year old working in an arms factory in Saitama Prefecture under the student mobilization program in August 1945. We had no newspaper or radio and had no way of obtaining information, so the Emperor's surrender broadcast was entirely a surprise. An old radio, the only one in the unit, was placed in the center of the open space. We listened reverently at the order, "All face inward." But the content was incomprehensible. Some took the message to be, "Rouse yourselves for the final battle on the mainland."

Eventually the real intent was made clear to us. Leaflets dropped from navy aircraft, however, urged us to "resist to the end" and confused us. To us, inculcated with "the invincibility of our divine land," there was more credibility in the order to "fight to the last soldier" than in the surrender.

After a while we heard from somewhere that "students in Tokyo have rallied as a group in opposition to the surrender." We were also told that if we didn't join in, our names would be dishonored in perpetuity. I hurried to start taking measures to procure weapons and food and to transport personnel. I was earnest in my determination not to sully my honor. My efforts ended up going for naught. There were a few students among the group that finally committed suicide after holding out at Atagoyama in Tokyo's Shiba district. That was an actual fact.

I am amazed at how naive and ignorant I was. This was an episode from my youth.

Ōmori Takuji, sixty (m), retired,
Tokyo

Who Knows How to Commit *Seppuku*?

After being burned out of my house in the Yokohama air raid, I had evacuated to Fujisawa, where on 6 July I received my draft notice. I was to enter the Kōfu Eastern Section Sixty-third Unit at 1300 on the seventh. Kōfu was hit by an air raid on the sixth, and the Kōfu Regiment suffered significant damage. Without enough weapons and uniforms for the new draftees, it was a scraggly looking unit that was assembled.

On 26 July, we arrived at Chikura on the Bōsō Peninsula and began work on defensive positions. Our orders for 14 August were to go to the seacoast, which was overgrown with reeds and weeds, to dig foxholes from which rifles and machine guns could be fired. On the fifteenth, we soldiers heard about the Emperor's broadcast when we returned to the houses where we were billeted.

On the nineteenth, our commander ordered all of us ranked above non-commissioned officer to gather at the primary school. He said, "Now, I will teach you how to commit *seppuku*. Is there anyone here that knows how to commit *seppuku*?"

For an instant we held our breaths, steeped in doom. A captain went up to the teaching platform and, taking off his uniform and undershirt, grabbed his saber with both hands and pressed its tip against his belly.

"Wait!" the commander said, stopping him. The entire company took a breath and relaxed our tensed-up shoulders in relief. The next day we were ordered to transfer to a different location, which we reached by night train. I was the paymaster. Borrowing the bathhouse, I handed out the final pay by candlelight.

Shimura Yūsaku, eighty-five (m),
retired, Tokyo

A Southern Island Vacation

After the fall of Iwo Jima the farthest frontline of Japan became the southern Ogasawara Islands. I was among those sent to Meijima supposedly as part of an attempt to defend and keep the distant islands. We were sent drifting off from Hahajima on a landing barge with a few rifles in hand. Just like the novel *The Shipwreck Account of Fifteen Boys,* we were twenty boys isolated and without support. We lived in a hut with a thatched roof of coconut leaves, and, wearing loincloths, dived into the sea and scavenged for fruit in the jungle. We sipped tepid water from the marsh. With our boyish curiosity, we searched for unusual plants and classified them. We satisfied our hunger by eating brightly colored fish, shellfish from tidepools, octopus, and slow-moving seabirds.

Our languid vacation on this southern island was shattered on 15 August by a huge seaplane that looked like a motor-powered sailboat with wings. Circling over us at such a low altitude that we could see the ruddy faces of the crew, they told us in English through a powerful microphone, "Japanese boys, the War is over." Whether as a warning or as a joke, they dropped a few bombs, causing all the frightened birds on the island to fly up like so many leaves blown off branches in the wind. Restraining my friend's rash attempt at countering with a small rifle, we rushed barefoot down to the beach of sharp coral fragments and hid in a natural cave. Our faces were all darker than coconut leaves. After that we saw daily the silver wings of the bombers glittering against the pure white cumulonimbus clouds and deep blue sky as large formations of them headed for the mainland. Gazing up at them naked, I came to the realization that Japan had fallen.

We were repatriated by a destroyer stripped of its guns. Though defeated, the screws left a wake that seemed to push us along. I gazed absently at the red bluffs on the green island and whispered, "Farewell, Meijima, until I come again."

Nakagawa Yoshio, fifty-nine (m),
company employee, Niigata

Why Soldiers Deserted After War's End

I received my draft notice without warning in mid July of 1945. I had just entered the sciences division of the Number 5 High School, and this notice was entirely unexpected. I was only seventeen years and eight months old. Having contracted typhoid fever, I was in bed and suffering from a high fever when I received my notice. An older friend from middle school who had entered high school at the same time wrapped me up in a padded quilt and carried me through the city of Kumamoto, which air raids had turned into a wasteland. He put me on a train for home. I underestimated the situation, thinking I wouldn't pass the physical and would be sent home right away, since I wore glasses and was skinny. At the physical exam, the examiner slapped my rear and scolded me, saying my typhoid fever would get better when I became a soldier of the Japanese Empire. When I said I was nearsighted, I was told that my bullets would hit their target if I shot from the heart. I was made an army private right off.

Two or three days after I joined the army, our march began. After we walked for two days straight, our unit was formed in Uchinoura, Kagoshima Prefecture. The next day we crossed over the mountains and took our post at the detached defense garrison on Birō Island at the mouth of Shibushi Bay. It was a small island shaped like a rice ball, which was to be defended by a company made up of infantry and artillery soldiers. Should there be a battle on the mainland, the island would no doubt be blasted by warship bombardment and we would all be killed. As first-year soldiers, our daily training consisted of carrying mock explosives and lying down on the tiny beach to be overrun by the enemy tanks in the landing.

There were three different reactions to the defeat in our unit. The first group was relieved that the War was over. I was one of them. The second group burned with a desire for revenge—but not revenge against the enemy. Now that the War was over, the officers were just men like everyone else. The soldiers who had been bullied by their superior officers now started to bully them back. The third group wanted to return to the mainland as soon as possible and desert. As soon as we landed on the mainland, they deserted en masse. This was treated as desertion in the face of the enemy during the immediate postsurrender period. A search party was sent out, and the deserters were arrested and punished.

Why had they deserted? An officer explained it to me, a member of the search party, in this way. "The soldiers who deserted were senior-level privates about thirty or thirty-five years old who had fought in China and had engaged in sinful acts such as raping women. They thought that once the American forces landed, their troops would behave the same way. They were so intent on returning quickly to their hometowns to hide their wives and daughters that they deserted." In fact, most of the deserters were captured in their hometowns. A large number of the deserters were caught and brought back to their companies. Some came back on their own as well.

They were sent to the heavy imprisonment cell. We felt sorry for them that they had to be locked up now that the War had ended. We heard that they were allowed just one small rice ball per day. The storage building of the local grade school was their prison.

In mid September we were disarmed and our company was discharged. A few days before, the new soldiers were told to line up in the hallway of the school. Our superior officer said he was promoting us one rank from that day. None of us was pleased by this.

Nakahara Seiichi, fifty-nine (m),
president, Meiji Junior College,
Hachiōji

Chapter 9

Japan Under Occupation

The successful Allied Occupation of Japan remains one of the extraordinary achievements of the twentieth century. Consider the situation in 1945, when Douglas MacArthur flew into Atsugi Airfield to begin his stewardship of the enemy country. The four years from the Japanese attack on Pearl Harbor in 1941 to the American A-bomb attacks on Hiroshima and Nagasaki in 1945 spanned one of the bloodiest and most bitterly fought wars in modern history. Until the final surrender on August 15, the entire Japanese nation had been mobilized into what promised to be a last-ditch battle against American invaders, to be waged with the same ferocity that marked the Japanese military's suicidal defense of its island empire throughout the War. The surrender declaration, however, left the entire nation in a state of suspended animation. Passively, Japan awaited its conquerors.

Unique in the history of such postwar occupations, the occupiers turned themselves to the task not merely of pacifying a defeated enemy, but of attempting to change its entire political and social system, to recast it in the American mold of true-blue democracy. To a great extent, this effort succeeded. Flaws there were. Yet for all the backings and fillings of postwar policies in both nations, the American-dictated constitution enacted in 1947 remains the law of the land in Japan, countenanced if not zealously protected by a majority of the Japanese public. It is unlikely that it will easily be revised. For all the bitterness of wartime hostility, a kind of working alliance was forged between the two nations. This has stood the test of time, despite the constant tug-of-war over trade and security issues, which in themselves stem from the political overprotection the Americans gave to a Japanese economy that would soon prove itself to be the world's most dynamic.

After the first weeks of the Occupation, the general reaction among the Japanese people was one of relief that Japan was not being despoiled as its armies had despoiled the captive nations of East Asia. After this, through the early years of the Occupation, the overriding concern among the Japanese was how to cope with everyday life. Tens of thousands had not yet returned from surrender, internment, or rigorous captivity in countries which Japan had once occupied. Once back, each family was faced with the task of survival in a time when starvation threatened the entire country. The American occupiers, therefore, had first to feed the defeated country and thereafter to attempt to get Japan's economy, if not its polity, back on its feet. Japanese in whatever walks of life had to accustom themselves to living under foreign rule. This was the fate that Japan's leaders had successfully fought against since the Meiji Restoration in 1868. Running on a bare subsistence economy, most Japanese were far from thinking about problems of future politics or governance. For the time they were content to have their basic political structure, headed by a now titular Emperor, confirmed by U.S. Occupation decision. SCAP—the acronym for Supreme Commander for the Allied Powers—became the shogun.

It was easy for the Japanese to personify the Occupation in the form of Douglas MacArthur. His arrogant, self-centered political style readily lent itself to this proconsular role. People in the countryside, in fact, began to think of MacArthur as the Emperor's surrogate. Working in Japan at that time as a member of the Occupation, I recall meeting a village patriarch and asking him his opinion of General MacArthur. Back came the reply, "The Emperor couldn't have picked a better man for the job."

The letters describing the period reflect this perception, as well as the general sense of shock and release following the War's end. However amiably the American troops seemed to behave, the Japanese soon found that living under a foreign occupation was no picnic. The best of the country's remaining creature comforts, like large hotels and first-class railway carriages, were reserved for the *shinchūgun,* literally, "advancing garrison troops," as the occupiers were officially called. The Japanese who had to deal directly with their occupiers found much to criticize as well as to praise; and in this sense the Occupation got mixed reviews. But for the nation as a whole, the rough-and-ready beneficence of the American Occupation occasioned great and widespread relief.

Sold in Manchuria, I Escaped Home

I was in southern Manchuria just after the surrender. The house I lived in was plundered and destroyed, so I spent several nights on the concrete rooftop. Wearing clothes left by my brother, who had volunteered for the Youth Air Corps, I shaved my head, rubbed soot onto my face, put on the canvas shoes with holes in them that had been distributed at my girls' school, and took refuge at the former youth school along with about twenty neighbors. Only the school's outer walls were standing. At night we staved off the mosquitoes by burning the weeds we cut during the day. We spent one night after another in the ruins of the building, hammering straw matting to the doorways and spreading matting on the ground. The only information we had was from the overseas Japanese management agency. Day after day the only news was about Japanese women forced to sacrifice their virtue.

Two or three months later, repatriation procedures were begun. Listed on the document were only three names, those of my parents and my younger brother. Where was my name? I was left there, alone.

I spent a month with the local people to whom I had been handed over. In the middle of the night one night when the stars glittered, I ran away, barefoot and taking only what I was wearing, not knowing where to go. I saw a light. I banged on the door as hard as I could. "Who is it?" "Help! I've run away. I was sold to a Manchurian."

The Japanese person who answered took me to a friend's house right away. I don't know what would have happened if the person had not been Japanese. I was very fortunate. Fearful that someone would track me down, I dreamed of returning to Japan and spent several months helping out with the work of that household.

A fellow Japanese made all the arrangements for me to return home. In August 1947, I retraced the journey of my childhood memory, and after changing trains several times I arrived at my aunt's house. I have not forgotten the joyous reaction of my aunt. This contrasted with my mother's speechlessness and blanched look at the appearance of the daughter she had thought was never to return. I was unable to shed tears of joy at seeing my mother again.

Now that forty years have passed, I no longer feel the bitterness toward my parents that I had during my adolescence. I see that time as having been a trial for me. My mother who had abandoned me suffered a stroke five years ago. She is now bedridden. Fortunately, all my brothers are alive and have good families and we are all faring well.

Chiba Tomoko, fifty-seven (f),
photography shop, Iwate Prefecture

A Japanese in the Eighth Route Army

In January 1946, I left Jinan in north China. Most of our group were on foot, walking in a long line along the tracks toward Qingdao. Traveling with our procession were disarmed Japanese soldiers, retreating. They walked alongside, ignoring us.

At a village called Jinlingzhan, our belongings were looted by the local peasants. With great shouts, they plundered the baggage of the withdrawing Japanese, which had been loaded onto large carts. Before our departure we had been ordered never to cross any Chinese people, so we had not reacted when during our trek we were spat upon and yelled at by mobs calling out "Eastern devils!" ["*Dongyang kui!*"]. But this time it turned into a rock-throwing fight. Some of the Japanese were injured.

Just then some Eighth Route Communist Army soldiers appeared from nowhere. They drove away the looters. They retrieved our belongings from those who ran off into the fields. After things quieted down, the soldiers flanked our group and escorted us. When dusk approached, they shot rifles into the air to ward off any further looters until we arrived safely at our quarters for the night.

When we entered the warehouselike facility, the soldier who seemed to be the company commander told us, "I am sorry that you met with such trouble today. The peasants in that area were on the receiving end of all sorts of violence, from pillaging to rape, at the hands of the Japanese army during the War. Please keep that in mind and be tolerant. I hope you will return to Japan safely as soon as possible."

With these words, he disappeared into the night. He was unmistakably a Japanese.

Maejima Daijirō, seventy-three (m),
retired, Shizuoka Prefecture

Some Troops Protected Civilians

On 15 August 1945, some fifty Japanese living in Qinglong Village in Rehe Province were ordered to gather for an emergency meeting. "You must all know that Japan has lost the War. The army will protect you now. Let us all return to our homeland, helping one another so that we will leave no one behind." This is what we were told by the company commander of the Kwantung Army. We departed immediately for Pingquan station, carrying the children on our backs or pulling them along by hand.

Day after day we proceeded over mountains where there were no roads. Soaked by the relentless rain, slipping in the mud, fording rivers up to our necks in water, we desperately sought the soldiers' help so as not to lag behind. We finally reached the airport at Jinzhou on 10 September, just as the autumn winds began to blow. The Qinglong Village Company had been disarmed by the Soviet troops at the airport. Leaving them, we were put into the Jinzhou Fuji National Grade School, which served as our internment camp. I heard rumors that the Japanese troops were being sent to Siberia.

My younger daughter, who had been carried on the shoulders of soldiers many times during river crossings, died of malnutrition in Mukden. But my older daughter and I were able to return safely to Japan.

Every year when 15 August comes, I recall the words the company commander spoke forty-two years ago and the kindness of the soldiers. I heard that there were many soldiers from the Kantō area in the company. I decided to take pen in hand, hoping that this will be read by some of them.

No children were left behind from the Qinglong Village in the depths of China. No orphans.* We were very fortunate to have had the aid of the soldiers during our painful ordeal.

Tanaka Tokiko, sixty-four (f),
housewife, Nagasaki

---

*Thousands of children were left behind by their families during the evacuation of Japanese families from China. Many of these "orphans" visited Japan in groups during the 1980s, in search of their relatives.

Forty-five Days Marching Over Da Hinggan Ling

Early in the morning of 9 August 1945, Soviet troops crossed the Argun River and invaded the Sanhe district of northwest Manchuria. Major Dan Eikei, commander of the Manchuria 208th Unit stationed in Naramuto, gathered the leaders of the Sanhe district border police, the military, administrative agencies, and the civilian population. "Rest assured," he said emphatically, "that we will unconditionally protect your lives and possessions." At that time my father was the accounting supervisor of the Hinggan settlement organization. Under these emergency conditions, I was dispatched by horseback to inform the settlement next to ours, Sanhe cooperative farming village.

A large unit of the Soviet army was proceeding toward Hailar. Our path of retreat cut off, we started off to evacuate toward Da Hinggan Ling to the east. Crossing over Hinggan Ling was a big adventure—even professional exploration parties often failed. During extreme wartime conditions, a group of 427 Japanese, including women and children, crossed over this mountain range. It was a large-scale forty-five-day escape march of over eight hundred kilometers. Along the way we suffered great difficulties, including bombings by Soviet aircraft, as we crossed rivers in the vast marshlands. We had to kill the cattle taken along by the settlement organization for food. It was the longest distance traveled by retreating Japanese in Manchuria.

That we were able to do this without a single casualty was considered miraculous. But there was a reason for this. It was due to the actions of army personnel experienced in making wartime judgments and to the Sanhe border police (led by commander Okada Yoshiki), who fulfilled their duty to protect civilians. Of course the existence of the settlement organization's cattle and horses staved off starvation. Compared to the civilians, the army lost scores of precious lives.

> Ōba Shōzō, fifty-five (m),
> company employee, Hokkaidō

Two Small Lives Vanished on the Plains

With the collapse of the Kwantung Army, Japanese residents in Manchuria were turned from rulers into refugees in one stroke. Many tragedies resulted. This is one of them.

In August 1945, as part of the unit in Dongan, the eastern border district, we were in retreat toward the Manchurian interior pursued by Soviet gunfire. There was no command structure among us. Civilian Japanese who had fled from the border district joined the desperate evacuations, exhausted and on foot.

I think it was near Linkou. As we left a mountain path, we came across a middle-aged woman with an absent expression, presumably a member of a settler family. She was sitting alone on the roadside burning some dried grass that she had piled up.

As I attempted to pass by, I caught my breath. Four little legs were sticking out from under the dried grasses. Unable to comprehend this odd scene, I went over to her and asked, "What happened?" Keeping her face averted, she replied, "They can't walk anymore. I've killed them and I'm burning them."

Forced to flee the wartime fighting at the border, she had managed to get this far. Having reached her limit, physically and mentally, she had killed her two young children, who were a hindrance. Now she was burning their bodies. She must have been driven insane. There were no words I could say as she stared, face wan and eyes dry of all tears, at the bodies of her children. They wouldn't possibly be cremated by this feeble fire of dried grass.

I wonder how the Kwantung Army, retreating in total collapse, looked in the eyes of these settlers. They had gone to the border area to cultivate the land under the state's policy, trusting in the absolute protection of the army.

The sullen way this woman answered me, without shifting her gaze, may have been her final attempt to show her resistance to the military.

Tamada Jin'o, sixty-five (m),
former company employee,
Fukuoka Prefecture

Feast From Cemetery Memorial

In 1946 the Huizhou highway from Huizhou to Zhangmutou in south China was full of soldiers on their way home to Japan. But those who were sick and not allowed on the boat down the Dong Jiang had to depart as early as

4 A.M. These soldiers walked slowly. Their eyes full of tears, they dragged swollen legs like logs. Those of us who left at 7 A.M. soon caught up with them.

Chinese Nationalist soldiers were assigned as security guards to protect this group from bandits. To encourage our men, they put up signs along the roadside reading "Keep it up; your father, mother, and children are waiting for you." I heard that these soldiers had lost their brothers in battles against the Japanese forces. This was General Chiang Kai-shek's way of implementing his stated policy "to recompense injury with kindness." After four days of marching twenty miles a day we finally made it to Humen port at the entrance of the Canton River.

One day, a peasant came to us and asked for the loan of a soldier. When we asked him what for, he said he wanted the soldier to carry a load to his father's grave. It was dangerous for us to go out and we were mulling over our concerns about sending a soldier off alone when an old veteran volunteered to go. "My life," he said, "has been saved from a war I thought I would die in. No need to worry, no need to worry." Then he went off with the peasant.

Our soldier hadn't returned at sunset, so we went to the edge of the village to look for him. We found him walking back in good spirits with a large load on his carrying pole. "Everybody eat up!" he cried. The basket was full of good food.

We heard the story from this soldier. The peasant's father had been killed by a Japanese soldier during the invasion of Guangzhou. Today was the anniversary of his father's death. "Father," he said, "you must be full of resentment that you were killed. But Japan has lost the War. Now the Japanese are pitiful prisoners. Today, for an entire day, I'm making a Japanese soldier work as a coolie carrying our load so that all your relatives can visit your grave. So forgive them, and rest in peace."

Eating the chicken, eggs, and moon cakes that he had brought back from the offerings to the departed, we listened silently to the soldier's expressive report. I wondered what a Japanese peasant would have done. In contrast to this kindness, I saw a dozen or more bloodthirsty local Chinese intent on finding the Japanese soldiers who had killed their family members. They were waiting at the fence by the boarding gate for the boat.

Tsuguhiro Masaru, sixty-four (m),
former textile weaver,
Hamamatsu

A Soviet Family in Sakhalin

There were many Japanese who experienced tragic circumstances in Sakhalin, where I was at the end of the War. Many of them despised the Soviet Union from personal rancor. Under Soviet rule, parents had to work desperately to feed their families, while waiting for repatriation orders.

In the spring of 1946, a Soviet family of four moved into the unit next door to us in the coal miners' row house where our family lived. The sons were twenty-four or twenty-five and fifteen, about my age.

This family was dirt poor. They said they had come from Siberia. They had practically no dishes or furniture. Their meals were plain, consisting of black bread, pickled herring, and cabbage soup. We children sang Russian folk songs like "Katushka" and "Firelight" and clapped our hands together, saying "*Kharasho*" ("That's good") to each other through the thin walls of the closets where we slept. We were scolded by our parents for making such a racket.

In the spring of 1947 the long-awaited orders came for our repatriation. There was a limit to what we could take with us, so we left all our household goods to the Soviet family next door. They were pleasantly shocked that we Japanese had so much. Saying *dasvedanya* (good-bye), we parted from that family.

Shortly after the repatriation ship *Hakuryū Maru* left Kholmsk, I caught my breath when I saw many loaves of the black bread that had been distributed at the internment camp thrown overboard and floating on the water. From somewhere aboard the ship I heard a voice yell, "Those Ruskie bastards," as a loaf of black bread flew down. Remembering the Soviet family who worked so hard to be able to buy a little black bread, I was full of mixed feelings.

> Kamiya Hiromi, fifty-five (f),
> self-employed, Sapporo

Straggler Soldiers

In the latter part of January 1947 I was riding on a demobilization train from Sasebo to Ueno in Tokyo. I was going home—my heart was full of yearning for my hometown. The faces of my wife and children floated up before my eyes and receded. Outside the train window were cities in ruin. It was a desolate sight. Having entirely lost my sense of time and space while detained in Siberia, I had no idea where we were traveling.

At a small train station, a man of about twenty-four or twenty-five got on our train. He was wearing a suit and seemed to be a company employee of some sort. "This is a special car for us demobilized soldiers. There's no seat for you here," someone warned him. "What do you mean, you straggler soldier?" the young man spat out.

We had all been worried about how our fellow countrymen would accept us prisoners who had been held in Siberia. This one phrase pierced our hearts like a nail. Everyone stood up in the car, and the atmosphere turned nasty.

"Throw him out the window!" "Shove him off at a railway bridge!" Angry voices swirled around. Some were so enraged, they said that going to prison for killing "this bastard" would be better than what we went through in Siberia.

Hearing the disturbance, an officer came rushing into the car. He had no insignia on.

"Won't you leave this to me? You've come back all this way, almost to the gates of your hometowns. You don't want to commit murder now. I'll make him get down on his knees and apologize, so won't you be satisfied with that?"

His reasoning persuaded the men. The young man had turned pale and was cringing. He eventually knelt down on the floor of the train car and said something in a low, muffled voice. He kept his head down and didn't move.

Toda Shōsuke, seventy-two (m),
retired, Nihonmatsu

Photographs in Repatriation Lodgings

In 1954 my older brother returned to Japan on the last repatriation ship. I went to Maizuru to meet him. What I can't forget seeing at the lodging for the returnees were hundreds of photographs—faces of children whom families had inquired after. The children in those photos were those same orphans left in China who are now visiting Japan in search of their relatives. My heart aches for them.

If the search for relatives had occurred ten or twenty years ago, the identification rate would have been greater. That is something to regret. We had heard that my brother was sentenced to twenty years of detention as a war criminal. My mother had often wept, saying "I won't be able to see him again while I'm alive." Fortunately, he was able to return after nine years imprisonment. So he was able to see our mother again.

I can't bear to think about the parents of those lost children who died full of sorrow. How regretful one feels about the orphans who were left behind, their relatives now unknown.

I would like to inform those orphans that many people made earnest efforts on their behalf. They tried to find out about their children by passing out inquiry sheets to each person who returned to Japan, asking them if they knew about their children.

Shibahara Kenzō, sixty-one (m),
company advisor, Hitachi

The Reason I Don't Sing the National Anthem

I was in Shibushi, Kagoshima Prefecture, at the time of the defeat. I thought of committing suicide but was unable to go through with it. "I'll be reborn seven times and attack America," I vowed. With this, I permitted myself to continue living.

For two years I had thought of nothing but "dying for the Emperor." When I entered the military, I said in my farewell greeting to those who saw me off, "I will die for my country." Since then, I had had no thoughts of my parents or my siblings. I applied to be sent to the front as soon as possible, but I was sent to Shibushi. When the surrender was announced, I was still alive.

Feeling ashamed about returning home, I took the last train of the day. When it arrived at the station, I walked through the wicket in the dark. Suddenly I heard a voice call out my name, "Hideo! Hideo!" It gave me a start. It was my father who appeared before me from the darkness. "I'm so glad you're home, so glad you've come home." He wept as he said this to me.

It was after eleven o'clock at night. I couldn't figure out how my father had known to meet me at the station. When I asked him, he replied that since 15 August, for three months, he and my mother had taken turns meeting all the trains as they arrived at the station. They had done this for three entire months.

I was speechless. I had never experienced my parents' love as strongly as I did at that moment.

To think that I had contemplated suicide. How undutiful that was toward my parents. For the two years of my absence my mother had not neglected to set a tray for me at each meal. She had gone to the shrine four kilometers away every day to pray for my safe return.

The Emperor was not a god. The War was an invasion. To me the Imperial Army had seemed a divinely inspired force. But its actions resulted in tragedy. I pledged in my heart never again to sing "Kimigayo," the national anthem.

Yamaguchi Hideo, sixty-four (m),
former high school teacher, Sasebo

When MacArthur Landed at Atsugi

The offices of the governor and other administrators of Kanagawa Prefecture were extremely busy preparing for MacArthur's arrival at Atsugi on 30 August 1945. At that time I was posted in the prefectural transportation section as a police officer. Officials were making plans for evacuating women and children, preparing lodging quarters for Occupation forces, and providing stores of food, particularly meat and fruit. The troops could be quartered in warehouses and offices could be renovated, but it wasn't easy to get toilets and beds. We managed to have some beds delivered from a hospital in Niigata, but they were all unsatisfactory. In the end the problem was solved by the American forces bringing what was needed from the U.S. mainland.

We were deeply grateful to be told that food for the Occupation forces would also be provided by America. Thus what we had gathered should be distributed to Japanese who were suffering from lack of food.

The order to provide vehicles was a problem for us. We were told to have 120 trucks, buses, and automobiles in the Atsugi area and 150 trucks in Yokohama. In those days, almost all of the cars that were still running had been requisitioned by the Japanese military, and they were mostly running on firewood and charcoal. We made arrangements with the army and navy and somehow managed to collect the vehicles by the due date. But only a few of them were fully operational. Most of them ran for a while, then broke down. The Occupation forces couldn't meet their schedules, and we were ordered to provide repairmen within forty-eight hours. But with so many people burned out of their homes, it was hard to gather enough mechanics. As a final resort we sent demobilized troops from the army repair shops. On the second day this was found out, and we were scolded roundly.

We made an emergency offer all around the Kantō region that we would pay three times the going rate and provide new work clothes to the workers. With this we finally gathered the mechanics. We breathed a sigh of relief. But we didn't have the necessary parts. Losing patience, the Occupation forces issued a strict order: "At noon tomorrow we will requisition all of your vehicles that are running smoothly."

We explained the facts of our situation and pleaded that it was absolutely necessary that we retain twenty vehicles for transporting food to citizens and five vehicles for the governor and other officials to do liaison work on matters dealing with the War's end, and we received permits for them signed by the commanding officer. When we told the Occupation forces honestly about our actual circumstances, they usually reacted with understanding. I rarely saw any of the stiff unreasonable attitude one might associate with an occupying army.

Hagitani Tomihisa, seventy-nine (m),
retired, Yokohama

The Fate of Mixed-Race Children

On 15 August 1945, the Greater East Asia War was concluded. What I cannot forget are the mixed-race children who were the by-products of the War.

American soldiers filled towns all over Japan. Children were born to these American soldiers and certain Japanese women. Many were not raised by their parents but were raised in an orphanage. The children were given the surname of the founder of the orphanage, Dr. Kusaba Hiroshi.

Kusaba Tetsu was of mixed Japanese and black American heritage. He committed many robberies after leaving the orphanage. He died of cirrhosis of the liver in his thirties. When he was a boy, he excelled in all types of sports. He was a very cute boy.

Kusaba Hitoshi was part Caucasian. He had a low IQ. After leaving the orphanage he became a band member in a hotel. I heard that he died of cirrhosis of the liver in his twenties. I wonder if the parents who abandoned them know what happened to these unfortunate children.

Kusaba Yoshino was a lovely girl. When she was in grade school she was adopted by an American family and went to live in America. I would like to think that she has become a mother herself by now and is lovingly raising her own children.

Satō Yasuko, fifty-two (f),
poet, Tokyo

A Lost Youth Serving Out a Sentence

The Sunshine 60 building flourishes in Tokyo's Ikebukuro. The tallest building in Japan, it is used by young people as a lively meeting place. I wonder how many people know about what used to be in the spot where this building now stands. This is a hallowed place where war criminals sighed in distress and soldier comrades were summarily executed.

I am saddened that most people generally assume that war criminals did horrible things during the War. When Japan lost the War, the victors convened what was euphemistically called an International Military Tribunal to suit themselves. With great speed they unilaterally judged the vanquished. Among those were many war buddies of mine. They were given the death penalty merely because their names had become known or because they happened to have been at a particular location.

I can understand feelings of criticism against Prime Minister Tōjō, who advocated fighting the War. The preponderance of those penalized at these trials, however, were lower-ranking soldiers who were at the scene.

In my youth, I dreamed of becoming a locomotive engineer in Kaohsiung, Taiwan. Bracing myself upon hearing that we were at war, I signed up to be an army civilian in 1942. I worked as a guard for three years at the internment camp in Kuching on Borneo. In June 1945, conscription became applicable to Taiwanese, and I was drafted as a private second class. Then came the defeat. I never dreamed that a military tribunal for abuse against prisoners of war awaited me. All that I had done was to slap a POW who had disobeyed orders, instead of reporting him for heavy imprisonment.

I was sentenced to fifteen years in jail. Prison life was dismal. Without any knowledge that guarding prisoners of war was subject to international law, my comrade was given the death penalty in what the court claimed was an impartial verdict. After I was released from prison, I took out Japanese citizenship. Despite having served that long sentence, I have been refused a veteran's pension. I feel deeply resentful that my youth was lost.

Hayashi Mizuki, sixty (m),
company employee,
Miyazaki Prefecture

Throwing Stones at Korean Children

"Look, it's Koreans! It's the Koreans' children!" Yelling out, the boy who was our local chief bully, stopped playing and started throwing stones. The children who were called Koreans all ran off. They were each carrying a tin can. One of them dropped his. Inside the can were tadpoles. Once they fell onto the ground, the tadpoles no longer moved.

I wonder if I threw stones then. The memory is so far back that I can't fully recall, but I'm sure that along with others I was one of the children that chased away the Korean children.

In front of the Americans, we kids were pathetic children of a defeated country. "Gibu me chocolate." "Gibu me chewing gum," we begged them in our English. We knew how to say "Gibu me cigaretto," too, asking for cigarettes from the American soldiers so we would be rewarded by the adults. Yet while we were children of the defeated nation, always hungry, we also knew how to discriminate according to nationality. We had unwittingly acquired this from watching our grownups.

The blank page of a child's heart can be dyed in any color. Hearing that some kindergarten children stand at attention in front of the national flag, I recall the days when we chased Korean children, stones in hand, and my heart is pained.

Sasaki Fumiko, forty-seven (f),
part-time worker, Ushiku

Fear After the Fighting's End

In a flash the rumor spread around town. "American soldiers are landing. All women, even girls, will be raped." This was Fukuoka just after the end of the War. I was in grade school. Leaving my mother and one older sister at home, three sisters and I, who were in girls' middle school and grade school, were evacuated to a family acquaintance's house in Fukuma in the same prefecture. This was at a chaotic time when the transportation network was in disarray. Waving our arms, we asked for rides from military trucks that left clouds of dust in their wake under the hot sun. Somehow we managed to get to our destination.

We stayed with the family until the rumors died down. The food that we ate—it was just rice mixed with barley and potatoes and bamboo shoots simmered in soy sauce, day after day—tasted so delicious. At night we went with the neighboring children to a cave in the mountains, taking with us some roasted soybeans in a basket. A pair of eyes shone from inside the cave. I wonder what happened to that young soldier who said "Thank you" to us.

On the day before my navy officer brother and others who were in Yokosuka at the War's end were to be demobilized, a group of American soldiers with tattoos on their arms barged into their barracks. As they were about to ransack the Japanese soldiers' few belongings, my brother's friend shouted, "What are you doing?" One of the American soldiers shot off his gun and hit the Japanese soldier's arm.

Although the War had ended, both sides must have been carried away by fear and suspicion. I feel that I can understand Mr. Yokoi's and Mr. Onoda's long-term escape from the world.[*]

> Inoue Tokuko, forty-eight (f),
> housewife, Kawasaki

---

[*]Reference is made to the two Japanese soldiers who hid themselves for more than two decades after the War, in Guam and the Philippines, before they finally surrendered. Mr. Onoda's letter is on p. 147.

In the Teachers' Room After the Defeat

Shortly after noon on 15 August I stood dazed, leaning against the stage used for morning assemblies in the school playground. It was quiet. The noisy bombings had ended. I was overwhelmingly happy that the fear of air raids had disappeared. Yet I was apprehensive about what attacks would come after the surrender. In Daudet's "Monday Story" an order is given that French cannot be taught in the schools in Alsace during the German occupation [after the Franco-Prussian War]. I was concerned that we might be ordered to "stop teaching Japanese and teach English."

The notification from the Occupation forces arrived. It stated, "Ink out the following parts in Japanese language, Japanese history, and geography textbooks so that they cannot be read." We were to strike out all of those parts that we had particularly emphasized in our lessons in order to teach our pupils to honor the state in our belief in victory. I felt angry and wretched. But there was no way I could resist. The fifth-graders were actually having a great time inking out their textbooks. How was I to explain the reason for this to the students? Looking at the innocent children my spirits sank.

The Japanese language was not taken away from us. But with the announcement that the Occupation forces were coming to inspect us, we decided to burn all the valuable historic photographs, rare books, and documents depicting the Ise Shrine that we had in our teachers' room and library. Someone asked, "Could we take them home and hide them? It is such a waste to destroy them." "I hear the Occupation forces will also be going to the teachers' houses," the principal replied, "so please discard what you have in your own homes as well."

I wondered what was to become of education in the future. We all stood wordless, our faces downcast.

> Kawamura Fusako, sixty-five (f),
> former teacher, Ise

Why MacArthur?

In 1946 I entered first grade in Niigata, where we had evacuated. I was among the first class to enter school after the War's end. One day the teacher passed out some paper and told us, "Write down the person you most respect." I wanted to write down the Emperor, but I thought that I shouldn't write that. So I wrote down General MacArthur. The teacher collected our papers and we never heard about it again.

Why had I, at the age of six or seven, wanted to write down the Emperor?

And why had I misrepresented that feeling and written down MacArthur? This was one of the war experiences that I had.

Iwabuchi Hisako, forty-seven (f),
housewife, Hachiōji

Professor's Death From Malnutrition

Immediately after the War's end and some two years before the well-known death from malnutrition of Judge Yamaguchi Yoshitada, a professor of German at Tokyo Higher School named Kameo Hideshirō lived in Nishihara, Shibuya Ward, Tokyo, a few minutes' walk from my house. He had a son who was in grade school. Professor Kameo had given strict orders to his wife not ever to attempt to get anything other than the officially rationed items. Nor should she buy anything on the black market. After a while he began to suffer from malnutrition. His wife suffered the same fate. They were both bedridden. Hearing about his condition, some of his former students sent some food to them, but that didn't last long. The professor died. In the next room, partitioned off only by sliding doors, his wife, not knowing that he had died, remained alive for a while, but she also died.

The children were sent to orphanages and such.

Now much of the food consumed in Japan is imported. If we enter into a war again it will be difficult to ship food to Japan, and the citizens may end up like the Kameo family. It is mass ignorance that we haven't taken notice of this fact.

Gamō, Hideo, eighty-eight (m),
professor emeritus, Aichi
Educational University, Tokyo

Threatened With "Reverse Return"

In April 1948 the Nakhodka prisoner of war camp in Siberia was full to capacity with Japanese prisoners of war who had been sent from all over. At the time I was twenty-three years old, a master sergeant and the senior squad commander, thin and 173 centimeters tall. I wore strong glasses for nearsightedness. Assuming from this that I was an intellectual, the "active" in charge told me, "From tomorrow you'll give the commentary." An "active" was someone who had become an activist for the "democratic" movement after being interned. I stayed up nights reading the thick volume of Soviet Communist Party history, which I had never read before, so that I could deliver the commentary on it by day. Fortunately I didn't humiliate myself, but I felt I was walking on thin ice.

When I landed at Maizuru on 6 May on the *Meiyū-maru*, I was threatened by a Japanese-American GI as he slammed his desk with a rifle. "You're a Communist Party member, aren't you? We've already investigated you. Write down the names of the other Party members who were on the same ship. If you refuse, we'll send you back to Siberia."

Exhausted by his persistent interrogation and offensive Japanese, I became furious. Believing that we were fighting for the Emperor, after death struggles in which we had lost seven hundred men—including half of my classmates at the officer's training school of the Kwantung Army—and after spending three years at hard labor under frigid conditions, I was finally able to stand on the soil of my home country. Yet I was not given a chance to take a rest. I held my ground and insisted, "I can't answer what I don't know."

The day after I arrived home in Shizuoka, I received a summons from GHQ. In the Dai Ichi Building across from the Imperial Palace I was questioned politely but thoroughly about the placement of Far East Red Army troops, by an American military officer and a Japanese who appeared to be a former senior military staff member.

The Allied honeymoon had ended, and the Japanese-American military alliance in preparation for a Soviet–U.S. war had already begun. Were the "honorable military leaders" who had inflamed the country by denouncing "American and British devils" again attempting to deceive the young people and make them dance to their tune? Had they never thought of those who could no longer raise their voices: the settlers who were left on the border; the many soldiers, our war buddies, who had dreamed of their homeland but lay in the frozen ground of a foreign land; and the masses of Chinese who were killed in their holy war?

Swelling up with violent anger against the former senior military staff officer who was exchanging nods with great familiarity with the American soldier, I gave them some old information. But it was no use. They had more accurate and more recent intelligence.

Masuda Minoru, sixty-two (m),
high school teacher,
Higashimurayama

Chapter 10

Rethinking the War Experience

The writers of the letters chosen for this category were often responding to specific letters that had run previously in the series, or to the series as a whole. These correspondents represented a far greater cross section of the Japanese public—or at least of that segment of the public that wrote letters to newspapers. Many of these had no direct war experience. There was a large percentage of students. Generally more women than men contributed. Both male and female writers tended to be younger than the average. In sum, these letters amounted to a massive reflection on the War—and on war in general. The average Japanese in the 1980s had not done much thinking about World War II, so that the appearance of the Sensō series in *Asahi* was disturbing for many. Rather than focusing on single incidents, as their elders had, these writers were chiefly interested in how another war could be prevented.

A general note of regret and disillusionment pervades all the letters in this chapter. The very appearance of the Sensō series had forced many people to think about a subject that was regarded as nationally "unpleasant." It was awkward for many to talk about the sacrifices made by their fathers or husbands or to hark back to the general privations of wartime.

Some wrote about the origins as well as the progress of the War. Many felt that notwithstanding the destruction and loss of life Japan's cause had been just. Their country, they argued, was forced to wage war to save itself from encirclement by the Allied powers. There were complaints about the war crimes trials. Some felt that Japan was being cruelly and unjustly singled out for punishment, when in fact all the belligerents had committed shameful and criminal acts.

Not surprisingly, many of these letters deal directly with the matter of the Emperor's guilt. Recalling the sacrifices of their fathers and brothers on behalf of an Emperor who had ordered them to fight to the death, people questioned angrily whether he should not have been held responsible for bringing war on Japan.

A common thread running through all the letters here, together with the desire for peace, is a sensitivity to even the thought of war. No one wishes for an expanding Japanese army and navy. On the contrary, there is a pervasive note of "never again," whatever the feelings of individual or collective guilt. This helps explain the almost unanimous aversion of modern Japanese to any kind of significant rearmament. Without reexamining overmuch the needs and demands of the Japan–U.S. security relationship, most of the letter writers keep reiterating their opposition to the buildup of any kind of significant military force in Japan. This would in itself constitute an incentive to make war. There is a general tone of concern over the current behavior of Japan's political leaders—many of whom would support a revision of the postwar Constitution. A case can be made for this, but few of *Asahi*'s correspondents would agree. Whatever else MacArthur did in Japan, his flash of inspiration for inserting Article 9, the antiwar clause of the Constitution, caught a responsive spark among the Japanese people.

He Flung the Flag Onto the Ground

There is something that I have doubts about. Each year newspapers and television stations produce special reports on the War. Although these evoke the tragedy of war for the viewers, they do not often touch upon the Emperor, who must have been at the root of this War. Those who tearfully speak of the cruelties of war do not mention the Emperor by name. Why? The fact remains that, no matter how many times one reads history books, it is clear that this War could not have been carried out without the Emperor's orders. He held supreme command. It is true that legally the Emperor bears no responsibility for the War. In order for the country to accept this, however, some issues should have been clarified.

When I was in the fifth grade, my classmate "S" flung to the ground a small flag that had been handed to him, to show his defiance at having to welcome the Emperor. "The Emperor made my father die in the War," he said. "Why do I have to respect him?" His father had pledged loyalty to the Emperor, followed his orders, and had sacrificed his life at the front. Even in this young child's heart the feeling of resentment was deep.

How much have people's feelings about the Emperor changed from the antiquated attitudes of prewar times? It is our national characteristic that we are unable to talk easily about our actual feelings regarding the Emperor. This allows the possibility that we may repeat a similar tragedy.

Hakota Atsuko, forty-five (f),
housewife, Tokyo

Glory Only When We Can Discuss Freely

I fully agree with Ms. Hakota's opinion stated in her letter. It is impossible for us to speak the truth concerning our nation's War without mentioning the Emperor. Forty years have passed since the declaration was made at home and abroad that the Emperor was human. This was shortly after the surrender. Now that the Emperor and the citizens of Japan are working toward our future glory from this starting point, it is nothing short of an absurdity to treat the issue of the Emperor as taboo. Shouldn't we discuss freely and decently the reality of the past, transcending our various ways of thinking and living based on our trust in each other?

In the faraway past, I, too, was moved by seeing youths who shouted "Banzai to the Emperor!" and sacrificed their irreplaceable lives on the battlefield. The heroic way my war comrades died even now remains vivid in my mind. What made those young men accept that kind of death? Unless we Japanese bring these issues out in the open and go over them thoroughly, we will never be able to extricate ourselves from the War.

The subject of the Emperor should not be treated as something above the clouds. It should be discussed freely. I believe that this is what will bring glory to the future of us Japanese, causing the people to bless the Emperor as a truly human Emperor.

Yamatsu Sumiyuki, sixty-eight (m),
retired, Tosu

Freedom and Responsibility to Oppose War

Immediately after the surrender the Higashikuni cabinet advocated a "general penance of a hundred million." This postulated that the defeat was the responsibility of all Japanese, and that we should unanimously engage in soul-searching. By diffusing the responsibility onto the entire populace, however, we seem to have granted immunity to the leaders.

I have doubts about the recent proliferation of the view that all Japanese should bear responsibility for waging this War. It goes without saying that freedom and responsibility are two sides of the same coin. It is essential that we first examine what degree of freedom Japanese had during wartime.

Was it possible, for example, for someone who had received a militaristic education consistently from birth to criticize the War? Were such people able to acquire the knowledge to see through the deceptions of the Greater East Asia Co-Prosperity Sphere or the slogan "eight corners of the world under one roof" ["Hakkō ichiu"]? How could they have found out about the brutality practiced by the Japanese military? And was there any freedom to resist the draft or leave the military? Can we hold responsible people who were uninformed and instilled with the idea of a divine war? This seems tantamount to expecting godlike omniscience and omnipotence from them.

Not only is it unproductive to carry logic to such extremes, it can also be considered harmful, in the sense that it obscures the place where true responsibility lies.

> Sugimoto Kōji, sixty-one (m),
> former civil servant, Yokohama

Father Did Not Permit My Return Home

A half century has passed since I received a red-card draft notice and joined the military. To the villagers gathered at the train station at Yukuhashi, Fukuoka Prefecture, I pledged, "I will die in battle protecting the Emperor by standing in front of his horse." At the time my mother was bedridden. I left my parents and my job and devoted my entire youth to the defense of the fatherland.

The fear, starvation, and indignities of military life would have been unthinkable in normal situations. We had to endure this because of the supreme command, "Consider your superior's orders to be the direct orders of the Emperor," which was included in the Imperial Rescript to Soldiers and Sailors. Because of this Emperor's order, many thousands of soldiers died at Guadalcanal, Saipan, and Iwo Jima. Okinawa was devastated. Hiroshima and Nagasaki were blanketed with deadly ashes.

I was barely able to keep alive in north China. When I came back to Japan after the surrender, I was unable to go home. My late father was a leader in the village. He did not permit the return of his son who had been defeated in the War.

I thought that when Japan surrendered unconditionally the Emperor would be deposed. Even if he couldn't abdicate during Mr. MacArthur's rule, there were many later opportunities for him to abdicate. In Konoe Fumimaro's "Konoe Diary" ("*Konoe Nikki*"), he wrote: "In the case of defeat in war, one solution would be for His Majesty not merely to abdicate but then to enter the Ninnaji or Daikakuji temple and pray for the souls of the officers and soldiers who died in the War. Naturally, I will accompany His Majesty."

Three million died in the War—Japanese civilians as well as military officers and soldiers. All fought not under orders of the military clique but under the Emperor's orders.

First of all, the Emperor should take responsibility. This is the starting point for the morality of postwar Japan. This is why I adamantly refuse to sing the national anthem, "Kimigayo," with its prayers that the imperial family will flourish.

Furumiya Toshio, sixty-nine (m),
city assembly, Machida

Preserve the Tragic Remains

A fourth-generation Japanese-American visiting from a high school in Hawaii told me recently that the battleships sunk at Pearl Harbor still remain where they settled. I have heard that Germany, too, has war ruins preserved in partitioned sections. Japan, by contrast, has only the Hiroshima Atomic Bomb Dome, and the tragedy is steadily fading from our memory.

The city of Hiratsuka, where I live, was reduced to rubble by firebombing attacks in the waning days of the War. But all that has now been overshadowed by the gaiety of the Tanabata Festival. Remains of the War cannot be found anymore. In the forty years since the defeat, we have lost the sensitivity to know how stupid and cruel war can be. We have been lulled into forgetfulness.

"Divine War," "American and British Devils," "I won't desire anything until victory is won"—At the time, we thought that this was right, and it never occurred to us to have any doubts. In observing the Japanese who after the War's defeat did an about-face and adapted to new ideals, I became aware that the change was not so much due to a concern about good and evil as it was to a national character that shifts with every whim. So to cast doubt on any argument that espouses killing, no matter how reasonable the logic may appear, we should preserve the ruins, the artifacts, and our impressions of the War for all generations to come.

Satō Shigeru, fifty-one (m),
teacher, Hiratsuka

Treating Battle Dead Like Curs

Whether it be between nations or between peoples, war is a clashing confrontation of hate. While there may be variance in degree, responsibility for it must lie with both sides. But in the last World War, the victorious nation one-sidedly imposed all responsibility for the War on the other and then convened judgment. Even now, they have yet to take responsibility for the barbaric use of the atomic bombs to kill masses of noncombatants. They justify their action by saying that it hastened the end of the War.

Japanese now enjoy the prosperity that has come after recovery from the misery of a one-sided defeat. Yet many are under the illusion that Japan alone bears responsibility for the War. I feel sad when I see the strong tendency toward censuring those of us who were participants in that War.

What should we think of the high-handed attitude the United States takes toward Japan's trade surplus that has arisen with the growth of our economy? The Japan–U.S. relationship is now very close. Nevertheless, U.S. hatred for Japan's economy grows ever stronger. If we consider that in the prewar days Japan and the United States were in a state of extreme political and economic confrontation, it is altogether too easy to imagine how much hatred the U.S. must have had for Japan then.

No people starts wars from preference. But since our country had taken this drastic step, we had no choice but to fight. The young people of today who live in peacetime conditions cannot possibly understand the state of mind of people living in wartime conditions. The various acts of cruelty and ignominy that we are told about were the monstrous acts of war (although we cannot blame them all on war). The acts of the occupying army in former Manchuria and in parts of the home country are also evidence of this.

That is why war is so frightening and so stupid. And it is right to desire that war should never be waged again. For this very reason, I wish to see a reversal of that trend toward spreading irresponsible denunciations against our country's past. We should not treat the deaths of those compatriots who fought so desperately in defense of our nation as no more than the deaths of curs.

Taguchi Hisago, sixty-seven (m),
retired, Fukushima Prefecture

Were Battle Deaths Like Deaths of Curs?

When I read the comments of Mr. Taguchi [preceding letter] I felt compelled to reconsider what I had always thought. It is certainly the case that those people who criticize war, including those of us in the younger generation who have never known war, have tended to lack sympathy toward those people who participated in the War. We are apt to jump to conclusions.

But in our love for Japan and hatred of war there is no difference whatsoever between us and Mr. Taguchi's generation. In fact, this is the very reason we want to make clear what caused Japan to tread the road to war. In order to do so it is necessary to expose to the light of day excesses Japan committed before and during that War. While that is certainly not a pleasant task, it is something that we Japanese must do for ourselves.

"No people starts wars from preference." What is it, then, that made the people start the War? "But since our country had taken this drastic step, we had no choice but to fight." Why did you have no choice but to fight? Rather than an abstraction called the "country" that took the drastic step toward War, was it not really something else that had borrowed the name of the country as a pretext?

Please do not give up on those of us in the younger generation as incapable of understanding war. Please teach us about all your experiences and all that you know. And then let us think about this together. We have a responsibility to strive to understand, just as the people of Mr. Taguchi's generation have a responsibility to strive to make us understand. If we are lax in this effort, then someday a different generation of Japanese may repeat those same mistakes. Already, today can no longer be called the "postwar period" but perhaps has again become a "prewar period."

Imagawa Nobuhiro, twenty-four (m),
credit bank employee, Sagamihara

Are We Thinking Deeply About the War?

Last summer, twenty of us joined together to issue a private publication of a record of wartime experiences, *Praying for Peace.* We called on many people to contribute manuscripts. From that process, I was left with two impressions.

My first impression is that Japanese do not seem to have thought very deeply about that fifteen-year War. A number of people said, "Since we lost, it was a bad war." I wondered if the mentality that wants to alter the word *invasion* to *advance* [in textbooks describing the War] might have a broad base of mass support. The comments to the contrary expressed in this column may be in the minority.

I avidly read the discussion published on 27 November about "the reasons for the Pacific War." If this kind of argument and research had been made repeatedly by people since immediately after the defeat, Japan's postwar period might have been shaped differently. Even today, there are many elderly people who believe that it was pressure from foreign countries that forced Japan inevitably toward war.

My second impression is what young people often say who do not know war: "You say that you are victims of war, but were you not also oppressors?" Whenever people say that, we who have experienced the War tend to wince and become tight-lipped. But that is all the more reason I want to tell young people about the realities of war.

When in a situation where everyone is made to think uniform thoughts and to engage in identical behavior, how many people can realize the horror of it all? The stares of those who are mercilessly on the lookout for nonconformists wear down one's power to think. War is one example of this.

The seeds of such behavior can again be seen in the peaceful Japan of today. Is it the excessive sensitivity of those of us who have experienced war that makes us see its shadow looming in the examination hell of competition for entrance to schools and in "bullying" among schoolchildren? The oppressors are always those ordinary-looking conformists found in every group.

Fujiwara Toshiko, sixty-three (f),
retired, Tokyo

Internal War Responsibility

A number of letters have been printed here that stated that the "people" did not have responsibility for the War. While it is true that they bore no political responsibility, each person in the nation should still have had the duty to take responsibility for and to strive to overcome the issues raised by the War. Because war is an extreme situation, it exposes issues that we tend to forget in our daily lives.

Why do humans fight wars? And if war breaks out, does it then become all right to kill people? In the postwar period we should have been thinking about what is nationhood and what is authority. Unfortunately, since Japanese in the postwar period felt they bore no political responsibility for the War, they neglected to engage in meaningful reflection. While there was also the tragedy of the American Occupation policy's reverse course, was it not our failure to pursue internal reflection that has resulted in equivocation over taking political responsibility for the War, the breakdown of the policy to limit defense expenditures to one percent of the GNP, and the attempt to revive the National Secrets Act?

I wish that those of you who participated in the War would reflect more—so that you can lay bare your true feelings. That is essential if those of us in the younger generation are to join you in bearing responsibility for the War on our own account—instead of seeing it as the concerns of mere strangers.

Tsunoda Tsutomu, twenty-six (m),
part-time worker, Tokyo

A Crime to Conceal Truth

I don't remember what triggered it, but beginning in middle school I became greatly interested in the War. Since then I have read the war memoirs of many different people. To my mind, it is a dangerous way of thinking to equate pacifism with judging the War to be a stain on Japanese history. We should not conceal it with a thick veil. There is no way one can oppose war without knowing what it is. There was just so much diversity in the human drama played out on the battlefield and on the home front and in the blend of emotions engendered, that I feel that we cannot describe that period with the stereotype "war equals crime."

The true character of war is certainly none other than mutual killing. It should never be allowed to happen again. It is for this very reason that I want to know: What was truth for the officers and soldiers on the battlefield? What did they see and what did they feel as military men and as human beings? Isn't it a crime to consign to oblivion the facts carved into history, along with the sullied reputation of the Japanese military?

You who have endured the land, sea, and air battles, please tell us the living facts. Otherwise our generation has no means other than history to learn of your experiences.

Kawabe Misa, twenty (f),
student, Yokohama

In Place of My Departed Father

I remember my father, who around 1935 crossed over to China with his dreams of youth, where he was then drafted. He had family in China. He even had a Chinese name. When he was driven by a desire to see his birthplace and return to Japan, he recalled that his Chinese friends were kind enough to say he could come back anytime. At another time, he said that a friend had pleaded with him for medicine even though he had repeatedly denied having any. Finally, feeling he had no choice, he had wrapped some tooth powder in a slip of paper and passed it along, only to be surprised to be told later that the child had recovered, thanks to his gift.

When the news came of Japan's defeat, his superiors had all fled, leaving only soldiers like my father (a private second class) and a few slightly higher-ranking soldiers. The soldiers who had treated the Chinese so brutally were now mistreated by the Chinese. Drinking sake, my father would often tell us children stories about those days. Before I was born, he told my mother, "I did lots of terrible things in China. A man like myself can't possibly have children with all their limbs intact." I wonder if he had thoughts that he could not repeat to us. I have submitted this contribution in place of my father, who died from illness sixteen years ago at the age of fifty-six.

I who have never known war am the recipient of my father's blood, and I know that I am living in a line that extends from that War. I, too, will hand down those stories to my own children. Perhaps that is the responsibility of us Japanese.

Nagaoka Eiko, thirty-six (f),
housewife, Tama

A Gift to the Next Generation

I was born in 1948. When I was a child, I used to hear stories of the War from my father and mother, and from my grandmother on my mother's side. While my father talked about the battlefield, my mother talked about seeing her home burn down in the bombing raids. At great risk to her life, she seized her younger brother's hand and crawled through the flames to escape. And my grandmother told me that once, while fleeing with her husband, she was distressed when a half-naked woman gone mad from shock demanded the kimono she was wearing. In every case, they seemed to speak almost inadvertently about something they preferred not to talk about at all.

The household that my parents set up on their own was truly poor, consisting as it did of a woman burned out of her home and of a man who had returned barely alive from Guadalcanal. My father had brought back a single khaki blanket, worn almost to a dust cloth, when he was demobilized, but it was like a treasure to them. Even though I was a small child, I concluded that war must be a tragic thing. My grandmother died three years ago, while my father and mother are now over sixty. As time passes, the number of living witnesses to the War is declining.

Now that forty years have gone by since the War, perhaps they can view it a little more dispassionately and speak out against war in their own words. While they perhaps do not want to remember, I wish those people who are living witnesses would relate their war experiences without attempting to glorify them. That would be the best gift they could offer the next generation.

Katō Mieko, thirty-eight (f), housewife, Toyota

How to Make Use of Sacrifices

In his letter, Mr. Taguchi says, "Do not treat the deaths of those compatriots who fought so desperately in defense of our nation as no more than the deaths of curs." I think that their deaths have ultimately been "treated like deaths of curs." I sympathize completely with Mr. Taguchi's thought that "war is so frightening and so stupid." I, too, cannot forget those many war dead who sacrificed themselves in the War. I pray from the bottom of my heart for their souls' repose in the other world.

Many who experienced the War and many families of the war dead believe, like Mr. Taguchi, that they "fought desperately in defense of our nation." I can understand their desire to believe that the deaths were not in vain, that they were meaningful. That belief is probably the only thing that keeps them going. How can they ever come to accept the deaths of their beloved husbands and sons? But were their deaths truly meaningful? If the War had been brought to a conclusion earlier, fewer people would have been sacrificed, and the atomic bombs probably would not have been dropped. No, if the War had never been waged, all that would never have happened.

Mr. Taguchi said, "they defended our nation." But did they really? A Japan that was being criticized from all over the world had withdrawn from the League of Nations and commenced on its own a war of aggression. While I have no intention of denying my patriotism, I believe that we must draw a sharp line between right and wrong, even when it concerns our own country.

In Germany, Nazi war criminals are being sought out even now. In Japan, in the period before and during the War, education was "education with a purpose." It was geared only toward nurturing people to follow the national authority. The seeds of criticism were not cultivated. So, while I understand people's desire to believe that the war deaths were not in vain, I think the practice of praising the war dead as departed heroes worthy of religious veneration is extremely dangerous. That is treading the same path as teaching the young that discarding one's life for the nation is a praiseworthy act.

Those who died in battle are not special. I believe they are the same as those who died in the air raids and the atomic bombings. Those people who died on the home front had not engaged in killing others. I have no intention of denying individuals the right to worship at Yasukuni Shrine. That is for individuals to determine for themselves and it is their right. But I am opposed to protection of this shrine by the national government.

I hope that the people will take an interest in government and society so that they will never again have to say, as was said at that time, "When I realized what was happening, it was too late."

Serizawa Nobuo, forty-four (m),
company employee,
Saitama Prefecture

Shock of One Person's Death

In the United States two passenger planes recently collided in midair, while in the Soviet Union a passenger ship collided and sank, each resulting in many deaths. Both of these accidents were heavily reported by many newspapers.

At about the same time as these two accidents, battles have been joined in the Iran–Iraq War that have probably resulted in far more casualties. But reports about these events are limited to minor mentions on the newspapers' international pages.

This was also true in Japan during the War. The city news pages daily reported by name the dead and injured from accidents. But even though there were probably no days when the number of dead and injured in the battles then raging totaled zero, the only reports given were general summaries of battle actions.

If there had been no restrictions on reporting, if a detailed report of each frontline soldier's death could have been made, giving his name, the people would have averted their eyes from the horror. The War could not have been continued.

People who have not had experience of war may conclude that the people of that day who endured the deaths of millions were insensitive or had a low level of ethics. But people are more shocked by one dead body lying directly in front of them than they are by words that describe a million deaths. As long as there are politicians who can manipulate that weakness, eliminating war will not be an easy task.

Kimura Akio, sixty-nine (m),
self-employed, Ogōri

War Mentality in People

As I have continued to read this column on the War, I have been made acutely aware of the huge gap—practically a case of split personality—between the mental state of humans placed in extreme circumstances and that of those living a peaceful everyday life. When as a soldier I was driven back by the enemy and went into hiding with civilians in a cave, I might have strangled a baby with my own hands if it had cried. The military is a collective organization that countenances any inhumane, demented, and violent behavior—as long as it promotes combat operations.

The soldiers who offered themselves to war and paid the greatest sacrifices at the same time exhibited cruel behavior on the battlefront. Those men were in the position of both victim and oppressor. They have no choice but to remain silent. The people who actually prosecuted and fought the War saw their destiny linked to the fate of the nation, as a kind of aesthetic awareness. After the end of the War, they never questioned their humanity but just slid back into obscurity, living an ordinary citizen's life.

As the fifteen-year War was beginning—around the time the conscription examinations were held—I used to wander over to the brothels with my childhood friends. We had come to a tacit mutual feeling that, before entering the military, we should satisfy our urgent desire at least to sleep with a woman before going off to die. Because it was in the nature of soldiers in those days to be poor and ignorant, it was impossible to feel humane love toward a woman. In the autumn of 1944, the young flight crews at the Matsuyama Naval Air Corps drank sake at the base canteen until they rolled down dead drunk. They were trying to shake off their fear of dying.

Soldiers are not the only ones who engaged in war without a sense of their own identity. At the Tokyo war crimes trial, every one of the War leaders gave testimony that they had only been fulfilling their loyalty and duty to the nation. Thus they denied responsibility for the War. The raw experiences in this column force us to struggle with our own war mentality to see how we should act as human beings to preserve peace.

> Kumagaya Tokuichi, seventy (m),
> machinist, Yokohama

The Guilt of Soldiers Who Returned Alive

"As soon as wartime friends meet, they instantly go back forty-two years in time. Although they are sixty- and seventy-year-old men of advanced age, their backs straighten right up, their voices grow younger, and they turn to talking about war buddies who have died. These are people who cannot forget their wartime experiences."

This comment was made by Mr. Suzuki Tokushirō, sixty-three, the president of a trading company in Kōriyama, Fukushima Prefecture, whom I recently met. While on his way to the Philippines, the transport ship Mr. Suzuki was on was torpedoed by an American submarine. He was forced to remain on Taiwan, where he awaited the end of the War.

"In our same unit," he recounted, "there were more than two hundred men who continued on to the Philippines on the remaining ship. They were caught in the mountains of northern Luzon. Beset by starvation and fever, they fought against the overwhelmingly better-supplied U.S.–Philippine forces. They were completely destroyed."

Mr. Suzuki was a member of the Seventy-sixth Regiment in the Nineteenth Division formed up in Nanam, Korea. He had no choice when it came to "the path dividing life from death"; he took the path of life and lived these forty-two years. Although he was a soldier for barely two years, perhaps because it was a time of the sentimental experiences of youth, it is impossible for him to push the War off into the oblivion of distant memory. What is more, he says, his feeling of guilt looms larger with age. "We are sorry that we alone have survived."

Mr. Suzuki says that he and his wartime friends will depart from Narita Airport on 14 February to go into the mountains 1,500 meters high located 250 kilometers north-northeast of Manila. There they hope to find their departed war buddies' bones and effects and bring them back.

"I cannot die with a clear conscience leaving them in a foreign land. I won't be able to face them in the other world. Of course, a week-long trek in the mountains will be hard on this old body of mine."

The agitated feeling of guilt held by the officers and soldiers who returned alive cannot be dismissed as ordinary sentimentalism. These former military men bear the War on their backs like a heavy load. After listening to Mr. Suzuki's story, I am left to ponder: Just whose sin is this?

Ōte Mikio, forty-seven (m),
corporate officer, Tokyo

The Danger in "Beauty of War"

More than twenty years ago, as a seventeen-year-old girl, I first encountered *Kike wadatsumi no koe* [*Hearken to the Ocean's Voice* (translated 1968), a book of reflections and poems by young suicide-mission pilots, published after their deaths]. In those days I became infatuated with the book. No other book did I read over and over, totally immersed in it. But contrary to the book's intentions, I realize now that my reveries about the book were extremely dangerous sentiments.

Someone said, "There is no beauty in war." But hasn't war, which has existed from ancient times somewhere on our planet without cessation, always been beautified by someone? Those intellectual young men were forced into the military, partway through their studies or immediately after graduation. In their twenties they were driven to die, contrary to their own intentions. That seemed to this seventeen-year-old girl to possess a thrilling beauty. I was infatuated with their gallant uniformed figures. What I was feeling was perhaps the same emotion that the young people of that earlier time had felt burning in their own bosoms. And the idea that not a single one of those young men who left memoirs was still alive in this world made the thought sweeter yet.

There is certainly no beauty in the stories about what really happened in the War that those survivors are writing to this column. They have finally overcome their reluctance and taken up their pens after more than forty years. An unavoidable fight by a tyrannized people who risk their souls may be justified. But it defies the imagination, to think of the lives shattered in that War, which was instigated by the military men's abnormally swollen and crazed mental state. Even today, wars continue to be waged somewhere in the world. With war now consisting of murderous weapons that can destroy the earth many times over, I wonder if there are any humans who can still find beauty in war?

Koyama Yoshie, forty-three (f),
business owner, Kamakura

Don't Repeat the Sins I Committed

The prewar education system suppressed freedom of thought and conscience, ignored basic human rights, and intently pressured the entire country toward war. But it did not spring up suddenly one morning. Rather, it was the result of change piled upon change, a little at a time, in an effort to reach a goal. I did not know what I could do concerning these gradual steps toward war and so just looked on. I have nothing but feelings of remorse and shame for my vacillation and inconstancy—as an educator—in support of this militaristic education. It is a fact that today, again, defense expenditures have broken through the barrier of one percent of the GNP, and a national secrets bill has been proposed. These are actions that infringe upon our Constitution, which abolishes war and protects freedom of thought and conscience.

I want us to face up to the fact that when we overlook these minute changes, we are in danger of repeating the errors of the past. The proclamation of the new Constitution after the War left us disoriented at the enormous switch in values. It took some time to make the change within myself, so that I could use the spirit of the Constitution as the basis for education. I feel responsibility for the considerable setbacks in education that occurred in this interim period.

I do not want to see my past mistakes repeated by others. For this, we must take pride in our country's Constitution. We must make it the basis for education and stand up with a strong will against anything that infringes upon it, even if it appears trifling. When I recall that there were people in the prewar period who resisted war to the death—even in the face of powerful national authority—I feel most acutely the depth of the sins that I committed in my position as an educator. War is a horrible act that suppresses the conscience and thought of the people and tramples on their basic human rights.

> Mogi Yoshio, sixty-eight (m),
> former middle school principal,
> Tomioka

Distrust by the Shōwa Single-Digits

Near the end of 1940, the homeroom teacher approached "O" in the sixth-grade elementary school boys' classroom and suddenly began slapping him right and left. A stunned "O," a frail boy, staggered first to the right, then to the left, returning to an upright position after each blow. This punishment, inflicted without any discussion, was delivered because "O" was wearing long pants when everyone else had on short pants. The boy's parents had finally been able to acquire a coupon issued under the controlled economic regulations. They had used it to buy him a pair of long pants, since in a few months he would be going to an upper-level school. The teacher had inflicted the punishment without even bothering to hear the circumstances.

In the school, students were divided into groups according to which middle school they desired to attend. Those applying to enter the top-rate schools were seated in the front and center, with the next group positioned around them. Those going for the third-rate schools and all the rest were discriminated against. The atmosphere was such that anyone who so much as dared to make a complaint about the system might be beaten half to death.

Very shortly after the War was over, we used that classroom for a class reunion. The words that came from our homeroom teacher were, "From now on it is the age of democracy. . . ." I stared fixedly at his face. Since then I have never felt the desire to attend a class reunion, even though I get the announcements. After having had loyalty beaten into us in our youth and then having the War end in the midst of this type of education, we who were born in the Shōwa single-digit years [1926–34] watched as those same adults that had been teaching loyalty then turned around and commenced shouting about democracy without any understanding of the import of the term. It can be inferred from this that a large majority of my Shōwa single-digit cohorts came to harbor a deep distrust of those in all levels of authority and leadership.

Ikezaki Kazuo, fifty-eight (m),
business owner, Matsudo

Three Antiwar Positions

Opposition to war can be classified into three positions. The first is, "I hate war, so I am opposed." The immediacy of this declines as the generation that actually experienced the War grows older. In addition, one who takes this position is unable to resist those people who say, "Even if you hate it, there are some wars that are necessary anyway." So "I hate it" is not so much an argument or a statement of position as it is an expression of feeling.

The second is, "I am opposed to war because it does not pay." For example, say these people, can our country survive a war when it is poor in resources and energy and has no more than thirty percent self-sufficiency in food? It is certainly true that our great navy was unable to protect ships that were carrying much less than ships now transport. But the problem with this statement is that one cannot then effectively respond to the counterthrust "Would you not oppose a war that did pay?"

The third opposition argument is, "Japan should not engage in war." This sentiment is guided by the reactions felt toward the past wars that Japan was caught up in. It is a position that goes beyond the people's "feelings" or their "calculations." It recognizes that war is immoral, and that it is the road to peace that should be trod even at the expense of economic prosperity. This is the people's "logic."

I do not believe that Japan can abolish war by opposing it on its own. But a policy can be adopted that prevents us from drawing close to war. While keeping military expenditures low may be criticized, we can always point with pride to the large outlays going toward international economic assistance and cultural exchanges.

I know that people may say this is just theorizing in vain. But even while some say the peace Constitution is an idealistic daydream, we have been able to defend it and to build Japan up to its present state of economic prosperity.

Kawaguchi Ikuo, sixty-one (m),
retired, Hirosaki

Welcome to the New Breed

My older brother died in Manchuria in about October of the year the War ended. He was returned to the soil in Manchuria but also sleeps in our own family grave. It has never occurred to me that he might also be at the Yasukuni Shrine.

While man can be ever approaching God, he can never achieve the same level as God. I am annoyed at the national policy allowing people who have died in battle to be easily made over into gods, and I am irate when I see that this is being used for political purposes. But at the Chidorigafuchi Cemetery for the war dead I am able to bring my hands together respectfully in prayer.

In the letters to this column on the War, I wonder how many of the writers have been referring to themselves rather than someone else? As long as these people are around, we can assume that all is well, but what worries me is what will happen in ten years. It seems that something has been put into motion with that time frame as a goal. It would appear that in an attempt to return to prewar Japan, forces are directly interfering with those aspects of society that are controllable, beginning with compulsory education.

In ten years' time, how many of the people who are speaking out will still be alive? Among those of us who desire peace there still exists another version of ourselves, a heritage of a time when we waged war. I welcome the appearance of a new breed of Japanese who have no connection to what we older Japanese went through, and I hope there will be more persons with this new way of thinking.

The new breed of Japanese would have been considered to be useless under the code of old Japan. But they are better not only for Japan, but also for world peace.

Hagiwara Hisao, sixty-three (m),
architect, Tokyo

The Reason I Am for Promotion of "Peace Studies"

"There's something called 'peace studies' now." So reported my son, home from college. Now that's more like it! I think it's wonderful to have "peace studies." I said, "That's more like it!" because the university he attends is unsurpassed in terms of its internationalism, admitting students from foreign countries who arrive to study when September comes around.

In earlier letters coming from young people they asked such things as why do wars occur and who starts them. I too have wanted to know in specific detail for some time, as if I were attending an imperial council meeting, what were the circumstances behind the decision to engage in war. At the very least, I had thought that universities could establish something like a course on "war studies," which would use the historical facts of war to conduct research into everything from basic theory to specific policies for maintaining peace. But of course, "war studies" would too easily give the impression that what is being taught is the know-how needed to conduct war. That is why I think that "peace studies" is a great concept. Upon further inquiry I discovered that it had been in existence for two or three years, but I hadn't heard about it because it was not a compulsory course. It may become compulsory sometime in the future.

War is said to be the method of last resort for resolving conflicts between nations. At the root of conflict is the contest over national interests and rights. Nevertheless, I sometimes wonder if the people who could be termed the intellectuals of each country can readily engage in fighting that ends up in killing people. During the War, when I was a girls' school student, English classes were suspended because English was the language of the enemy. Such borrowed words as *poketto* [pocket] were awkwardly replaced by native terms such as *monoire* [place to put things]. While we didn't think anything of it at the time, looking back it seems really foolish. The first step toward peace is to know about war. This is the reason I favor the promotion of "peace studies."

> Sakuraba Mieko, fifty-six (f),
> housewife, Fuchū

Progress of Mankind

Resistance to the rising sun flag is often seen in Okinawa. This is probably because memories of wartime miseries are associated with it. But these Okinawans cannot make progress if they insist on criticizing the rising sun flag forever. Rather than continuing to harbor in their hearts the somber images of war, I think they should instead strive to the utmost to prevent such a thing from ever happening again.

The rising sun flag is the source of unceasing sadness and pain for other people as well. But from these circumstances came the new Constitution and reforms leading to the Japan of today. That our lifestyle is so much more affluent than it was during the War is proof that Japan has made great progress. This is a wonderful thing. We must now take this Japan our predecessors have built and make it splendid. Although I do not know anything about the horrors of war, I must etch in my heart the stories that have been told about wartime Japan and then progress forward. This progress is toward peace and it is the progress of mankind.

> Kojima Yuki, fourteen (f),
> student, Kitakyūshū

Tired of Boasts

"You're fortunate not to know war," we're told. We've heard stories about the War over and over again, but it wasn't as if we were listening to them with gratitude. Secretly, we thought, "There, they've started up again." Because we are living a happy life, it is hard for us to comprehend that older people suffered hardships in the past. This is because we haven't had the opportunity to experience the extreme circumstances of war.

And yet, when adults attempted to admonish us with stories about the War, our aversion only mounted. As we grew up, we came to detest the repetitive lectures on the War; we had only contempt for the boastful stories. To us they exhibited no self-reflection about the War. When we point that out to adults, they respond that their education and ideology were different from those of present times. What is more, they say that the young people these days are effete and that the present-day prosperity owes its existence to the War. What an inflated assessment of the War! It might be that if there had been no War people might be living a much brighter life—with a low cost of living and a full line of welfare benefits.

Both countries involved in a war are undeniably perpetrators and victims. But I think in Japan the feeling of being victimized, including by the atomic bombings, is overwhelmingly strong. Now that those born after the War constitute the majority of the Japanese population, shouldn't we think more about responsibility for the War? Isn't that better than just telling stories about wartime experiences?

Suda Atsuko, thirty-one (f), housewife, Fuji

Listen to the Agony of the Adults

Ms. Suda, you say that you are "tired of boasts" and that you didn't listen to stories about the War with gratitude. But please keep in your mind that war is a frightening thing. Be thankful for the mere fact that you haven't experienced such extreme circumstances. For you young people the peace that we have now is a "given." But for us older adults peace in itself is something to be thankful for.

Those who talk to you about the War may unfortunately sound boastful. But won't you reread the letters in this column? No one has made any boasts. Please listen carefully to the adults' voices, which practically moan in agony. Please accept with good grace these letters as alarm bells sounded to the next generation by adults who lost their valued compatriots to war. Why? Because they had been ignorant, because they didn't have the freedom to oppose. Please learn from them so that you will not have to send *your* beloved children and grandchildren off to the battlefield.

The leaders who make war begin first with education. It is heartbreaking for me to recall those days. Believing that it was the honorable thing to do, I waved a small rising sun flag and stood at the edge of our village to send soldiers off to die on the battlefield in the name of the Emperor. We had no freedom of expression. We had no power to resist. But now we are fortunate to have freedom of expression. Shouldn't women study so that we can work toward preserving world peace through words and not by relying on weapons?

Takamura Mieko, fifty-seven (f),
housewife, Matsumoto

Able Only to Improve Over Past Mistakes

During the War, my teaching was based on belief in the national policy of the Greater East Asia Co-Prosperity Sphere. When doubts arose in my mind, I thought that they were due to shortcomings in my own way of thinking. With the defeat, I realized that my doubts had been correct. When I thought of how misguided my teaching had been during wartime, I resigned myself to not being able to return to teaching upon my repatriation from Korea. Yet during the year that I looked for work, I observed that the teachers from before the War had stayed on in the schools. Since that was the case, I thought that I had every right to be reinstated. So I decided to apply for the teacher's eligibility certification.

I acknowledge that my teaching during the War was misguided, and I don't make excuses for it. What was wrong was my ignorance. When I started over again I vowed that I would not teach according to the policies of the state or the Ministry of Education. I would teach according to my own convictions. I believe that I was able to do so until I reached mandatory retirement.

Sakai Manabu, seventy-five (m),
former high school principal,
Fukuoka

As a Christian

I became a history teacher in April 1941, just before the start of the Pacific War. I taught the imperialistic view of history as directed by the Ministry of Education. Although I was a Christian, I took my students to pray at the Shintō shrines for victory in war. It was not as if I didn't feel any doubt in my heart, yet at root I was ignorant and cowardly.

I may be asked why I didn't take responsibility at the time of the defeat. I was then taking care of my mother and younger siblings—and transforming of one's consciousness is not something that can be done immediately. It is a fact that it never occurred to me to resign from my post. One of my fellow teachers was demobilized in October after the surrender. Watching the morning meeting of the teaching staff begin with clapping our hands in prayer to the shrine in the principal's office—a force of habit from wartime—he was shocked. "You're still doing this sort of thing?" he said. The Imperial Rescript on Education was so ingrained in us that it amounted to brainwashing. Our eyes were not opened to this situation until the abolition of state Shintō was ordered in December 1945.

With the renunciation of the Emperor's divinity the following January and the promulgation of the new Constitution and the Fundamentals of Education Act, I finally started to realize the immensity of my responsibility as an educator regarding the War. Since then, as a sign of my penance, I have continued to this day to whip this worn-out horse of a body by telling myself that I must inform my students about my own sinful experience. In my classes on world history I do not wish to repeat the teaching of fallacies to students who will shoulder the next generation. They must not repeat the same mistakes we have made.

Itabashi Toshinori, seventy-one (m),
part-time high school instructor,
Shimodate

"Have You Finished Your Military Service?"

"Have you finished your military service?" This was a question I was asked one night several years ago on a train crossing the European continent. When I explained that there was no military draft system in Japan, the fellow expressed surprise and disbelief. He asked me how my country can be defended without a conscription system.

In Japan we have the Self Defense Forces. These troops are made up not of draftees but of those who enlist as volunteers. It is all on a considerably smaller scale than the military forces of the Greater Japanese Empire during World War II. In addition we have the military framework of the U.S.–Japan Security Treaty to maintain the security of the nation. I haven't experienced war nor the draft system, but if my country were invaded, I would probably carry a rifle and fight, I explained.

It appeared to me that the young people in Europe felt national security to be a more immediate concern. They thought about it much more than the young people of Japan. Patriotism seems to be rather weak among Japanese youth as well. People often say that when you go abroad you become a patriot, and I was no exception. Yet I don't want to be blindly patriotic. That would merely be egotistical self-love. I feel it is our duty as citizens to make our country into something that is worthy of our love. Just because Japan has become an economic power doesn't necessarily mean that it has become a nation worthy of our love. Isn't it necessary for us to start by recognizing that Japan is a developing country in terms of efforts to make it a country worthy of our love?

I have an acquaintance who works for the Self Defense Forces, and I occasionally go to visit their facilities. The Ground Self Defense Force's tanks, armored trucks, and firearms and the Maritime Self Defense Force's escort ships and minesweepers are imposing and awesome. Whether one thinks they are impressive or whether one views them with fear as weapons to kill people, seeing is believing. People should look at the actual tools for war. Doing so will make us become familiar with the internal circumstances of the Self Defense Forces and more directly involved in the issue of defense expenditures.

Akazaki Jun'ichi, thirty-one (m),
company employee, Kawaguchi

A Plea to Adults

Almost all young people nowadays seem to have the awareness that war is a bad thing, something that must be avoided. This hasn't come from our own experience, however. So it is a fact that our feelings about this issue are weak. The wars that are actually being fought in other countries seem to be happening in another world. The stories we hear from those who have experienced war lack immediacy. As a result we merely harbor feelings of hatred toward war as an argument in our minds. These feelings are not enough to rouse us to action. They won't impel us to do our utmost to avoid the road to war.

When the young people of today become responsible for Japanese society, we may become wrapped up in a war without realizing why. That possibility is what I fear most. Compared to today's adults, most of us young people have no practical ideas about how war can be avoided. At school we learn about the process by which Japan entered into the War, but most of us forget it right away.

I would like to say this to the adults of today. There is a limit to imparting impressions of the horror of war. This alone is not useful. I would like you to think deeply about education to prevent war. I make this plea because, frankly, I am afraid that if my generation begins leading society as we are now, we could very well become embroiled in a war.

> Usami Satoshi, nineteen (m),
> studying for university entrance
> exams, Utsunomiya

We'll Be the Ones Who Go to War

If war should break out, I will be drafted to be a soldier. That means I won't be able to go on dates with the girl I love or fool around with my friends. I'll have to stop my studies, which have recently finally started to become interesting to me. My body that I have gotten into shape to play sports, the dreams that I have nurtured in my heart, my very life—the one thing that I should be able to do with as I want—all these will no longer be mine.

There's something that I find even more unbearable. I will be thoroughly trained in how to kill people by the higher-ups, then sent off to the battlefield. And I will end up killing people with my own hands. I'll be selling my soul in exchange for medals. If there were no war, the person I kill and I might have become close friends. I will have to kill someone like that.

War is an issue that concerns each of us as individuals. This is because the ones who receive direct harm in war are not those who first espouse war, but those of us who are forced to go along with their decision.

Takahara Hiroshi, eighteen (m),
student, Yokohama

Are We at Peace Now?

Needless to say, I haven't experienced war. My parents were just children, so they hardly remember the War. From reading books and looking at photographs I think I fully understand the horror of war. We should never engage in war again.

Recently I've begun to wonder if this world is really at peace. Certainly, compared to the time of World War II it is vastly more peaceful. I feel that what we have now is a false peace, although those who experienced the War may express disagreement with this. Japan is unmistakably at peace, but what about the world as a whole?

The Iran-Iraq War, the effects of defoliants on Vietnam, South Africa's race problem, the African nations suffering from drought, the continuing Cold War between the U.S. and the Soviet Union.... It seems to me that conditions all over the world are such that war might break out at any moment. I wonder what real peace is. Can someone tell me?

Sugitani Akie, thirteen (f),
middle-school student, Matsudo

Counted the Number of Fingers on My Son

What I feared most when my oldest son was born was whether he had five fingers and toes on each of his hands and feet. I was afraid that retribution for having killed many enemy soldiers in battle might be delivered onto my own child. Their death cries and the expressions on their faces have not faded from my memory. At the crucial moment of "kill or be killed," I fought with my instinct for survival. I lost all sense of reason or cultivation.

Those whom I killed must have despised me greatly. Having incurred so much hatred, I have lived my life attempting to run away from the torments of my conscience. I had numbed my conscience by giving myself the excuse that those who face each other as enemies on the battlefield openly acknowledge that there will be casualties. I had been inflamed with battlefield psychology—a frightening code of ethics.

One of my elders told me that the resentment of those who were killed can be so deep as to pierce one's very marrow. Their killer will be cursed until his grandchildren's generation. I counted my child's fingers and toes from this fear that I could not divulge to anyone. I have lived tortured by the after-effects of battle. My resentment at this will not disappear.

Yabe Teruo, sixty-seven (m),
farmer, Yamaguchi Prefecture

Build a Magnificent Monument to the War Dead

I was deeply touched by the meaningful proposal at the conclusion of the 15 August editorial in this newspaper, which stated, "What if the government and Liberal Democratic Party, rather than sticking to concerns as to what occurred in the past, shift their thinking to seek a way to truly mourn the war dead?"

What if the government and Liberal Democratic Party listen to this suggestion without bias and discontinue their current Yasukuni Shrine–only doctrine.*

---

*This refers to Japanese government officials' practice of publicly visiting the Shintō shrine of Yasukuni in Tokyo, which was the focus of Japan's prewar and wartime militarism.

Taking the U.S. and Soviet Union as examples, can't we transcend religious sectarianism to build a memorial to the unknown soldier in the Imperial Palace Plaza, a symbol befitting a peaceful Japan? Can this be deliberated among all the citizens of Japan?

This would not violate any articles of the Constitution. Nor would it offend any other nations. It would allow the Emperor and other members of the imperial family to attend services there. This would be a place where state guests from foreign countries can lay a wreath without disgrace when they visit Japan. Please carry this out without treating it as the ramblings of an old man. Should this plan be realized, I would be able proudly to join my friends from the South Manchuria Railway and my navy buddies from the days of the Manchurian Incident, who left before me, when the time comes in a few years for me to be placed beneath the ground.

This would not have the effect of making war more likely. Even those young people who don't know war would reflect upon those touching and priceless lives sacrificed in the War, each time they bow their heads in front of the monument. They would strengthen their aspirations for peace. And, I believe, this will nurture in them an immovable spirit, and they will then be ready to face the muzzle of a rifle and give their lives to preserve the peace of Japan, their homeland. Peace cannot be defended by mere lip service. Only with the resolve to face the muzzle of a rifle can it be defended.

Twenty years ago at the International Trade Fair Center in Harumi, an Australian buyer whom I didn't know asked me where the memorial to the unknown soldier was. I took him to the cemetery for the war dead at Chidorigafuchi and prayed with him. On the way back, after thanking me for my kindness, he spoke to me dejectedly.

"I fought against your country's navy as a naval officer in the last war, and I had great admiration for your valor. In particular, I felt that the attack on Sydney Harbor by the small submarines led by Lieutenant Matsuo of your navy was splendid, even if he was the enemy. The attack ended in failure, but we courteously buried the remains of the dead. We pulled up the submarine, and it is displayed honorably, along with a memorial tablet. The Australian young people who see this memorial are inspired by this. It strengthens their resolve to defend their country; and they carve into their hearts the name of Lieutenant Matsuo, Japanese Naval officer. That meager memorial at Chidorigafuchi is not consistent with Japan's prosperity. I was disappointed, thinking about the people who martyred themselves for their country." Saying this, he shook my hand heartily and parted.

Kii Shūichirō, eighty-five (m),
war history scholar, Tokyo

Requiem Echoes in Mountain Temple

The other year I visited a small temple in a tiny village in the Izu mountains. I saw a solid row of photographs of soldiers pasted on the room divider above the sliding doors in a small room. It was at the side of the priest's quarters in the main hall.

"These are all the soldiers who went to war from this village. They left and didn't return."

After saying this, the priest sat in the middle of the room and quietly played his *shakuhachi* [five-holed bamboo clarinet]. It was a tune that permeated the soul.

The soldiers in the photos were all youths wearing navy or army uniforms. Some looked like mere boys. The pictures of these twenty-seven dead soldiers bring to mind the many women—their lovers, mothers, and younger sisters—who wept for them. What is even sadder is that these photographs in the room facing the sea have listened to the requiem played on the *shakuhachi* for forty years.

At a time when the suggestion of a monument to the war dead is evoking much comment about the separation of religion and state, in this mountain temple there was a much more direct way of transmitting the sorrow of war.

Arai Emiko, forty-eight (f),
housewife, Yokohama

Animations Are Dangerous

Every year, in commemoration of the anniversary of the end of the War in August, newspapers and television stations produce programs about the tragedy of war. They appeal to viewers that such tragedies should not be repeated. But that is a once-a-year occurrence. It is no match for the influence on the younger generation of the animated science-fiction videos broadcast every day.

These animated characters are drunk on absolutism. Love brings them back to life even after they die. They are not contaminated by radiation.

They have a multitude of weapons that could hardly be produced even by pouring a hundred percent of our GNP into their development. The beautiful battle scenes in the films are skillfully drawn by animators with a full command of technology.

These are nightmares. I am afraid of the generation raised on these animations. I feel that the people who create such cartoons are dangerous. I am not suggesting that we ban them or restrict them from being televised. Freedom of expression is important. Do the producers and advertisers, however, truly realize the social consequences of these films?

I am one of those who were called "children who don't know war."* I am of the Astro Boy generation. Astro Boy is a character created by Mr. Tezuka Osamu, a man who experienced the War. This animation series was loaded with criticism of atomic testing. It depicted the futility of fighting and appealed for the promotion of communication. The first television animation series created in Japan was that kind of work. But what do we have now?

> Kaneko Naomi, thirty (f),
> not employed, Yokohama

---

*"Children Who Don't Know War" ["Sensō o Shiranai Kodomatachi"] was a popular song in the sixties.

Animations Are Not Dangerous

This is in response to Ms. Kaneko, who wrote "Animations are dangerous." Among the many works of animation there are those that can be taken as being dangerous, but please understand that those are not all there are. There are main characters who lose their loved ones one after another in war, then finally suffer a mental breakdown or kill someone they value by mistake. I don't think anyone would glorify war after watching such programs. The miracle of the main character brought back to life through love—it is a way of showing the strength and importance of love, not a glorification of war.

What you called "beautiful battle scenes" I would call "realistic." Isn't it possible that with the developments in animation technology it will actually become easier to express the wretchedness of war?

There are current science-fiction animation works with an infinite variety of themes, including those with quality content as a new awakening of mankind and communication throughout space. Before prejudging all animations as bad because they have battle scenes that glorify war, I would hope that you would grasp the themes expressed in these works.

Ichikawa Satoshi, eighteen (m),
high school student, Kasukabe

Tell Us More

In the eyes of those of an age to have experienced the War, I am one of the "young people these days." Being indulged by the wealthy society we have now, I had neglected the War.

This I memorized from my textbook: "The atom bombs were dropped on Hiroshima and Nagasaki by the United States. The War ended on 15 August 1945. Children had been evacuated to farming villages, and young soldiers lost their lives in special attacks units. War is meaningless, and therefore we must never start a war again." Along with this, in the bottom of my heart remained the question, "Who was it that started the War? Why must we search our souls when they started the War by choice? Shouldn't *they* be the ones to take responsibility and search their own souls?

Reading this column, however, I think that, rather than just being taught passively about the War, I have been touched by the War in a direct manner. My previous way of thinking has changed, a little at a time. I think that I have come to understand something of the weightiness of the War.

Those of you who know firsthand about the War, please teach us more. You have a duty to tell us about the War, just as we have a duty to learn about the War. Tell us more about the War so that when the generations change and we become the ones to tell about the War, we will be able to fulfill that duty with conviction. Among my friends are many who have turned their backs on hearing about the War. But won't you believe that there is a time when we will face up to the War? We promise that we will not treat the War merely as a past event, but will respectfully transmit the experience as your descendants.

Kobayashi Noriko, seventeen (f),
high school student, Machida

A Road We Cannot Sidestep

In our country, where wartime leaders remained in power in the postwar period, people associated with them have suddenly become active. Ominous signs have reappeared. At this time we have a great duty to face up anew to the actual circumstances of the War and impart this knowledge to future generations. Those with experience of the War are advancing in age. So unless we do it now it will be too late.

In this series, there have been dark recollections of the atrocities committed by the Japanese forces in the war zones. We read about the tyranny over the weak at home, which had been concealed until now. Those making their confessions must feel that what had felt stuck in their hearts has been cleared away. They have had the opportunity to release with a single stroke what they had locked up in their hearts for so many years. The confessions about the atrocities committed in the occupied areas were without question made because of the natural sense of guilt felt by human beings. It is narrow-minded nationalism—consisting merely of self-righteousness and arrogance—to view these confessions as disgracing us Japanese. Attempts to conceal, feign innocence, and idealize only deepen others' mistrust and hatred of all Japanese.

These confessions are evidence of self-reflection and atonement. They allow those in the former occupied areas to realize anew that the majority of Japanese are loving, sincere, and upright people with a conscience. They will serve to aid in forging lasting international understanding and exchange; and they will lead to a sure road to promoting our national interest. Though it may be painful, we cannot sidestep this road.

> Okada Chūken, sixty-nine (m),
> professor emeritus,
> Ibaraki University, Mito

Why Do You Cover Your Ears?

Among the writers to this column there are some whose reactions consist of "Again? I don't want to hear anymore," and "They are boasting." No matter how a story is told, we mustn't overlook the truth hiding there. Fastening only on the surface, on the way something is presented, will not allow the reader to see the truth. No one wants to hear, see, or recognize what is sorrowful, painful, or shameful. But if it is the truth, we cannot avert our gaze from it.

When I was about twenty years old, I visited the Peace Memorial Museum in Hiroshima. I was overcome by the urge to strike out at all the Westerners who happened to be there at the same time. There is no "correct reason" or "righteousness" that can justify dropping an atomic bomb.

The Pacific War was a tragedy. Those who participated in the War state, "I live in disgrace." For the younger generation *disgrace* is probably an obsolete word. How were those participants who are "living in disgrace" able to sublimate this war within themselves? No matter how many decades pass, they are likely to continue to weep bitter tears in the depths of their memories. By having them speak to us in this column, we ought also to weep bitter tears and search our souls.

The topic of the evils of war cannot be exhausted. We should not become tired of hearing of it. Those who say they are just want to cover their eyes and ears. They are people who, coddled in the leading-edge civilization of the world, have no understanding of the pain of past history or awareness that they have any responsibility for it. We must not become like this.

> Taguchi Tomiko, forty-three (f),
> housewife, Kuki

For Us Young People

I have had occasion to read what many people have written about the War in this column. Unlike what we usually think of as war, I found in their letters entirely different, much more abhorrent and tragic realities, which might only be explained by saying that people's souls became corrupted. The reality of war differs from American movies. It is something completely other than the wars in animation films and comic books. On an actual battlefield it is harder to see "righteousness." We thought we knew this, but we really had no conception of it. That is why the letters were a shock to me.

As I read the letters in this column, I thought there might be some people—no, many people—who think, "There were many awful things that were done in that War. But . . . " Their thoughts range from "That fellow who went into enemy territory was a hero" to "It was wrong because we lost—if we had won. . . . " If despicable things had not been done, would it now be necessary to do our soul-searching regarding that War?

The first lines of "War," sung by the American singer Bruce Springsteen, go like this: "War! What is it good for? Absolutely nothin'."

War serves no useful purpose. But people tend to forget that and think it is a means to some kind of end.

Let us learn our lesson now, before it is too late. Having lived with old, painful memories shut up inside you for so long must in itself have been an ordeal. To expose them now can't be an easy thing to do. Even so, I take it upon myself to beseech you to do so, for all of us young people.

> Senda Yuriko, eighteen (f),
> high school student, Yachiyo

To Give Meaning to Deaths

Is there another newspaper column into which so many deaths have been carved? Since last summer, how many deaths have become printed words? It is said that our prosperity today has risen from those priceless deaths, but I wonder if that is really so. Is it acceptable for us to give meaning to those deaths in such a form and rest easy with that?

Reading this column I feel strongly that we haven't made the best use of those priceless deaths. That war was not one of victims defending their homeland, as stated by a mother who was running from an incendiary bomb; nor was our military one that protected the people. I do think that all lives and deaths are meaningful and that those who take over the next age should not allow those people to have died in vain. When I recall the history that I learned in school, I can't help but think that in terms of education, which can be considered to be the country's journey toward the future, we have treated those deaths as having been in vain.

"War" is taught in classes designed to regurgitate what is written in textbooks. There is none of the horror that we have read about in this column. Children are said to be students from the foreign land of the future. By telling these children the truth and by so connecting our precious peace to the future, the enormous number of deaths will live on with great meaning.

> Muramatsu Hiroaki, twenty-six (m),
> local civil servant, Shizuoka

Index

Frank Gibney was born in 1924 and raised in New York City. He graduated from Yale College, in absentia, in 1945. He served in the navy as Lieutenant, USNR, from 1942 to 1946.

Through his career, he has held the positions of foreign correspondent and associate editor of *Time* magazine, senior editor of *Newsweek*, and editor and publisher of *Show* magazine. Gibney was in charge of Encyclopaedia Britannica's Japanese and East Asian companies from 1966 to 1976 in Tokyo. He is presently Vice Chairman, TBS-Britannica, and also Vice Chairman of Encyclopaedia Britannica's Board of Directors.

Mr. Gibney is President of the Pacific Basin Institute in Santa Barbara, California. He is the author of twelve books including *The Pacific Century; Japan: The Fragile Superpower;* and *Korea's Quiet Revolution.*

Beth Cary is a translator and interpreter based in the San Francisco Bay Area. Born and raised in Kyoto, Japan, she has spent some twenty years living in Japan. Educated at Wellesley College and Sophia University in Tokyo, she was Assistant Director, Center for East Asian Studies, Stanford University, and Assistant Director at The Japan Society of Northern California.

Her published translations include *A Spring Like Any Other (Itsumo to Onaji Haru)* by Tsujii Takashi [Tsutsumi Seiji] (1992); *Inspector Imanishi Investigates (Suna no Utsuwa)* by Matsumoto Seicho (1989); *Blind Man's Buff (Mekura Oni)* by Enchi Fumiko in *The Mother of Dreams and Other Short Stories: Portrayals of Women in Modern Japanese Fiction* edited by Makoto Ueda (1986).

Beth Cary's father, Otis Cary, served with Frank Gibney as a language officer in the U.S. Navy during World War II.